HENRY L. STIMSON
and Japan

Manchuria has become to the watchers on the fire tower of the Far East what Constantinople was to Europe for half a century, and for much the same reason. It is a great opportunity geographically placed where three nations meet, and such an oyster has seldom been opened without war.
HUGH BYAS, Tokyo correspondent, *New York Times*

Manchuria . . . shows every sign of becoming the cockpit of Asia just as Belgium has been that of Europe.
NOEL H. H. CHARLES, Japanese specialist in the British Foreign Office

ARMIN RAPPAPORT

Henry L. Stimson
and Japan, 1931-33

The University of Chicago Press

CHICAGO & LONDON

Library of Congress Catalog Card Number: 63-18847

The University of Chicago Press, Chicago & London
The University of Toronto Press, Toronto 5, Canada

_____

PREFACE

To MANY observers of the international scene, the Japanese
conquest and occupation of Manchuria was, as the *London
Times* noted, "the *fons et origo* of the whole catastrophe"
which subsequently engulfed eastern Asia and led to the great
war in the Pacific. Why the United States and Great Britain
did nothing effective to halt Japan is a crucial question which
has troubled students of international history from that day
to this. In the following pages I have tried to answer the
question as far as the United States is concerned by examining
the policies of the principal decision-makers and the moods
of the people. To a lesser degree, I have tried to do the same
for Britain, although my efforts were necessarily limited by
the paucity of official documents and private papers. I have
tried, also, to include some account of Japan's position. In a
subsequent volume I plan to carry the narrative to the end
of the decade.

I am indebted to many people who smoothed the path of
my research in libraries and archives at California, Harvard,
Columbia, Swarthmore, Yale, Newberry, the Library of Congress, the National Archives, and the Department of State.
I am especially grateful to the Honorable William R. Castle,
who graciously made his diary available to me in the scholarly
surroundings of his own study. Special thanks go also to Mrs.
Corliss Lamont for collecting the scattered papers of the
American Boycott Association for my use, and to the Honorable Stanley K. Hornbeck for reminiscing aloud for my benefit, to E. Taylor Parks for sharing his matchless knowledge of
the Department of State Archives, and to McGeorge Bundy
for permission to use the Stimson material in Yale University
Library. Peter Buzanski helped at various stages of the re-

search, Nobuya Bamba assisted with translating Japanese documents, and Benjamin H. Hazard saved me from numerous errors in the spelling of Japanese names. My colleagues at Berkeley, Robert A. Scalapino and Delmer M. Brown, graciously took time from their busy schedules to read the entire manuscript. My wife, Marjorie S. Rappaport, spent many hours testing the book against the rules of grammar and syntax.

A grant from the American Philosophical Society made possible the research, and funds from the Institute of Social Sciences at the University of California provided for clerical assistance and for the services of a research assistant. To both go my deepest appreciation.

                                                                    A. R.

University of California
June, 1963

CONTENTS

HENRY L. STIMSON
and Japan

CHAPTER ONE
in which
the world reacts

Had Bethman-Hollweg been at the [League of Nations] Council table and blurted out his phrase about the scrap of paper, he would not have been rebuked. He would have "evoked a spirit of conciliation" and would have been invited to a secret session in order to join in the hunt for a happier formula. And the result would have been hailed as a diplomatic victory.

SIR ALFRED ZIMMERN, 1932

O N THE evening of September 17, 1931, the counselor of the Japanese legation in Peking discussed with the American minister to China conditions in eastern Asia. During the conversation, Counselor Yano Makoto [1] assured Minister Nelson T. Johnson that there was no chance of Japanese military occupation of Manchuria. Why occupy, he said, when peaceful economic penetration produced the same result at less cost? Except for some young army officers, he continued, even the military opposed occupation.[2] Twenty-four hours later, Japanese troops of the Kwantung army [3] were on the move in Manchuria. At 10:00 P.M. on September 18, a squad of Japanese railway guards, while patrolling the South Manchurian Railway some three miles south of Mukden, heard an explosion about five hundred yards away and saw some Chinese soldiers fleeing from a section of damaged track. They pursued, were fired on, and returned the fire. The tinderbox was lit. Rapidly, elements from Mukden and other garrisons along the railway fanned out from their barracks. Within three hours, Mukden, Changchun, Antung, and Koupangtzu were taken. Three days later the troops occupied Kirin and the civil administration in Southern Manchuria was in Japanese hands.[4]

There is every reason to believe that the Japanese counselor had been sincere in his assurances. He, his colleagues in

[1] Chinese whose names are commonly used in the Western style are so designated throughout this book. All other Chinese and Japanese names follow the oriental pattern of surname first.

[2] Memorandum by Nelson T. Johnson, U.S. minister to China, in *Papers Relating to the Foreign Relations of the United States, 1931* (3 vols.; Washington, 1946), III, 95–96 (hereafter cited as *F.R.* [followed by the relevant year]). For an excellent account of the civil-military dispute in Japan relative to Manchuria, see Nakamura Sadako, "The Manchurian Affair" (unpublished Ph.D. thesis, University of California, 1963). Nakamura's work covers Japanese policy toward Manchuria from 1931 to 1933, with an introductory section tracing antecedents from 1905. It is based on a wide variety of Japanese sources, printed and manuscript, some never before used by scholars. The work is heavily tinged with antimilitarism and is critical of the uninhibited actions of the Kwantung army. See also Yale C. Maxon, *Control of Japanese Foreign Policy: A Study of Civil-Military Rivalry, 1930–1945* (Berkeley, 1957).

[3] So called because it garrisoned Japanese-leased Kwantung Territory in southern Manchuria.

[4] Robert H. Ferrell analyzes the outbreak of the fighting in "The Mukden Incident: September 18–19, 1931," *Journal of Modern History*, XXVII (1955), 66–72.

4 In Which the World Reacts

Manchuria, and the Foreign Office in Tokyo were taken com
pletely by surprise. They were fully aware, of course, of the
army's dissatisfaction with the conciliatory policy of the Foreign Office toward China. War Minister Minami Jiro had
said so as recently as August 4 in an address to a conference
of army and divisional commanders in Tokyo.[5] Well known,
also, was the army's restlessness and its chafing to take positive
action on the mainland. Late in August, at an inspection
of reservists in Tokyo, officers had talked openly of an impending crisis in Manchuria, and three days before the fighting a
company commander in Fushin had predicted an outbreak
within a week. Reporters in Tokyo frequently asked members
of the government when war would begin.[6]

But Foreign Minister Shidehara Kijuro had been satisfied
that the military impulsiveness had been effectively curbed,
at least temporarily, to give the government time to work
out Sino-Japanese problems peacefully.[7] Both the emperor
and Prince Saionji Kimmochi, the last of the elder statesmen,
or genro, deeply concerned over reports of lack of discipline
among the younger officers at home and abroad, had ordered
Minami to tighten the reins. Dutifully, the war minister had
given his promise to curb the impetuous officers, especially
in Manchuria and Mongolia, where the dangers of outbreak
were greatest.[8] Neither the emperor nor Saionji nor Shidehara knew at that time, however, that the emissary chosen
to carry the instructions to Mukden was General Tatekawa
Yoshitsugu, carefully selected by the chief of the Military
Affairs Bureau of the War Office because of his sympathy

[5] Takeuchi Tatsuji, *War and Diplomacy in the Japanese Empire* (New
York, 1935), pp. 342 ff.
[6] The Japanese consul in Mukden in August worried over the possibility
of an outbreak. See J. C. Vincent, the consul in Mukden, to State Dept.,
Aug. 20, 1931, *F.R., 1931*, III, 1–2. See also *International Military Tribunal
for the Far East*, pp. 2004–2006 (hereafter cited as IMTFE), and Nakamura,
p. 76.
[7] See the British ambassador in Tokyo (Lindley) to Marquess of Reading,
Oct. 1, 1931, *Documents on British Foreign Policy, 1919–1939* (Second Series,
Vol. VIII [London, 1960]), ed. by R. Butler and J. P. T. Bury, p. 698 (hereafter cited as *British Documents*).
[8] Diary of Prince Saionji, ed. by his secretary, Harada Kumao, p. 65 (typescript in University of California Library). Shidehara had for some years
successfully frustrated the demand by the militarists for action in Manchuria.
See Nakamura, p. 7.

with the aspirations of the military.[9] There is reason to believe that he permitted himself to be taken to a restaurant
on his arrival in Mukden on the evening of September 18
to delay delivery of the orders. Thus the army could move
without directly disobeying the imperial wish, but it had
to move at once.[10] There was not even time to secure permission from Honjo Shigeru, the commanding general, who
was at headquarters in Port Arthur. He learned of the fighting at 11:46 P.M. and promptly ordered reinforcements to
Mukden from neighboring garrisons. At 3:30 A.M., he left
Port Arthur, arriving at Mukden at noon the next day.[11] It
seems likely that had the Chinese not damaged the track, an
incident would probably have been provoked by the Japanese
army.[12] Actually, the damage was negligible.

The story of the army's dissatisfaction with the civil government and its devotion to a mission was an old one. For some
years before 1931, many officers had been revolted by the
Foreign Office's soft policy in China. Successive Chinese steps
threatened Japan's power and prestige on the mainland, yet
Shidehara, they believed, did nothing but conduct endless
negotiations. Building parallel lines to the South Manchurian

[9] Saionji, Diary, p. 74.

[10] *Ibid.;* see also IMTFE, pp. 2004–2006.

[11] There were rumors in Tokyo that some of the officers in Manchuria were
displeased with Honjo because of his mildness. These reports lend support to
the view that the officers in Mukden, chiefly Colonel Doihara Kenji, commanding the Special Services Section (Political) of the Kwantung army and
called by some the "Lawrence of Manchuria," Colonel Itagaki Seishiro, and
Lieutenant Colonel Ishihara Kanji, moved first and then informed Honjo.
See IMTFE, p. 18986. Honjo, however, before committing suicide in 1945,
took full responsibility for what had happened in 1931. See his "True Nature
of the Manchurian Incident," an account of his command from August 1931
to August 1932, IMTFE, Exhibits 2401 and 2403.

[12] There is some doubt that the Chinese damaged the track. William Lang-
don, American consul at Dairen, believed that the Japanese manufactured
the story and did it themselves. See *F.R., 1931,* III, 86. That something was
being planned for that night was suspected by Morishima Morito of the staff
of the Japanese consulate in Mukden. At 9:00 P.M. that evening, he thought
it strange that not one responsible officer could be located. See IMTFE,
Exhibit 245. The Kwantung army in the summer of 1931 was prepared to
move in Manchuria and was seeking some pretext to begin an attack. See
Nakamura, p. 69, n. 129, and pp. 70 ff. The British military attaché reported
that the "attack was a set piece, break in railway served as a pretext and was
conveniently arranged at a point which put the Japanese railway guards in
a favorable position for dealing with the only Chinese troops worth men-
tioning in the vicinity of Mukden." See *British Documents,* pp. 708–10.

Railway and a port to rival Dairen,[13] boycott of Japanese
goods, anti-Japanese education in the schools, infringements
on rights of Koreans in Manchuria and an assault on a group
of them near Changchun, all gave evidence of attempts by
the Chinese to assert their political and economic independence of Japan and impair Japanese rights in Manchuria.
China under Chiang Kai-shek's leadership was showing signs
of rejuvenation and already the Chinese war lord in Manchuria, Chang Hsueh-liang, and Chiang were drawing together.[14] Such an alliance menaced Japanese hegemony in
Manchuria. Most excruciating to the army was the execution
on June 27, 1931, of Captain Nakamura Shintaro, a Japanese
army officer traveling in Manchuria in civilian clothes presumably to investigate conditions for future colonization but
suspected by the Chinese of military spying. It was the army's
task to prove Japanese mastery and punish Chinese effrontery.

The army despised the Foreign Office for its subservience
to the zaibatsu [15]—the capitalists, financiers, and industrialists
—whose interests, it was believed, dictated the weak China
policy. They subordinated Manchurian considerations to
their own selfish designs. Fearful lest a strong hand alienate
the Chinese market, they chose to act cautiously. Worried
that the Western powers would object to a firm policy with
a consequent loss of international trade, they permitted Japanese honor to be besmirched. Manchuria had to come first.
There was the lifeline, the base for continental expansion,
the buffer against the Soviet Union—there where Japanese

[13] T. A. Bisson, "Railroad Rivalries in Manchuria between China and
Japan," *Foreign Policy Reports*, VIII (April 13, 1932), 29–43. The South
Manchurian Railway suffered heavily from newly built Chinese competing
lines, and officials of the railway whipped up army sentiment. Okawa Shumei,
director of the company's East Asia Research Institute, campaigned in Japan
early in 1931 for military action; Count Uchida Yasuya, the railway's president
and an ardent nationalist, played an important role in the preliminaries.
In the spring of 1931, a Sino-Japanese conference to resolve railroad problems failed. The railroad, a government instrumentality whose president was
appointed by the prime minister, helped to finance the Kwantung army.
See Ambassador Joseph C. Grew to State Department, Mar. 24, 1933, Manuscript Diplomatic Correspondence of the State Department, File 793.94/6144,
National Archives (hereafter cited as D/S File). Grew learned this from a
Japanese book by Komai Tokuzo, a member of the Privy Council of Manchukuo, *Recording of the Founding of Great Manchukuo* (Tokyo, 1933).

[14] Sara Smith, *The Manchurian Crisis* (New York, 1948), p. 17.

[15] The four greatest industrial and banking combines were Mitsui,
Mitsubishi, Sumitomo, and Yasuda.

blood in two wars had fertilized the soil. Manchuria must be the cornerstone of Japanese policy.

The capitalists and their political servants needed chastening. They were accused of sacrificing the traditional Japanese ideals for profit. While the zaibatsu grew richer, the peasant farmers and lower middle classes became poorer. The resulting inequalities threatened to destroy the concept of one family united by loyalty to the emperor. Parliamentary government was disgraceful. Politicians, eternally wrangling, placed party above country, and patriotism was dying. The army, whose junior officers were largely sons of lower middle class parents and whose soldiers came from peasant families, alone could end the hold of the wealthy and the politicians on the life of the nation and restore the old ideals.[16]

To this end, numerous nationalist and patriotic organizations were formed—the Cherry Society, the Blood Brotherhood, the Patriotic Labor party, and many others. They together with older groups—Black Dragon Society (Amur River Society), National Foundation Society, and others— aimed to overthrow the parliamentary system, substituting for it a government by the military which would be free to pursue a bold course. In March 1931, an attempt was made, but it failed. Yet the goal remained constant. The attack in Manchuria in September 1931 may be considered a "resumption in another direction" and in the same spirit of the March plot.[17]

By the fall of 1931, the army was desperate and determined. It had been steadily losing prestige at home. Ever since the misadventure in Siberia in 1921, public estimation of the military had fallen. Successive civilian-minded governments had confidently cut appropriations. Equipment was shabby, even rations had been niggardly. Soldiers were considered social parasites by moneyed families, who frequently refused

[16] F. C. Jones, *Japan's New Order in East Asia, 1937–45* (London, 1954), p. 7.
[17] The words are those of Royal S. Wald in "The Young Officer Movement in Japan" (unpublished Ph.D. thesis, University of California, 1949), p. 80. Wald describes, in superb fashion, the aspirations of the officer groups and narrates details of the March plot on pp. 58 ff. Delmar Brown, *Nationalism in Japan* (Berkeley, 1955), pp. 190–91, contains some material on the societies; the best account of the societies is Richard Storry, *The Double Patriots* (Boston, 1957), chaps. i–iii. Edwin Reischauer, *The United States and Japan* (Cambridge, Mass., 1950), pp. 169 and 201–202, is excellent.

to permit their daughters to marry officers. Now, with a disarmament conference in the offing, the final blow might be struck by the government. It might well acquiesce in a reduction of the army's strength, much as had been done at London the previous year when Japanese delegates accepted an inferior navy.[18] A powerful and successful move in Manchuria was calculated to restore the army's prestige and forestall a cut in strength by timely demonstration of the need to maintain a great establishment. The army would become the darling of the nation and, at the same time, perhaps, create in Manchuria an ideal political, social, and economic order.[19]

News of the fighting reached Tokyo early on the morning of the nineteenth.[20] The newspapers informed the public, and Minami, who had got the word from Mukden shortly after midnight, carried the report to Premier Wakatsuki Reijiro and to the emperor.

The reaction of the government was a mixture of shock and chagrin. "It had finally happened" was the way Prince Saionjo's secretary put it.[21] Wakatsuki was terribly distressed that the army had moved without imperial sanction.[22] Shidehara, who had stood in dread of such an incident, saw a decade of laborious diplomacy brought to nought.[23] The Gaimusho [24] had demonstrated at Washington in 1921 and at London in 1930 its willingness to settle international problems peacefully. Japanese delegates had initialed the Pact of Paris, thereby pledging to engage in no offensive war. Implicit in all these diplomatic moves was Japan's intent to become an active partner with the Western powers in the quest for peace. As for relations with China, Shidehara had fully expected

[18] General Araki Sadao's views, expressed during interrogation in 1946. IMTFE, Defense Document 674. See also Takeuchi, *War and Diplomacy*, p. 342, and Shidehara Kijuro, *Gaiko Gojunen* [Diplomacy: Fifty Years] (Tokyo, 1951), pp. 166–68.

[19] Some time later, Ambassador Grew reported this view to be held by many observers. *F.R., 1934*, III, 645. Counselor of Embassy Edwin L. Neville held similar views, which he reported to the State Department from Tokyo on October 13, 1931. D/S File 793.94/2050.

[20] The Foreign Office received a report from the consul general in Mukden, while the War Office heard the news from the military in the field.

[21] Saionji, Diary, p. 74.

[22] *Ibid.*, p. 79; see also the account in Aoki Tokuzo, *Wakatsuki Reijiro* (Tokyo, 1958), pp. 91–93.

[23] IMTFE, p. 1390.

[24] The Japanese word for Foreign Office, occasionally used by Westerners.

that all difficulties would soon be resolved. Even the nasty Nakamura affair had been on the verge of a settlement. All of these hopes and efforts now appeared to have been undone by the army's rash move. The minister in Switzerland cabled his fears of an aroused and hostile world,[25] while Minister Shigemitsu Mamoru warned from Peking that anti-Japanese feeling was greater than during the time of the Twenty-one Demands.[26] The old Marquis Kido Koichi commented bitterly that if not stopped, the army would cause the nation serious damage. "It is a national calamity," he said.[27]

At 10:30 the same morning, the Cabinet met. After voicing grave concern over the course of events, the premier instructed Minami to confine the army's operations and prevent the spread of fighting. Two days later at a second meeting, the Cabinet voted to refuse the Japanese army in Korea permission to reinforce Honjo.[28]

The Cabinet's decisions, however, were meaningless. Although Minami promised to issue the necessary orders, he had no wish to impede the operations of the army in Manchuria.[29] After a conference with the chief of staff that afternoon, he informed the press that the Kwantung army itself must decide what action is necessary and that it need not consult the Cabinet. At another General Staff conference on the following day, he virtually sanctioned reinforcements from Korea without Cabinet approval, and while he suggested that the situation not be aggravated, he seemed not to oppose enlarging the scope of operations if that were necessary.[30] But even had he wished to halt the army, he was powerless to do so. The army was, for mobilization and operations, responsible to the chief of staff. Neither the war minister nor the Cabinet had any control over it except in administrative mat-

---

[25] Japanese Foreign Office Documents, S 1.1.0.–23, p. 7 (microfilm in University of California Library; hereafter cited as JFOD). See also consul general in Mukden to Foreign office, Sept. 19, 1931, for similar fears. JFOD, PVM 34, pp. 13–14.

[26] JFOD, PVM 34, p. 135.

[27] Diary of Marquis Kido, Oct. 1, 1931 (microfilm in University of California Library).

[28] Saionji, Diary, p. 76; Takeuchi, *War and Diplomacy*, pp. 350–51.

[29] From Mukden, Consul General Hayashi reported the army's determination to solve Japan's problem in Manchuria by the sword and not permit a diplomatic settlement. JFOD, PVM 34, pp. 15–17.

[30] Takeuchi, *War and Diplomacy*, pp. 351–52.

ters. The chief of staff had to submit his war plans only to the emperor, and as far as Manchuria was concerned, there was no indication that he wished to stop the army. As a matter of fact, the Kwantung army had virtual *carte blanche* by a regulation of April 1919 which authorized the use of force to protect the railroad.[31] And while it is true that the war minister could have withheld supplies from the army as part of his administrative function, Honjo had enough matériel in September of 1931 to act independently for some time.[32] And so he and General Hayashi Senjuro, commanding in Korea, did act. On the twenty-second, the Korean garrison crossed the Yalu River in response to General Honjo's urgent summons and the following day the Japanese consul general in Mukden reported that the Kwantung army was enlarging operations.[33]

Curiously enough, both these facts brought forth no public censure by the government. Indeed, it began to look as if Wakatsuki and Shidehara, although no less distressed by the army's brash move, were not disposed to undo what the army had done. For one thing, public reaction to the military was decidedly favorable. Except for some pacifists, labor groups, and socialists, the exploits in Manchuria excited the Japanese masses. Manchuria was a magic word and mention of it stirred the embers of patriotism. Easily recalled were the victories in 1895 and 1905 and the heroism of the Mikado's soldiers. The Japanese public was pleased to see the chastening of the Chinese. Their newspapers had been filled with stories of Chinese arrogance and effrontery, particularly the Nakamura murder, which on September 27 was to reach an emotional climax in a public memorial service which was attended by ten thousand officers and men, and where, amidst hundreds of wreaths, was a white banner bearing words of homage in the blood of members of his class at the Military Academy.[34]

[31] IMTFE, p. 2415.
[32] IMTFE, p. 1392.
[33] JFOD, PVM 34, p. 132.
[34] Takeuchi, *War and Diplomacy*, p. 362; Brown, *Nationalism*, p. 191; Erle R. Dickover, "Survey of the Movements and Reactions of the Japanese People Since the Outbreak of the Manchurian Incident," D/S File 793.94/5939. A pacifist movement, associated with the International League for Peace and Freedom, existed in Japan. There was also an active League of Nations Association and a National Association for Disarmament.

Moreover, neither the premier nor the foreign minister wished to convey the impression at home or abroad that the government was any less prepared than the army to defend Japan's interests in Manchuria when threatened. All factions and all parties agreed on this question. Disagreement over method there was, to be sure. The army, supported by the party out of power, the Seiyukai, advocated rapid and forceful action, while the party in power, the Minseito, stood for slower and diplomatic means.[35] Back in July, in a public address, Wakatsuki had disclaimed any intent to surrender Japan's right in Manchuria, although he repudiated territorial aggrandizement.[36] And from the language of Shidehara's testimony at the War Crimes Trials in 1945, there is no doubt that he, too, believed Japan had to control Manchuria.

Japanese rights and interests in Manchuria were vast. Never in history had one nation enjoyed such great economic and administrative privileges in the territory of another sovereign state. A network of treaties, chiefly those with Russia in 1905 and with China in 1915, gave Japan the right to build railroads; settle land; dig coal; operate hotels, banks, factories, port facilities, and utilities; and station troops in certain areas. By 1931, Japan had 1,200,000,000 yen invested in the widest variety of operations, operated 690 miles of railroads, and controlled 1,400 square miles of leased territory. One thousand Japanese companies were engaged in business there, and 200,000 nationals lived in the area. The importance of Manchuria to Japan's economy cannot be overestimated. Industry in the Island Empire rested on Manchurian lumber, coal (7,000,000 tons a year), and iron (200,000 tons per year). One-half million tons of steel were manufactured by Japanese firms in Manchuria alone. Manchurian grain and, particularly, soybeans helped feed Japan. The soybean was to Japan what the peanut became to the American South after the work of George Washington Carver. From soy were made flour, cheese, milk, soup, rubber, linoleum, fertilizer, and oil important as a vegetable fat.[37] No politician in his right

[35] Takeuchi, *War and Diplomacy*, p. 339, n. 7.

[36] *Japan Chronicle*, July 22, 1931. Shigemitsu, the Japanese ambassador in China, also ardently defended the army. See the report of his conversation with British Ambassador Miles Lampson in *British Documents*, pp. 812–13.

[37] C. W. Young, *Japan's Special Position in Manchuria* (Baltimore, 1937),

12   In Which the World Reacts

mind could have foresworn such great benefit, and the
zaibatsu might have been thinking better of Manchuria as
a market as international tariffs during the Great Depression
cut into international trade.[38]

These factors conditioned the policy pursued by the government in relation to the League of Nations and the other
powers. After an extraordinary Cabinet meeting, on September 22, Shidehara's representatives in Washington and
Geneva informed the United States and the League of Nations that the army had acted in self-defense to protect Japanese rights, that Japan had no territorial ambitions, that the
army would withdraw and operations would come to an end
as soon as the rights were secured, and that Sino-Japanese
difficulties would be resolved between the two powers.[39] On
September 24, there emerged from another Cabinet session
a long statement defending the army's action with another
promise of withdrawal, another disavowal of territorial designs, and a second statement that mediation was not needed.[40]
But even while assurances were being given that Tokyo had
the situation well in hand, the Cabinet approved the occupation of Kirin and appropriated the funds necessary to transfer
troops from Korea to Manchuria.[41]

These statements and policies by Tokyo provided sufficient
proof to China that the outbreak was more than a local incident, that it marked instead the opening of a power struggle
for the control of all Manchuria. On September 19, the Chinese government had proposed a Sino-Japanese commission
to iron out the difficulty of the previous night, but within a
few days the rapid and determined advance of the Japanese
troops and the inability or unwillingness of Tokyo to check
it caused China to withdraw the proposal[42] and appeal instead to the League of Nations and to the United States.

passim; Japan Year Book, various years; John Orchard, *Japan's Economic
Position* (New York, 1930); *Business Week,* Sept. 30, 1931, p. 37; Institute of
Pacific Relations, *Conflict in the Far East, 1931–1932* (New York, 1932), p. 29;
Foreign Policy Reports, VII (December 23, 1931), 381 ff.
[38] F. C. Jones, *Manchuria Since 1931* (London, 1949), pp. 144–45.
[39] *F.R., 1931,* III, 53–54; Takeuchi, *War and Diplomacy,* p. 356, n. 69.
[40] *F.R., Japan, 1931–1941,* I, 11–12; Takeuchi, *War and Diplomacy,* p. 356;
IMTFE, Proceedings, pp. 9350, 2241; *F.R., 1931,* III, 64.
[41] IMTFE, Exhibit 2408.
[42] Shigemitsu to Shidehara, Sept. 19 and 24, 1931, IMTFE, Exhibit 246.

Alone, China could not cope with the Japanese military machine. Chiang was moving in the direction of strengthening and unifying the republic, but the problems facing the generalissimo were staggering. He had weathered a series of rebellions but still there were bandits, Communists, and war lords who spread disorganization in Hunan, Kiangsi, Fukien, and other areas. Although he had consolidated his position as president of the Executive Yuan, chairman of the State Council, and commander-in-chief of the army, navy, and air force, southern China, supported by Japanese gold, was in open rebellion against his authority.[43] The Yangtze floods had devastated central China, leaving millions homeless. It was, indeed, the worst year since the revolution of 1911. China needed help—from the West if Manchuria were to be saved.

And Manchuria had to be saved. Ninety-five per cent of its people were Chinese.[44] It was tied to China culturally and politically. It was Chinese territory, Chinese soil. Any rights enjoyed by Japan flowed from grants by China in treaties. The treaties, many signed at bayonet point, did not confer upon Japan the right to occupy Chinese territory, kill Chinese citizens, seize Chinese property, or tell China it could not build railroads on its own soil.[45] The determination to resist Japan's land-grabbing even if help did not come was shouted by thousands of people in China—students in Nanking, mobs in Shanghai, and demonstrators before Japanese businesses in Peking. Chiang expressed the mass sentiment in a speech on September 23 when he said: "For the moment we await the judgment of the world and we must suppress our indignation and remain calm but if the League of Nations and the signatories of the Kellogg Pact fail to uphold justice, the National Government is prepared for a final and supreme

[43] See *F.R., 1931*, III, 8. Also *Christian Science Monitor*, Sept. 19, 1931, and *Japan Chronicle*, Sept. 16, 1931. Eugene Chen, a leader of the Canton group, had secured a Japanese political advisor on a visit to Tokyo in July 1931. American consul at Canton to State Dept., July 27, 1931, D/S File 793.94/1789; see also *Current History*, 35 (1931), 235 ff.

[44] There were thirty million Chinese in Manchuria in 1931 as against three million in 1905.

[45] See the illuminating article by Arthur N. Holcombe in *Current History*, 35 (1931), pp. 349 ff., for an analysis of Chinese claims to sovereignty over Manchuria; also W. W. Yen, "What Manchuria Means to China's Future," *New York Times*, Mar. 27, 1932.

struggle. I shall lead the army to fight for the preservation of our race and to uphold the dignity of our people." [46]

The League of Nations had been in operation for eleven years and had demonstrated its usefulness for settling political disputes on two occasions. In the Mosul dispute involving Turkey and Iraq in 1924–26 and in the Greek-Bulgarian frontier clash in 1925, it had successfully resolved differences which might have led to war. But these were relatively minor matters concerning small nations, and it was expected that some day a situation would arise involving a vexing question between great powers and provide a real test of the League's capabilities.[47] The outbreak in Manchuria was not, at the outset, viewed as the test. To the statesmen at Geneva, the Far East was peripheral, if not remote. They knew little of the depth of the Sino-Japanese controversy, of the treaty rights of the Japanese, and of the annoyances by the Chinese. Their eyes focused on Europe, on Germany and the Treaty of Versailles. The challenge, they believed, would come from a violation of that treaty. Eventually, these attitudes underwent a change. The stakes and the scope of the struggle in the Far East became more apparent. There dawned the realization that the sanctity of treaties everywhere was under attack and that the rule of law was being breached. The test had, indeed, come,[48] but the awareness lagged behind. There was the tragedy. Perhaps it was too much to expect them to see that the road to China, to Southeast Asia, to Singapore, to Pearl Harbor, and "to the beaches of Dunkirk lay through the wastes of Manchuria." [49]

From the very first it was quite clear that the men at Geneva hoped the incident might pass unnoticed or at best that the League would be required to take only a minor part in restoring peace. On the morning of September 19, just before the scheduled meeting of the Council, a number of the chief delegates of the leading states got together privately and decided against bringing up the matter.[50] This, of course, proved

[46] Quoted by Nelson T. Johnson to State Dept., *F.R., 1931*, III, 41.
[47] Felix Morley, *The Society of Nations* (New York, 1932), pp. 433–34.
[48] Hugh Wilson, *Diplomat Between Two Wars* (New York, 1941), pp. 261–62.
[49] Quoted in R. Bassett, *Democracy and Foreign Policy* (New York, 1952), p. 5.
[50] Prentiss Gilbert, the consul in Geneva, to State Dept., Sept. 20, 1931,

impossible. Two nations were fighting, both members of the League. The newspapers reported armies marching and soldiers dying. The affair could hardly be ignored. It was suggested, therefore, by these same delegates, that the Japanese representative, Yoshizawa Kenkichi, himself inform the Council of what had taken place. Presumably, there was a feeling that anxieties could best be allayed and doubts assuaged after a careful and reasonable explanation by the party in control of the situation. Here lay the clue to the position the League was to take in the next few weeks. Japan's intentions were not questioned; Tokyo would be considered to be acting in good faith. The situation would improve if Japan were given the opportunity to work things out without interference.

Although without specific instruction and lacking many details, Yoshizawa rose in the Council chamber on the nineteenth to assure his fellow delegates that all would be well: the army would withdraw and hostilities would cease as soon as order was restored. He spoke frequently during the ensuing days until the Council adjourned on the thirtieth, always on the same note. Japan was in the process of withdrawing, direct negotiations between the disputants would settle all problems, a League commission of inquiry was unnecessary, his government had no designs on Chinese territory, the situation was well on the way to improvement.

These assurances seemed to satisfy the Council completely. The president, Señor Lerroux, publicly announced his pleasure with Japan's promises in the Council on the nineteenth and twenty-fifth and in the Assembly on the twenty-ninth. The only action taken consisted of a request to Tokyo and Nanking on the twenty-second urging both countries to end hostilities and withdraw their troops. Informal discussions of sending a fact-finding mission to the Far East came to naught. Sleeping dogs were permitted to lie quietly and peacefully despite efforts by the Chinese delegate, Alfred Sze, to arouse them. The Chinese were naturally distressed by the Council's apparent calm and confidence in Japanese pledges. Sze kept pointing out that operations were being enlarged, not constricted; advance, not withdrawal, was the order of the day.

F.R., 1931, III, 18–19. See also Walter Lippmann, *The United States in World Affairs, 1931* (New York, 1933), pp. 192–93.

He demanded the appointment of a neutral commission of inquiry and pressed for League of Nations observers to supervise Japanese withdrawal. He threatened to invoke Article XV of the Covenant, thereby requiring the Council to investigate, report, and render a recommendation binding on both parties.[51]

Chinese insistence was tiresome and unavailing. Sir Eric Drummond, the secretary general, refused to permit China to drag the League deeply into the dispute. There was enough danger in dealing with the single item of withdrawal. On the thirtieth, the Council adjourned after adopting a resolution calling on both parties to restore normal relations. The hope was strong on that last day that by the time the Council met again, on October 14, the dark clouds would have passed and the threat to peace would have been laid to rest.[52]

Escape from responsibility, however, was not so easy. In the first few days of October, the Kwantung army moved steadily southward. Newchwang was entered on the fifth, and three days later, twelve planes flying at two thousand feet dropped thirty-six bombs on Chinchow. Sze demanded that the Council be reconvened immediately to deal with the new Japanese aggression. Drummond, along with the members of the Council, were unquestionably disturbed by news of the bombing.[53] Still, the secretary general hesitated to call the session together in advance of the scheduled date. More information was needed, he claimed. It was true enough that the reports of the attack were sketchy, but more than likely Drummond simply wished to delay confronting the Council with a problem grown more difficult. To appease the Chinese and in the absence of something better, on October 9, he cabled notes to Tokyo and Nanking reminding them of their pledges not to aggravate the situation.[54] This action hardly satisfied Mr. Sze. He believed that some strong move would have to be taken by the Council to stem the rising anti-Japanese spirit in China before the celebration of the national holiday on the tenth. People in Nanking were in a belligerent

[51] Gilbert to State Dept., Sept. 26, 1931, *F.R., 1931*, III, 72–73.
[52] For details of the deliberations and discussions in Geneva, see Smith, *The Manchurian Crisis.* The story may also be followed in the dispatches from Prentiss Gilbert in *F.R., 1931*, III, and *F.R., Japan, 1931–1941*, I, *passim.*
[53] *New York Times*, Oct. 9, 1931.
[54] *F.R., 1931*, III, 145–46.

mood. Some days earlier the foreign minister, who was suspected of softness toward Japan, had been badly beaten and cut by a band of students who invaded his house in Nanking. Students all over China were parading, demanding war on Japan. This latest outrage, belying Japanese pledges, had to be punished. Sze pointed out the dangers of throwing China into Russia's arms if help did not come from the West.[55] Drummond budged—barely. He consented to call the Council to meet on October 12 or 13, one or two days before the scheduled session.

So in Geneva passed the first phase of the conflict between Japan and China which was to continue, with only minor interruptions, until 1945. By doing nothing more than sending notes to both contestants urging them to do the right thing and by putting faith in Japan's pledges, the League was losing the opportunity to restore peace. Each day the Mikado's troops entrenched themselves deeper in Manchurian territory, and each step made more difficult the cessation of hostilities. Japanese emotions fed on the army's successes, making any surrender of territory more unlikely. More and more, public passions, whetted by the inflammatory speeches of patriots, swung behind the military. Liberals, such as Professor Yokota Kisaburo of Tokyo Imperial University, cried for moderation and branded the army's move as unwarranted, but their pleas were drowned in the chorus of jingo tirades.[56] The violent voices of men like General Tatekawa and Representative Mori Kaku were louder in advocating an even stronger, more bellicose policy. The Tokyo *Miyako Shimbun* flatly stated that the army must not permit the Foreign Office to settle matters.[57]

Why did the League Council believe peace could be gained by giving Japan time and confidence? Why did not the mem-

[55] This threat the Chinese kept constantly before the League. See a memorandum submitted to the State Department by J[ohn] C. F[erguson], Mar. 11, 1932, D/S File 79.94/4946; also C. V. H. Engert, first secretary of American legation in China, to State Dept., Oct. 23, 1931, D/S File 793.94/2312, and Sir Miles Lampson, British ambassador in China, to Reading, Oct. 8, 1931, *British Documents*, p. 724.

[56] See his pamphlet in *Teikoku Daigaku Shimbun*, Oct. 5, 1931, cited by Takeuchi, *War and Diplomacy*, p. 363, n. 98.

[57] Takeuchi, *War and Diplomacy*, p. 365; see also *Literary Digest*, Oct. 3, 1931, p. 11.

ber states realize that "war is something which must be stopped instantly or it cannot be stopped at all?"[58]

The answer lies in the many complex and elusive factors of which history is made and which lie behind the actions of nations. One thing may be said with certainty: the two great powers, France and Great Britain, which controlled the Council, sympathized with Japan, the strong, Western-type, industrial nation, efficient, enterprising, and cohesive. They despised China as weak and disorganized, torn by civil war and internal strife, incapable of ruling herself or of protecting the rights and interests of foreigners within her borders. Instinctively, they leaned toward Japan and were willing to permit her to work out her own solution. After all, they would have expected the same treatment had they been involved in a similar quarrel with a pesky neighbor or an obstreperous dependency. All the important London dailies reflected this attitude. They agreed that Japan's cause was just and that she served as the civilizing force in the Far East.[59] "The right of a government to protect its interests against barbarism and anarchy is a well-recognized one," intoned the *Daily Telegraph*,[60] while the *Times* viewed Captain Nakamura's death as proof of China's inability to protect foreigners.[61] Many British merchants who had themselves suffered for years from Chinese whimsy took vicarious pleasure from Japan's chastening action,[62] and some Englishmen saw a parallel between Japanese relations with China and England's problem with India (then clamoring for political concessions). They believed Britain might well follow Japan's example in treating with India. Arnold Toynbee, observing the scene in 1932, felt convinced that the governing classes (the "city," Big Business, the professions, the services, the "gentlefolk of

[58] The words are those of Chester Rowell to Nelson T. Johnson, Oct. 11, 1931, Rowell Papers (Bancroft Library, University of California).

[59] D. Morgan, "The League and Manchuria—the Facts," *Welsh Outlook*, 19 (1932), 42–43; K. Martin, "The English Press and the Manchurian Dispute," *Political Quarterly*, 3 (1932), 117–24; Bassett, *Democracy and Foreign Policy*, p. 32. Of the important English newspapers, only the *Manchester Guardian* expressed concern over Japanese acts.

[60] *Daily Telegraph*, Oct. 23, 1931.

[61] London *Times*, Sept. 9, 1931.

[62] E. M. Gull, *British Economic Interests in the Far East* (London, 1943), p. 111.

independent means") favored Japan.[63] The government in power, a coalition National Government, although headed by Labourite Ramsay MacDonald, was composed chiefly of Conservatives, who saw a greater threat from a chaotic China than from a rightist Japan. Indeed, a strong, conservative Japan might well serve as the bulwark against the ominous tide of bolshevism in the Far East which if successful in enveloping China would wipe out the billion-dollar investment in that country. And the possibility of a communist penetration of China did not appear fantastic. The Red leaders, Mao Tse-tung and Chu Teh, controlled large areas in northwestern China and Chiang Kai-shek himself seemed to be drawing closer to Moscow. Abounding in every principal capital were reports and rumors of the imminent resumption of Sino-Soviet diplomatic relations, of large-scale aid pouring into China from Siberia, and of a reconciliation between Nanking and the Chinese Reds. The danger of bolshevism in China appeared very real.[64] Furthermore, the British had, ever since the consummation of the Anglo-Japanese Alliance in 1902, looked to the Japanese to help safeguard their interests in the Far East; and, despite the abrogation of the alliance in 1921 (under American and Canadian pressure), the sentiment of friendliness for the old ally had not died. The immediate reaction of the British ambassador in Tokyo was that Japanese action in Manchuria would probably be good for British interests and Japanese assurances that they had no territorial ambitions "can, we believe here, be accepted as completely genuine." [65]

There were other important and immediate considerations which affected British policy. The depression had crippled industry, finance, and commerce. On September 20, gold payments were suspended; on the following day, the stock exchange closed. The public was so absorbed in the financial situation that no pressure was put on the government to act

[63] Arnold Toynbee, *Survey of International Affairs, 1932* (London, 1933), p. 523, n. 1.

[64] Numerous and frequent warnings to this effect came from the American legation in China (see D/S File 793.94/2312, 1886, 2384, 2885), from Americans traveling in China, and from missionary groups (D/S File 793.94/2110, 2129).

[65] See Lindley to Reading, Sept. 20 and Oct. 1, 1931, *British Documents*, pp. 667 and 701.

in remote Manchuria.[66] In addition, the navy was in sorry shape. Only one week earlier, mutiny had broken out at Invergordon among some sailors who protested recent pay cuts. The cancellations of the annual maneuvers followed. Under these conditions, no government could have dreamed of taking any action on the other side of the world even had it wished to do so. But the important point is that the British government did not have the wish; it was satisfied that the matter was on the way to being solved. Lord Reading, the foreign secretary, made that clear to the American ambassador when he indicated that he regarded the conflict as a local affair, and Undersecretary for Foreign Affairs Anthony Eden made it equally plain to the House of Commons. Even Lord Cecil, the British representative at Geneva, who immediately after the outbreak seemed intent on a strong anti-Japanese policy, receded from his earlier position. Japan was depended upon to wind up the affair as quickly as possible or at least as soon as her rights were secured and the punitive mission accomplished.[67]

The French, although following Britain's lead, saw no reason for meddling. Japan represented law and order, and the Parisian press, with the notable exception of the *Journal des Débats,* gave her open support.[68] Particularly the business and financial interests approved Japan's actions. Their commercial stake in China was slight,[69] but not so their investments, chiefly in Yunnan Province, and they saw in Japan the only restraining hand against the menace of bolshevism and confiscation.[70] It was even conceivable that if Japan pulled Manchuria away from China, France could do the same for Yunnan, which would further protect the colony of Indo-

[66] Ray Atherton, counselor of embassy in Great Britain, to State Dept., Sept. 29, 1931, D/S File 793.94/2051.

[67] Gilbert reported on September 25 the change in Cecil's position, *F.R., 1931,* III, 73; for Eden's statements on September 30 and October 5, see *Parliamentary Debates,* House of Commons, Fifth Series, Vol. 250, pp. 370, 819. Reading's position was reported by Charles G. Dawes, the ambassador in Great Britain, on September 24, 1931. *F.R., 1931,* III, 58.

[68] *New York Times,* Sept. 21, Oct. 10, 16, 1931.

[69] Roger Levy, *French Interests and Policies in the Far East* (New York, 1941), chaps. ii and iii.

[70] Special assistant to the ambassador to France (Dawson) to State Dept., D/S File 793.94/3017. Also Lippmann, *World Affairs, 1932,* p. 520, and K. Radek, "The War in the Far East: A Soviet View," *Foreign Affairs,* X (1932), 553.

China. No one seemed to realize that if Japan took Manchuria, Yunnan and Indo-China might also be on the agenda. Similarly, no one seemed aware that the Japanese move threatened the principle of collective security. Quite the contrary. Frenchmen looked upon Japan's position in Asia as analogous to France's in Europe. China was to Japan as Germany was to France. China claimed duress in the treaty of 1915, as did Germany in the one in 1919. China failed to carry out her treaty obligations; so did Germany. Japan had to send an army into Manchuria; France had to do the same in the Ruhr in 1923 and might well have to do it again.[71] Paul Claudel, the ambassador in Washington, unquestionably reflected the public and official sentiment when on October 12 he let Secretary of State Henry L. Stimson and Undersecretary William R. Castle know where his sympathies lay.[72]

What the other nations in the League thought of the crisis in the Far East never really mattered. Some showed little or no concern, although every country was to feel the effect in the long run. Italians, for example, were completely apathetic. They had practically no interest in eastern Asia. Rome's newspapers generally used the occasion to sneer at the League and pat Japan on the back for contributing to world order.[73] German comment was desultory and restricted to sympathy with China's efforts to break an unfair treaty.[74] Other states appraised the situation as it affected their own peculiar aspirations. Eastern Europeans, filled with fear of Soviet Russia, scouted the possibility of Russian intervention in Manchuria, which would occupy the Bear and permit its neighbors in Europe to breathe more freely.[75] There was even the suggestion some months later of a repetition of Polish action in 1904, when that country offered her help to Japan to fight

[71] One of the most brilliant and perspicacious journalists in Europe, William Martin, editor of the *Journal de Genève*, noted this in an editorial on November 19, 1931. See also Lippmann, *World Affairs, 1932*, pp. 520–22.

[72] Memorandum by William R. Castle, undersecretary of state, Oct. 12, 1931, *F.R., 1931*, III, 165. See also memorandum by the secretary of state, Oct. 12, 1931, D/S File 793.94/2161. The French ambassador in Tokyo shared Claudel's sentiments. See *British Documents*, p. 681.

[73] Ambassador in Italy to State Dept., Oct. 15, Nov. 10, 1931, D/S File 793.94/2118, 2870.

[74] Ambassador in Germany to State Dept., Nov. 19, 1931, D/S File, 793.94/2942.

[75] Minister in Latvia to State Dept., Nov. 21, 1931, D/S File 793.94/2810; Dec. 16, 1931, D/S File 793.94/3360.

Russia.[76] On the other hand, some Poles speculated on the connection between the Japanese move and German ambition to retake the Polish Corridor. If the League proved ineffective in this case, commented one Warsaw newspaper, nothing would stop Germany from breaking the bonds of Versailles and marching eastward.[77] The Dutch, keeping uppermost in mind the security of their vast East Indian empire, frankly applauded Japanese action as a bulwark against Russia. The real danger in the Far East, said the Dutch minister of colonies to the American ambassador at The Hague, is from the Soviet Union.[78] In every country, however, and particularly in the smaller ones, a strong undercurrent of uneasiness gripped many people who believed that the test case for the League of Nations had come, that if the League broke down now, collective security was dead and any talk of disarmament would be futile in the face of the inability of Geneva to guarantee the peace. It was perfectly clear to these people that no hope could be placed in the League, given the French and British attitudes. Only from the United States could real leadership be expected.[79] Hopefully, the leading Rotterdam newspaper predicted that the crisis would carry the United States irresistibly into world affairs. America was bound to extend the Monroe Doctrine to the whole world: "That doctrine will definitely disappear as a result of its generality— swallowed up by the Covenant of the League." [80] The hope, however, was to turn to despair as events in America unfolded.

[76] *Rigasche Rundschau,* Nov. 24, 1931.

[77] *Gazeta Warszawaska,* Dec. 4, 1931.

[78] Ambassador in the Netherlands to State Dept., Nov. 28, 1931, D/S File 793.94/3149.

[79] Minister in Bulgaria to State Dept., Oct. 10, 1931, D/S File 793.94/2289; see also Gilbert to State Dept., Sept. 26, 1931, *F.R., 1931,* III, 70–71.

[80] *Nieuwe Rotterdamsche Courant,* Sept. 25, 1931.

CHAPTER TWO
in which
Stimson remains calm and refuses
to press Japan

The chief lesson I have learned in a long life is that the only way you can make a man trustworthy is to trust him; and the surest way to make him untrustworthy is to distrust him and show your distrust.

HENRY L. STIMSON TO PRESIDENT HARRY S. TRUMAN,
SEPTEMBER 11, 1945

A MERICAN diplomats in the Far East had numerous indications during the summer of 1931 of the danger of an explosion in Manchuria. The staff of the embassy in Tokyo could read in the local press reports that changes were being contemplated for Manchuria and Mongolia.[1] More than that, they could smell an impending storm in the air. The legation in Peking received frequent warnings from consular officers in the principal cities that a crisis was imminent. John Carter Vincent relayed from Mukden the fears of his Japanese colleague,[2] and from Nanking, the seat of the Chinese government, Willys Peck sent a memorandum handed him by the Foreign Affairs Ministry which expressed the deepest concern for the future of Manchuria.[3] Conditions were bad enough for John C. Ferguson, an advisor of the Chinese government, to journey to Peking to tell Minister Johnson bluntly that the Japanese army would occupy Manchuria within a few months.[4] Of great significance, however, was the fact that the American representatives did not share the alarm of their informants. Johnson thought Ferguson's suspicions "incredible, fantastic." He did not even consider the interview or the Peck memorandum important enough to send to the department at once. As for the people in Tokyo, both the ambassador, W. Cameron Forbes, and his counselor, the experienced and knowledgeable Edwin Neville, viewed affairs with such calm as to proceed with plans for Forbes' trip to the United States.

The source of this remarkable confidence is not difficult to determine. It was summed up neatly some months later by a newspaper correspondent who knew the Far East. Writing in March 1932, Rodney Gilbert recalled the recent history of "Japan's conciliatory path toward China and the world. Twenty-four hours before Japan moved in Manchuria, almost any foreign observer would have said that liberalism was too firmly seated in Japan for any kind of reactionary

---

[1] Neville to State Dept., Aug. 1, 1931, D/S File Manchuria/69; see also Journal of W. Cameron Forbes, Series 2, Vol. 4, p. 176 (Library of Congress).

[2] Vincent to State Dept., Aug. 20, 1931, *F.R., 1931*, III, 1–2.

[3] Willys Peck, the consul general at Nanking, to Nelson T. Johnson, Sept. 12, 1931, *F.R., 1931*, III, 5.

[4] Memorandum by Nelson T. Johnson, Sept. 11, 1931, *F.R., 1931*, III, 3.

movement." [5] With this judgment American diplomats in Tokyo would have concurred. They believed that liberal forces were in the ascendancy in Japan. Before them lay sufficient evidence pointing in the direction Japan was traveling: a system of responsible government, acceptance of naval limitation, peaceful China policy, and adult male suffrage, particularly the latter, which, many were convinced, marked "a turning point in Japanese history as great as the Magna Charta's in England." [6] Military action would never be condoned by the Wakatsuki-Shidehara ministry and the Kwantung troops would not dare move in defiance of the civil authority. The assault on Mukden did not shake their confidence. Forbes did not change his plans. He left Tokyo for home on the nineteenth, satisfied by the Foreign Office's assurances that the conflict was nothing more than a local engagement. Indeed, both he and Neville considered his departure from Japan at that time a wise move in that it demonstrated confidence in Shidehara's promise that military action would be halted. [7] Their dispatches to Washington reflected their faith in Japan's leaders. [8] They did not question the genuineness of Shidehara's surprise at the army's move or the possibility that the military could not be curbed.

Given this attitude by the men on the spot and considering their views reported home, Secretary of State Henry L. Stimson's policy is not surprising. He stated it quite clearly in instructions to Hugh Wilson, the American minister in Switzerland, on September 22. "It is apparent," he wrote, "that the Japanese military have initiated a widely extended movement of aggression only after careful preparation. . . . The military chiefs and the Foreign Office are evidently sharply at variance as to intention and opinion. Consequently, it would be advisable . . . that nationalist feeling be not aroused against the Foreign Office in support of the army." [9] Three days earlier, in his first press conference after the outbreak,

[5] New York *Herald Tribune,* Mar. 27, 1932.
[6] Quoted by Robert Schwantes, *Japanese and Americans: A Century of Cultural Relations* (New York, 1955), pp. 100–102.
[7] Forbes, Journal, Series 2, Vol. 3, Sept. 24, 1931.
[8] Forbes to State Dept., Sept. 19, 1931, *F.R., 1931,* III, 11; Neville to State Dept., Sept. 19, 1931, *ibid.,* 13–14, and Sept. 22, 1931, *F.R., Japan, 1931–1941,* I, 4.
[9] *F.R., 1931,* III, 26.

he had been even more explicit in his conviction that the clash had been set in motion by military subordinates in defiance of orders from the Japanese government.[10] Privately, to Debuchi Katsuji, the ambassador in Washington, he gave assurances that Shidchara would not be pushed but would be left unhindered in his efforts to regain control over the military.[11]

The Secretary realized the complexities of the situation. Both sides had grievances, both had cause for complaint, neither nation was completely right or wrong. It was as difficult to determine the true aggressor as it was to decide "who first jostled the other man on a crowded subway train."[12] Before a lasting peace could be achieved in eastern Asia, both powers would have to settle all their problems. In Stimson's view, the Japanese military could not solve the problems in their way—by the sword. Only the civil authorities could resolve the difficulties—by peaceful negotiations. That was why he swung his support to Shidehara. All this did not mean that he was not troubled by the fighting or that he expected it to drag on. He let Debuchi know that if the situation did not improve and hostilities continued, certain treaties might be affected.[13]

The situation did not improve in the days which followed. Reports from Asia indicated that the Kwantung army was enlarging the scope of operations, and in a cruel and ruthless manner.[14] In his diary, Stimson expressed concern that conditions were growing worse;[15] still he kept his peace. Shidehara needed time, and time he would get. The Secretary continued to accept Debuchi's almost daily explanations that his government had disavowed the army's course, that it had no territorial designs on China, and that withdrawal would be effected when Japanese rights were secured. Then negotiations would commence.[16] Stimson's faith did not break, even

[10] *Ibid.*, 15–16.
[11] Sept. 22, 1931, *F.R., Japan, 1931–1941*, I, 5–7.
[12] The words are those of Walter Lippmann, New York *Herald Tribune,* Sept. 29, 1931.
[13] *F.R., Japan, 1931–1941*, I, 5–7; also Diary of Henry L. Stimson, Sept. 22, 1931 (microfilm copy in Yale University Library).
[14] *F.R., 1931*, III, 22, 25–26.
[15] Stimson, Diary, Sept. 21, 1931.
[16] *F.R., 1931*, III, 53–56, 64, 68–69; *F.R., Japan, 1931–1941*, I, 11–12.

though on one occasion, on September 24, he had in his hand a dispatch, which had just come from Mukden, informing him of a new military move at the same time Debuchi was making one of his usual explications. But Stimson considered Shidehara's task a difficult one and was willing to be patient. He knew the foreign minister and the prime minister personally and respected and admired them. While serving as chief of the American delegation to the London Naval Conference in 1930, he had been aware of the foreign minister's efforts to work with the West to reach a limitations agreement. He knew also of the long and arduous fight he had had to wage against the militarists at home before the treaty was accepted by the Diet. He did not question Shidehara's sincerity.[17]

During the first week after the outbreak, Stimson reiterated his position frequently so that American diplomats in Europe and in Asia could have no doubts regarding their government's policy. By telephone and cable he urged Hugh Wilson, Prentiss Gilbert, the consul general in Geneva, and Ambassador-at-Large Norman H. Davis to steer clear of any involvements in the plan supported by Drummond, Cecil, and some of the representatives of the lesser powers for a League of Nations commission of inquiry. Indeed, he pressed them to use their influence to scotch the idea. The oriental mind, he said, did not take to judicial inquiry. Such a move would only inflame nationalist opinion in Japan and jeopardize Shidehara's struggle with the military. He made clear his intention to leave the settlement of the Sino-Japanese question to the two contestants.[18] When all three reported the strong feeling in Geneva and throughout Europe that the United States should sit in the League Council, he flatly refused to give his consent.[19] This decision stemmed in part, no doubt, out of deference to the public feeling against participation in any political questions before the League and from fear of the political repercussions from the remnants of the

[17] *F.R., 1931*, III, 56.
[18] *Ibid.*, 48–49, 50–52, 60–61; *F.R., Japan, 1931–1941*, I, 10–11. He told the Czechoslovakian minister in Washington the same thing. Sept. 24, 1931, D/S File 793.94/1923.
[19] Stimson, Diary, Sept. 23, 1931; Wilson to Stimson, Sept. 24, 1931, D/S File 793.94/19441/2; also Sept. 23, 1931, *F.R., 1931*, III, 40; Gilbert to State Dept., Sept. 23, 1931, *ibid.*, 38.

"Irreconcilables of 1919" to so drastic a step.[20] More important was the fact that Stimson believed the League of Nations approach to the dispute too excited and vehement in pushing the plan for a commission. He feared America's sitting with the Council might be used by the League as a means of threatening Japan.[21] Finally, to Forbes, en route to the United States, the Secretary cabled his veto of the ambassador's desire to turn around and return to Tokyo. The situation did not demand it, he said,[22] so confident was he that all would be well if only the civilian authorities in Japan were given a chance to work matters out without interference.

Stimson's positive policy at this time was to support, by parallel but independent action, the moderate measure taken by the League in its resolutions of September 22. This he did on September 24 in identical notes to the two nations concerned in which he expressed the hope that both would withdraw from the zone of operations and negotiate between themselves all the outstanding problems.[23] As for the inevitable question, put to him at a press conference, of America's position on the Kellogg-Briand Pact for the Outlawing of War and the Nine Power Pact guaranteeing Chinese territorial integrity (both instruments having been signed by Japan and the United States), the matter, for Stimson, was academic, since Japan, in his view, had not violated either treaty. There was no war, merely an attack by unauthorized soldiers. There seemed no doubt that Stimson was fully aware of America's obligations under the treaties, but the occasion for acting was not yet at hand.[24]

The abandonment by the League of the plan for a commission of inquiry and its resolution of September 30 pleased the Secretary. Both nations had accepted the resolution, thereby pledging to withdraw their troops. Negotiations would follow, and all the intricate difficulties could be solved peace-

---

[20] In *The Far Eastern Crisis* (New York, 1936), Stimson recalled that he would have supported sitting in with the Council from the very beginning but the President was opposed (p. 60). However, his contemporary comments on the League's activities do not substantiate his recollection.

[21] Stimson, Diary, Sept. 24 and 25, 1931.

[22] Forbes, Journal, Series 2, Vol. 3, Sept. 27, 1931.

[23] *F.R., 1931*, III, 58.

[24] Stimson to Nelson T. Johnson, Sept. 25, 1931, *F.R., Japan, 1931–1941*, I, 10–11; Stimson to Gilbert, Oct. 5, 1931, *F.R., 1931*, III, 116–17.

fully and without interference. Meanwhile, Stimson quietly, privately, and impartially stimulated both nations to move speedily. The Chinese request to send American observers to Manchuria was firmly refused on the grounds that it might imply taking sides.[25] On his own, however, Stimson had the previous week sent two diplomats, Lawrence E. Salisbury of the embassy staff in Tokyo and George C. Hanson, the consul general at Harbin, to the theater of operations to make a full report. At the same time, he let the Chinese know that he fully supported the League of Nations resolution of September 30, was carefully watching developments, and remained hopeful that they would promptly pull back their forces.[26] To Debuchi and to Shidehara, he strongly recommended an immediate withdrawal of troops.[27]

Stimson's calm confidence received a mighty shock early on the morning of October 8 when news of the Chinchow bombings reached him. This apparently needless and wanton attack on unarmed civilians many miles from the Japanese railroad zone shook him.[28] The scope of the military occupation was being enlarged, not constricted, and Shidehara's pledges seemed empty. There were many disturbing signs pointing to a worsening of the situation. Shidehara had not reprimanded the army for the bombings; indeed, he himself stated that the incident was of little importance,[29] and he had as yet not really voiced any severe indictment of the military. Did this mean that the split between army and Cabinet was a fiction? Hugh Byas, reporting to the *New York Times* from Tokyo, thought this to be the case.[30] Furthermore, the prospect of withdrawal of troops was not bright. A bulletin issued by the Japanese General Staff declared withdrawal impossible as long as Chinese bandits continued to operate.[31] Information from Tokyo via Neville, from Nanking via Hallett Abend of the *New York Times,* and from Geneva via

[25] Stimson to Johnson, Oct. 5, 1931, *F.R., 1931,* III, 115, 116.
[26] *Ibid.,* 117–18.
[27] Memorandum by Stimson of conversation with Debuchi, Oct. 3, 1931, *ibid.,* 108–109; Stimson to Neville, Oct. 3, 1931, *ibid.,* 110.
[28] Stimson, Diary, Oct. 8, 1931. Chester Rowell, in a letter to his wife on October 11, compared Chinchow to Sarajevo. Rowell Papers.
[29] Neville to State Dept., Oct. 10, 1931, *F.R., Japan, 1931–1941,* I, 18–19.
[30] Oct. 10, 1931.
[31] Neville to State Dept., Oct. 8, 1931, *F.R., Japan, 1931–1941,* I, 14–15.

Gilbert corroborated the statement in the bulletin. There would be no move by the Japanese army *until* China assured the safety of Japanese property and nationals. Stimson's whole case rested on withdrawal followed by assurances on both sides.[32]

Still, Stimson believed all would be well. There were assurances which bolstered his faith in Shidehara and in his own policy. Neville reported that the General Staff bulletin was not a government pronouncement, that the vice-minister of foreign affairs had assured him that withdrawal would precede negotiations.[33] He pointed out the difficulty of Shidehara's position in view of the excited state of public opinion stemming from the Chinese boycott of Japanese goods. Again, he warned that only direct negotiations could settle the problem; there must be no outside mediation.[34] From Mukden, Consul General Myers sent word of the anarchic conditions in the capital, which almost demanded continued patrolling by Japanese troops.[35] And there was always Debuchi, calming the Secretary's fears by repeated avowals of his chief's good intentions. The foreign minister, he said in an interview with Stimson and William R. Castle on October 12, was confronted with an extremely delicate situation in combating the jingo element, but he would triumph and be free to pursue his peaceful China policy.[36]

But Stimson's patience was being tried. He accepted Debuchi's guarantees and said he appreciated Shidehara's difficulty, yet expected more rapid results. He began to think about prodding the foreign minister by injecting a catalyst into the situation. The policy of patient prying might have to be supplemented by lighting a fire under the people of Tokyo. He told Debuchi quite firmly of his displeasure over the bombing and cabled Neville to get an explanation from the Foreign Office for the aerial action fifty miles from the railway zone.[37] Again he urged the Japanese ambassador to

[32] Neville to State Dept., Oct. 5, 1931, *F.R.*, *1931*, III, 114-15; *New York Times*, Oct. 6, 1931; Gilbert to State Dept., Oct. 12, 1931, *F.R.*, *1931*, III, 158-59.
[33] *F.R.*, *1931*, III, 113-14; *F.R.*, *Japan*, *1931-1941*, I, 18-19.
[34] *F.R.*, *Japan*, *1931-1941*, 21-22; *F.R.*, *1931*, III, 147-48.
[35] *F.R.*, *1931*, III, 186.
[36] *Ibid.*, 166; *F.R.*, *Japan*, *1931-1941*, I, 22-23
[37] *F.R.*, *Japan*, *1931-1941*, I, 20, 21.

effect a withdrawal.[38] And he was prepared to go further. He was now in favor of resorting to the Kellogg-Briand Pact, which would emphasize the seriousness of the situation for the world and for the two powers involved by recognizing the imminence of a state of war. This action, he suggested, lay in the League's province. He instructed Gilbert on October 9 to get Drummond to call the Council into session as quickly as possible and discuss the invocation of the pact. America would act concurrently if such action were taken, he promised, and would even sit in on Council discussions, if invited.[39] But Drummond refused to rise to the bait. For one thing, the pact had nothing to do with the League. For another, a double jurisdiction would be created, he claimed, which would complicate matters. Either party would have the privilege of choosing for their points of reference the pact or Article XI of the Covenant. The discussion would be on two different planes, making any agreement impossible. Worse yet, invocation of the pact would virtually admit the existence of a war, which might lead to League action under Article XVI and bring into play international sanctions against one or the other of the parties. A real war might then ensue. Why should not the United States, rather, remind China and Japan of the dangers of a violation of the pact, which need be only a warning by one power and not involve the League and its machinery?[40] Now it was Stimson's turn to decline the bait. For America to invoke the pact would be to deprive it of the force of *world* opinion. That is, after all, said Stimson, where its strength lay—in universality of condemnation.[41]

No doubt Stimson's point on the matter of universality was sound, but it was hardly the real reason for his refusal to take the initiative. He still hoped for and expected a solution to be reached by direct negotiations between the two nations after Shidehara reasserted his authority over the army. His policy was still based on Japanese sincerity and good intentions. Any American move which might be interpreted as putting the onus on Japan would serve only to incur that nation's animosity. And surely, Stimson's leadership in invoking the

[38] Oct. 10, 1931, *F.R., 1931*, III, 153.
[39] *Ibid.*, 146–54.
[40] Gilbert to State Dept., Oct. 11, 1931, D/S File 793.94/2058.
[41] Stimson to Gilbert, Oct 12, 1931, *F.R., 1931*, III, 168.

Briand-Kellogg Pact would do just that. He was not going to let the League dump the crisis in America's lap.[42] Japan must have no reason to suspect Washington of any sentiments other than the friendliest. This explains Stimson's great care when he suggested to Gilbert, on October 13, the possibility of aiding direct negotiations through the appointment, by Drummond, of neutral observers who might give moral protection during the deliberations to Chinese overawed by Japanese military preponderance. He warned Gilbert to guard the source of the suggestion lest Japan be irritated.[43] This also explains his request, on the same day, to the Navy Department to order elements of the Asiatic Fleet away from Chefoo, which was across the Gulf of Pechihli from Dairen and on the supply route from Osaka to Manchuria, to scotch a report in the New York *Daily Graphic* that American submarines were lying in wait, ready to pounce on the Japanese.[44] This accounts, too, for his renewed assurances to Debuchi.[45]

In the end, Drummond backed down and agreed to discuss the pact when the Council reconvened. America's participation in the Council's deliberations was greatly desired, and it could be secured only on that condition. Stimson won a real diplomatic victory in shifting to the League's sphere of responsibility the question of the pact, thus relieving himself of any undesirable unilateral action and the accompanying onus.

So passed, in Washington, the first phase of the Sino-Japanese dispute. Years later, in recording his long public service, Stimson called Pearl Harbor the logical results of events begun in Manchuria,[46] but during this first month of the crisis that realization had not yet dawned. He operated on the same assumption which underlay the statement he made at the close of the London Naval Conference. At that time he spoke of "our good neighbors across the Pacific" and said that the treaty "insures the continuous growth of our friendship

---

[42] Stimson, Diary, Oct. 9, 1931; Diary of William R. Castle, Oct. 13, 1931 (in possession of Mr. Castle); New York *Herald Tribune*, Oct. 14, 1931; *New York Times*, Oct. 15, 1931.
[43] *F.R., 1931*, III, 176–77.
[44] Stimson, Diary, Oct. 13, 1931.
[45] *F.R., 1931*, III, 166.
[46] Henry L. Stimson and McGeorge Bundy, *On Active Service in Peace and War* (New York, 1947), p. 220.

with that great nation toward whom we have grown to look for stability and progress in the Far East." [47] One key to Stimson's failure to grasp at once the full and dire implications of the September 18 assaults lay in his misinterpretation of the course of events in Japan and of the nature of the structure of politics in the Island Empire. He underestimated the power of the military and overestimated Shidehara's strength.[48] But there were other important factors which affected his policy. For one thing, the complexity of the international problems which confronted him was staggering. Disarmament, debts, reparations, and the world depression all demanded his attention. In fact, in a letter to the British prime minister on September 25, he did not even mention the Far Eastern crisis in recounting the difficulties at hand but talked only of economic problems.[49]

In addition, the state of America's defenses would have precluded Stimson's taking any course calculated even remotely to involve the use of force. The navy, the first line of defense, was in no position to support a bellicose policy. Budget cuts were threatening to reduce the enlisted strength, close two shipyards and one training station, and place one-third of the fleet out of service (on an annual rotation basis). No new keels were to be laid in 1932–33, while six of the eleven destroyers authorized for construction in the current year were to be postponed or abandoned. Lack of funds in 1930–31 had prevented landing-force exercises and other strategic and tactical training; no improvement in this area was in the offing. The United States had one more battleship than Japan, but the Japanese had many more light and heavy cruisers and one more aircraft carrier. Their superiority would be increased within the next few years, by their regular annual building program, up to the strength allowed by the Washington and London naval treaties. Furthermore, their advantage was even greater than any numerical superiority might indicate because of the world-wide dispersal of the American fleet and the absence of American bases in the Far

[47] U.S. Department of State, *Proceedings of the London Naval Conference of 1930 and Supplementary Documents* (Conference Series, No. 6, Washington, 1931), p. 106.
[48] Schwantes, *Japanese and Americans*, p. 100.
[49] Henry L. Stimson Papers, Box 27 (Yale University Library).

East. Japan could concentrate her vessels in one relatively small area and in proximity to her home bases. American supply lines reached thousands of miles across the Pacific, with no strong way stations for protection. At Guam, Midway, Samoa, and the Aleutians there were no fortifications, and none could be built because of the restrictions of Article XIX of the Treaty of 1922. Corregidor was the only fort in the Far East, and, being thirty-five hundred miles from Hawaii and only one thousand from Japan, it could not be expected to resist.[50] As would any good diplomatist, Stimson was operating within his military capabilities, although later on, out of desperation, he moved in the direction of transgressing this cardinal rule. It was estimated that five years would be necessary to prepare for a war with Japan.[51] The Secretary in 1931 had only moral armaments. To have brandished a pistol without having been prepared to shoot would have been a most dangerous policy.

Finally, Stimson had to act under another stricture: the mood and will of the American people. Since the end of World War I, Americans had made clear their intention to avoid international complications which might require the use of force. No political commitments and no guarantees of armed assistance were the twin facets of the American credo in the twenties. In a speech on Armistice Day, 1929, President Herbert Hoover reflected the spirit of the American people when he remarked that "the European nations have, by the Covenant of the League of Nations, agreed that if nations fail to settle their differences peaceably then force should be applied by other nations to compel them to be reasonable. We have refused to travel this road. We are confident that at least in the Western hemisphere public opinion will suffice to check violence. This is the road we propose to travel." And a few months later he said: "The instinct of the vast majority of our people is that our contribution is not to be based upon

[50] *Annual Report of the Navy Department, 1931;* see also Annual Report of the Commander-in-Chief, Asiatic Fleet, 1931, Navy Department Records, FF6/A9–1 (310718) (National Archives), and New York *Herald Tribune,* Oct. 2, 3, 16, 1931. Admiral Montgomery M. Taylor, commanding the Asiatic Fleet, complained about the wretched condition of his ships. Taylor to Admiral W. V. Pratt, chief of naval operations. Dec. 17, 1931, Montgomery M. Taylor Papers, Box 269 (Library of Congress).
[51] Herbert Hoover, *Memoirs, 1920–1933* (New York, 1952), p. 368.

commitments to use force to maintain peace. . . . I believe
it is clear that the United States can more effectively and
wisely work for peace without commitments to use coercion
to enforce settlement." Moral support to preserve peace, yes—
and both the Nine Power Treaty and the Kellogg-Briand Pact
provided only for consultation in the event of a breach. As
for the Far East, few Americans, if any, were willing to sanction a firm course which might lead to involvement. Again,
the President spoke for the vast majority of Americans when
he said that "neither our obligations to China, nor our own
interests, nor our dignity require us to go to war over these
questions." [52] True, the United States had at the turn of the
century taken the lead in pressing for the preservation of
Chinese territorial integrity and for equality of commercial
opportunity, in the Open Door notes of 1899 and 1900, but,
again, never was it intended that force be used to implement
the policy. American economic and strategic interests in that
area were never considered great enough to warrant active
defense. Americans bought, sold, and invested in eastern Asia,
but in relatively small amounts. China and Japan accounted
for only 12 per cent of the total American export and 28
per cent of the total import. As for investments, $241,000,000
worth of Japanese and Chinese bonds were held on this side
of the Pacific, and approximately $700,000,000 in capital out-
lay had been put out by American businesses in those countries, only 1.5 per cent of the total United States foreign
investment.[53] Nor was American security deemed to be threatened in eastern Asia. The flag flew over the Philippines, but
those islands had been written off as a strategic liability by
the first Roosevelt and the movement to cast them adrift was
already well under way. Stimson, again, in good diplomatic
fashion, was operating within the limits of public opinion,
without which no foreign policy can be successfully pursued.

      During this first month of the crisis, the Secretary worked
under ideal conditions, unhindered and unencumbered by
the usual impediments which hamper a secretary of state.

[52] W. S. Myers, *Foreign Policies of Herbert Hoover, 1929–1933* (New York,
1940), pp. 156–58.
[53] Institute of Pacific Relations, *Conflict in the Far East, 1931–1932*, dis-
cusses the American stake in China and Japan; see also G. H. Blakeslee, "The
Foreign Stake in China," *Foreign Affairs*, X (1931), 81–91, and *Department of
Commerce Year Book, 1931* (Washington, 1932).

The President, preoccupied on the domestic front, gave all his attention to battling the ravages of the depression and gave Stimson a free hand, which the Secretary used liberally. He made policy virtually alone, although the President was kept fully informed.[54] Congress was not in session, and this liberated him from many of the most vexing and embarrassing predicaments which may descend upon a Cabinet officer from the direction of Capitol Hill. There were no questions to answer, no diplomatic correspondence to produce, no public investigations, no personal criticism, no challenges, no suggestions of how better it might be done. Stimson had these precious assets: freedom from pressures, time, secrecy. Yet he had complete approval from the public at large as well as from his own official family.

His subordinates in the department agreed unanimously with his policy of caution and moderation, of acting within American capabilities, and of recognizing Japan's legitimate interests. Although he worked most closely with his own special assistant, Allen T. Klots, and did not always confide fully in the other officers, he did consult with them and solicit their views.[55] The undersecretary, William R. Castle, while by no means a Japanophile, had long believed that Japanese preponderance was inevitable in eastern Asia. To him, Japan's role in that area was not unlike America's in the Western Hemisphere. While serving as American ambassador in Tokyo in 1930, he had said as much on many occasions, publicly and privately.[56] Much as United States security demanded control over Nicaragua, so did Japan need to exert hegemony over Manchuria, he believed; and he was convinced that America's interest in the Far East would be best served by a strong Japan as guarantor of order, progress, and peace. He made perfectly plain in conversation with a French editor

---

[54] Stimson, Diary, Sept. 30, 1931.

[55] William R. Castle to the author, June 4, 1956. Forbes complained bitterly that Stimson frequently bypassed him by negotiating with the Japanese government through the Japanese ambassador in Washington. Forbes, Journal, Series 2, Vol. 4, pp. 16–17. The British ambassador in Tokyo also believed that Forbes was ill-informed. See *British Documents*, p. 856.

[56] See, for example, his final speech as ambassador, May 6, 1930, reported in *Japan Times*, May 7, 1930; also his speech of Feb. 3, 1930, printed in *Trans-Pacific*, same date; also copy of an extemporaneous address made April 4, 1930, in D/S File 123 Castle/38. See also the editorial in *Jiji Shimpo*, May 23, 1930, for a very favorable appraisal of Castle by the Japanese.

in October that "if Japan is in Manchuria, it is owing to treaty rights conceding a police zone to her. It may be that Japan exceeded her rights in encroaching on the limits of the zone, but there can be no discussion about the fact that she was provoked by China to do so. If we want Japan to go back to her zone, we have also to bear pressure upon China to cease her bloody and endless provocations. The two things go hand in hand." [57] Although he admitted that Japan had played fast and loose with the treaties, he considered her "our one useful friend in the Orient." [58]

Stanley K. Hornbeck, chief of the Far Eastern Division, was no friend of Japan. He was appalled by the move of the army in Manchuria and his immediate reaction was to condemn Japan and brand her an outlaw. To Castle on September 25, he sent an editorial from the *Manchester Guardian* which urged invocation of the Kellogg-Briand Pact by the world powers and which warned that the attack threatened all nations. His comment was that the writer of the editorial had his head "well screwed on." [59] To Stimson on the twenty-fourth, he suggested that direct negotiations between China and Japan were not advisable, for in such a settlement Japan would have the advantage, thereby leaving irritations likely to lead to a real war.[60] But soon he came around to believing that the United States should keep out of the Manchurian muddle lest a precedent for intervening be set in an area where trouble was constant. Any co-operation by the United States with other powers for ending the fighting should be taken as part of the international peace movement rather than as an aspect of Far Eastern policy. By the end of September, he had gone so far as to agree with Castle that stability in Asia could best be achieved by Japanese control over Manchuria.[61]

After the Chinchow bombing, both Castle and Hornbeck gave their approval to the decision reached at a Cabinet meeting on October 9: [62] that the United States must not take the

[57] Stephane Lauzanne was the editor. See the account of the conversation in the *Far Eastern Review*, 28 (1932), 490.

[58] Castle, Diary, Sept. 29, 1932.

[59] D/S File 793.94/1981.

[60] D/S File 793.94/1978–1/6.

[61] Memorandum by Hornbeck, Sept. 24, D/S File 793.94/1889; also Castle, Diary, Sept. 29, 1931.

[62] Stimson, Diary, Oct. 10, 1931.

leadership in any move calculated to be considered anti-Japanese but should support League action.[63] Neither was enthusiastic for Stimson's plan to have the Kellogg-Briand Pact invoked by the League, with the United States participating in the discussion with the Council. Castle feared Japan might see the hand of Stimson guiding the Council, while Hornbeck saw no necessity for using the pact in view of Japan's anticipated withdrawal.[64]

As far as the public was concerned, support was almost universal and Stimson could operate without carping or pressure from press or interest groups, except for one dedicated and insistent executive of a peace organization—Dorothy Detzer. The Secretary had feared that his policy of giving Japan time would be endangered by an inflamed public opinion aroused by newspaper goading and by the numerous peace-society workers excited at the outbreak of fighting. To a friend he wrote, "I hope that our peace people at home will be reasonable about such a difficult situation. They are not always reasonable." [65] As for the press, he appealed to some of the senior Washington correspondents, whom he met privately in his home, for patience and self-control.[66] But his fears were groundless. Both press and public maintained a calm attitude and gave approval to his policy.

There seems to have been a general feeling that while the Japanese had suffered provocation by the Chinese, they ought not to have resorted to force.[67] It was believed, however, that the civilian authorities in Tokyo did not condone the army's action and would soon gain sufficient control to end hostilities and negotiate differences with China peacefully.[68] There was considerable sympathy for the Chinese, who awakened images of hard-working laundrymen in America or pitifully paid coolies at home drowned by constant floods and starved by

[63] Castle, Diary, Oct. 10, 1931.
[64] *Ibid.;* also memorandum by Hornbeck, Oct. 13, 1931, D/S File 793.94/2239. This action pleased Nelson T. Johnson, who had from the beginning plumped for invoking the pact. He did not agree with Stimson's differentiating between the military and the Foreign Office. See his dispatch to Stimson, Sept. 22, 1931, *F.R., Japan, 1931–1941,* I, 4–5. Johnson's counselor of legation strongly favored Japan; see Castle, Diary, Oct. 6, 1931.
[65] To Frederic Coudert, Oct. 9, 1931, Stimson Papers, Box 27.
[66] Stimson, *The Far Eastern Crisis,* p. 72.
[67] *Christian Century,* Oct. 7, 1931, pp. 1230–31; *New Republic,* Sept. 30, 1931, p. 167.
[68] *Christian Century,* Sept. 30, 1931, pp. 1196–97; *New Republic,* Oct. 7, 1931, p. 191.

perpetual famine. Almost every Christian American had some connection with the vast missionary endeavor in China, if only to the extent of a few pennies tossed into the collection plate on Mission Sunday.[69] But never were these sentiments made grounds for proposing rash action against Japan. Americans did not want to get embroiled in any foreign wars; they had enough to occupy them in staving off the numbing effects of the depression. The fall of 1931 found unemployment, foreclosures, bankruptcies, and bank suspensions at a high point.[70] The *New York Times* reported from Washington Stimson's view of the fighting and his confidence that the army would be bridled and gave him editorial support. It urged no pressure on Tokyo. Japan wanted peace, not territorial aggrandizement. The crisis was near solution, said an editorial, with the imminent withdrawal of the Japanese army to the railway zone. A commission of inquiry was unnecessary. Direct negotiations provided the only solution.[71] Senator William E. Borah was roundly castigated for a severe indictment of Japan which he made in a speech on September 24.[72] Even after the Chinchow bombing, the *Times* retained its composure. The situation does not call for threats or minatory gestures, ran an editorial, but for consultation and representation.[73] No sides should be taken or action contemplated in behalf of either country. On October 14, a news item announced an atmosphere of increasing optimism in Washington that the crisis would be settled amicably.

The New York *Herald Tribune* treated the affair in the same way. Editorial columns favored Japan; they pointed to the failure by the Chinese to provide adequate protection in Manchuria and warned that nothing must be done to weaken the hand of the civilian authorities.[74] And from its pages the

[69] There were about 5,000 Protestant and 3,000 Roman Catholic missionaries in China. They operated 307 hospitals, 750 dispensaries, 5 medical schools, and 13 colleges or universities.

[70] Both the New York *Herald Tribune* and the *New York Times* featured front-page items concerning recovery measures in their September 19 editions. News of the Japanese seizure of Mukden appeared in the left-hand columns of the first page.

[71] Sept. 20, 22, 25, 27, 29, 1931.

[72] Editorial, Sept. 26, 1931.

[73] Editorials, Oct. 10, 14, 1931.

[74] Sept. 23, 1931. A series of four articles by the Tokyo correspondent, Victor Keen, September 28–October 1, gave the background of the dispute with pro-Japanese overtones.

mighty and authoritative voice of Walter Lippmann rang forth in approbation. "The immediate need," he wrote, "is to . . . gain time in which to devise an arrangement which assures safety of the Japanese and Chinese respect for Japanese treaty rights. We must play no favorites. We must not support Chinese violations of treaties and we must show the Japanese we wish to settle the problem by pacific means." [75] Across the country, other newspapers voiced a "go slowly" policy.[76] No wonder Stimson recalled some years later how the press had striven "to protect me from having my elbow joggled during the ticklish times through which we were passing." [77]

Peace groups in the United States were, quite naturally, greatly upset that war had erupted in Asia, but within their councils there was great uncertainty about the wisest course for the government to follow. To fight fire with fire was repugnant to the majority of peace workers, and the only alternative was to hope, along with Stimson, for the eventual settlement of the controversy by peaceful negotiations after the civilians in Tokyo regained control over the army. At a meeting of the Emergency Peace Committee in New York on September 29, a resolution was proposed to form a committee to call upon the Secretary of State and urge him to abandon his timid and hesitant policy, which endangered the cause of disarmament and pacifism, and to stand on the Kellogg-Briand Pact and the Nine Power Treaty. There was powerful opposition to the resolution, for it implied advocacy of strong action, which itself might lead to more war. Only the unflagging and militant drive of the executive secretary of the Women's International League for Peace and Freedom, Dorothy Detzer, who had been the chief force in proposing the resolution, pushed it through.[78] The committee was appointed and, on October 5, called on Stimson but did not convey to him the Detzer view. Instead, the three delegates evinced

[75] New York *Herald Tribune*, Oct. 14, 1931. Privately he wrote to Stimson applauding the Secretary's wise policy. Oct. 1, 1931, Stimson Papers, Box 14.
[76] *Literary Digest*, Oct. 10, 1931, p. 11.
[77] Stimson, *The Far Eastern Crisis*, p. 72. The allegation by Sara Smith in *The Manchurian Crisis*, p. 79, that Stimson's reiteration of Japan's good intentions made impossible American public support for strong measures does not seem valid in view of the attitude of the press and public.
[78] See Report of the Executive Secretary of the Women's International League for Peace and Freedom, June–October 1931 (copy in Swarthmore College Peace Collection [hereafter cited as SCPC]).

satisfaction with his policy of peace.[79] Similarly, the National
Council for the Prevention of War went on record as approv-
ing Stimson's cautious and peaceful program.[80] Miss Detzer,
singlehanded, carried her own standard. She addressed an
open letter, in the name of her organization, to President
Hoover urging him to take action by "immediately demanding that 'the sovereignty, the independence, and the territorial and administrative integrity of China' be observed by
all parties to the [Kellogg-Briand] pact." [81] She also hounded
Hornbeck at the State Department, insisting that action be
taken and maintaining that the Japanese were guilty of clear-
cut aggression. How well she personified the paradox of the
militant, belligerent peace advocate! Hornbeck put her off,
artfully yet firmly, and there is no evidence that she unduly
distressed him or Stimson.[82]

Stimson's policy at this stage cannot be called pro-Japanese.
His support to Shidehara was geared to a broader purpose of
providing an equitable solution to the problems of both powers. His was a program of playing no favorites, of watchful
waiting, and of letting time and sanity solve the issue. Yet the
Japanese government and people considered him their good
friend and were extremely grateful for his confidence and
patience. His refusal to sanction a commission of inquiry and
his careful handling of the American press, to which was
ascribed its moderate tone, pleased them, although there were
rumblings of dissatisfaction over Stimson's reported plan to
invoke the Kellogg-Briand Pact and join in Council deliberations.[83]

The Chinese, on the other hand, felt betrayed. They had
hoped, from the very beginning, that the United States would
take the lead in driving the Japanese out of Manchuria. Not
much was expected from the League of Nations because of
Japan's powerful voice in the Council,[84] although, as a Shang-

[79] Stimson, Diary, Oct. 6, 1931.
[80] National Council for the Prevention of War, *News Bulletin*, X (October 1931), 1.
[81] The open letter was published in the *New York Times* on September 24, 1931. The original is in the Emily Balch Papers, SCPC.
[82] Annual Report of the Executive Secretary of the Women's International League for Peace and Freedom, April 14, 1932 (copy in SCPC); see also Horn-beck's memorandum, D/S File 793.94/1910.
[83] Stimson, Diary, Sept. 28, 1931; see also Tokyo *Asahi*, cited in *Trans-Pacific*, Oct. 8, 1931.
[84] Alfred Sze to Gilbert, Sept. 20, 1931, *F.R., 1931*, III, 18–19.

hai newspaper pointed out, all nations ought to be able to see the similarity between the Manchurian invasian and the Twenty-one Demands of 1915 when under cover of a world war Japan moved to dominate China.[85] But the United States, acting independently, was looked to for help.[86] Exactly what kind of help was never made clear. After considering the consequences of resorting to the Kellogg-Briand Pact, the Chinese apparently decided against it on the grounds that admission of a state of war might give Japan an excuse for a full-scale conquest of Manchuria.[87] As for the Nine Power Treaty, it seemed that they preferred American unilateral action to international action, although an occasional appeal to the treaty was made. They just expected, somehow, that Stimson would wave a magic wand. T. V. Soong, the finance minister, put it this way: "All that it [China] asks is that the United States government may take the first steps which it may find possible in order to ensure the prompt and complete withdrawal of the Japanese troops." [88] Chinese in the United States and in Hawaii made frequent appeals to the United States government not to leave the mother country alone to face formidable Japan.[89] Help was not forthcoming, however, and the Chinese were bitter. They were saddened, too, that America treated both nations alike, not differentiating between the aggressor and the aggrieved. How could Stimson act so calmly in the face of Japanese military ruthlessness? Could he not see the danger of world conflict if Japan were not stopped? Some Chinese suspected that the United States and Great Britain had given Japan the green light in Manchuria twenty-four hours before the attack.[90] There was a rumor in Europe, too, that they had struck a bargain with the Japanese at the London Naval Conference in 1930—free hand in Manchuria for a naval-limitations treaty.[91] Soong only believed that Stimson had been badly hoodwinked by Shidehara's plea that any firm action would play into the hands of the army and en-

[85] *Shanghai Pao*, cited in *Literary Digest*, Oct. 31, 1931, pp. 11–12.
[86] T. V. Soong, minister of finance, to Peck, Oct. 11, 1931, *F.R., 1931*, III, 170.
[87] The record of Chinese indecision on this point may be followed in *F.R., 1931*, III, 12, 24; D/S File 793.94/1854, 1903; and Nelson T. Johnson Papers, Conversations, 1931, Sept. 19, 23, 1931 (Library of Congress).
[88] Soong to Peck, Oct. 6, 1931, *F.R., 1931*, III, 126.
[89] See numerous memorials, D/S File 793.94/1810, 1819, 1835.
[90] Nelson T. Johnson to State Dept., Sept. 22, 1931, *F.R., 1931*, III, 27.
[91] *Journal de Genève*, Oct. 25, Dec. 19, 1931.

courage a military dictatorship.[92] But he did consider the Secretary in some way responsible for the failure by the League to take any really strong action against Japan, claiming that the Council's diminished interest in the crisis reflected Stimson's own satisfaction with Japan's pledges.[93]

Not only Soong believed this. Many diplomats in Geneva shared the view, [94] and William Martin in his *Journal de Genève* quite emphatically attributed the Council's weakness to Stimson's policy of giving Shidehara a chance to consolidate his position.[95] In London, the editor of *The New Statesman* similarly placed the onus on the United States for the failure of the League's commission plan. America's refusal to accede, he wrote, stiffened Japan's determination to resist.[96] There was some truth, of course, to this assumption. America's position counted heavily in Geneva. Without her concurrence, no program would have been effectual, and Stimson did let Drummond know at once of his objection to the inquiry idea.[97] He also promptly informed the British chargé in Washington of his disapproval.[98] But while his disapprobation unquestionably counted, there is no reason to believe it was the crucial factor. Neither the British nor the French nor Drummond himself was willing to support any action, a commission of inquiry or anything else, to which Japan was violently opposed,[99] and Japan was opposed to any interposition by any third party between herself and China. For various reasons already mentioned, no one in authority was prepared, as yet, to beard Japan. If there is any blame to be assessed at this stage, it must be evenly placed on the shoulders of all who might have acted but did not.

[92] Consul General Peck reported Soong's views to Nelson T. Johnson, who conveyed them to Washington. *F.R., 1931*, III, 134–35.
[93] Soong to Peck, Sept. 30, 1931, *F.R., 1931*, III, 104–105.
[94] Peck to State Dept., Sept. 27, 1931, *ibid.*, 80–81.
[95] Oct. 16, 1931.
[96] Supplement, Oct. 8, 1931, p. 421.
[97] Stimson to Hugh Wilson, Sept. 23, 1931, *F.R., 1931*, III, 48–50.
[98] Memorandum by Castle of a conversation with the British chargé, Sept. 24, 1931, *ibid.*, 63.
[99] Reading's caution, his lack of apprehension, and his acceptance of the Japanese pledge to withdraw were reported by Ambassador Dawes. *Ibid.*, 57–58. The British chargé agreed in regard to the unwisdom of a commission of inquiry.

WARREN'S

CHAPTER THREE
in which
Japan ignores the League of Nations
and the world

The vital interests of the Japanese . . . [are] in Manchuria and Korea. It is, therefore, peculiarly our interest not to take any steps as regards Manchuria which will give the Japanese cause to feel, with or without reason, that we are hostile to them, or a menace—in however slight a degree—to their interests.
THEODORE ROOSEVELT, 1909

THE COUNCIL of the League of Nations met on October 13 and immediately took up the question of inviting the United States to participate in the forthcoming discussions on the Kellogg Pact. This move surprised no one; it came as the logical culmination of the period of co-operation and of parallel but independent action by the United States during the preceding month. Active and positive collaborations had been desired and sought by Geneva from the outset.[1] Washington's views were easily as important as those of London or Paris. Hugh Wilson, the minister to Switzerland, met regularly with Drummond before and after sessions.[2] Before the Council reached a decision, American attitudes were solicited, and after a decision had been made, American support was eagerly awaited.[3] Neither Wilson nor Prentiss Gilbert, the consul at Geneva, had been asked to sit in with the Council because its deliberations concerned procedures under the Covenant, to which, of course, the United States had not subscribed. Now, however, the discussions were to be geared to the Kellogg Pact, to which America was a signatory, and so a basis for an invitation existed.

The decision to tender the invitation, made on October 15, was not reached without difficulty. So radical a departure from the norm as the participation by a nonmember state disturbed some of the delegates, who feared the effect of such a portentous precedent. Particularly upset were those who themselves had no seat on the Council or who represented smaller states and resented the usurpation of authority by the big powers on the Council who initiated the move. But the salutary consequences expected from active co-operation by the United States canceled the objections and assuaged the doubts.[4] The real trouble arose from Japan's strenuous opposition.[5] Tokyo made every effort to keep the United States off the Council, ostensibly on juridical grounds but really for political rea-

[1] Wilson to State Dept., Sept. 21, 22, 1931, F.R., *1931*, III, 22, 37; Gilbert to State Dept., Sept. 22 and Oct. 14, 1931, *ibid.*, 27-28, 35-36, 195.
[2] Wilson, *Diplomat Between Two Wars*, 260.
[3] *New York Times*, Sept. 22, 1931.
[4] Gilbert to State Dept., Oct. 27, 1931, D/S File 793.94/2362; also Nov. 9, 1931, reporting a conversation with Drummond, F.R., *1931*, III, 401.
[5] Gilbert to State Dept., Oct. 13, 1931, F.R., *1931*, III, 188; also Tokyo *Asahi*, Oct. 16, 1931.

sons. Shidehara and his colleagues in the Cabinet believed themselves immune from any strong League action as long as Washington and Geneva were kept apart and did not act in concert. No good could come from collaboration, which might well have the effect of stiffening the League's resolve by the mere presence of the great transatlantic power. It was not expected that the United States would act as a brake on the Council in view of the language Stimson used in his October 9 note to the League, in which he suggested that "the League . . . assert all the pressure and authority within its competence." These words Japanese newspapermen interpreted as hostile and aroused a sensation in the press.[6] It was also feared that Stimson might be inclined to push matters because of the impatience and bellicosity of the Chinese. Chiang Kai-shek had issued a virtual ultimatum to the world on October 12, promising to plunge the Far East into a terrible war "if [the] signatories to [the] League and Kellogg Pact fail to uphold their sacred duties," and the pronouncement was given front-page coverage in the *New York Times*.[7] Nor did Tokyo wish to see the Kellogg Pact invoked, and that was expected if America participated. Its whole case rested on the contention that no danger of war existed in Manchuria.[8]

Finally, however, the Japanese relented and withdrew their objections. They had no choice but to accept, wisely, the inevitable.[9] Their single dissenting vote could have no effect on a purely procedural matter which required only a majority, and continued opposition might serve to alienate American opinion, which had thus far, on the whole, been favorable to Japan. The accusation was, indeed, leveled at Debuchi at this time in a letter from Sidney L. Gulick of the Federal Council of Churches of Christ in America which stated that Japan's resistance to seating an American on the Council constituted an admission that her contentions could not stand the light of public consideration.[10] Probably, recognition of the unavoidable by Tokyo was made easier by the report from the

[6] Memorandum by Castle, Oct. 14, 1931, *F.R., 1931*, III, 191.
[7] *New York Times*, Oct. 13, 1931; see also Johnson to State Dept., Oct. 12, 1931, *F.R., 1931*, III, 188.
[8] Gilbert to State Dept., *F.R., 1931*, III, 232–33.
[9] Wilfred Fleisher in New York *Herald Tribune*, Oct. 17, 1931.
[10] Copy of the letter dated October, 1931, D/S File 793.94/2261.

Japanese envoy in Geneva, who earlier, in relation to the commission of inquiry, had advised consenting to American participation as a means of "clearing the air." [11] Castle's explanation to Debuchi of the phrase "assert all pressure" as merely "moral pressure" and his assurance that America respected the rights of the Japanese in Manchuria also helped the Japanese swallow the medicine.[12]

On October 16, the American consul at Geneva, Prentiss Gilbert, took a seat at the Council table in one of the most historic and dramatic moments in modern history. Eleven years earlier, the United States Senate had rejected the Treaty of Versailles and membership in the League of Nations. During the intervening period, the United States had drawn gradually closer to Geneva by taking an increasingly active part in the work of many commissions and committees, albeit only those of a nonpolitical, humanitarian, or technical nature. Consistently, America had refused to play a role in any political matter. Now, however, in a discussion concerning the gravest political question of war and peace, her representative was conspicuously present and the significance of the occasion was grasped by the whole world. Nations, big and small, from east and west, north and south hailed the event and rejoiced.[13] At last, the end of American isolation and the beginning of her association with the rest of the world appeared at hand. The attitude at Geneva was "as a sort of feast of brotherhood set forth before the prodigal propounders of the League returned after years of absence." [14] As Gilbert and his associates on the delegation passed through the corridors they were showered with congratulations. The Panamanian delegate ventured "to express the hope that the co-operation of the United States of America may soon be transferred into a valuable association on a footing of equality with the other states here represented—such an association as the world has been awaiting and desiring for many a year." Aristide Briand, the president of the Council, in the official welcoming address uttered the same sentiments: that the transitory collaboration

[11] JFOD, 5.1.1.0–23, pp. 6–7, 10–11.
[12] Memoranda by Castle, Oct. 14 and 17, 1931, *F.R., 1931*, III, 191, 220.
[13] See the report from the American minister in Rumania, Oct. 24, 1931, D/S File 500.C1/80; also Amsterdam *Telegraaf*, Oct. 16, 1931.
[14] Lansing Warren in *New York Times*, Oct. 17, 1931.

will be transformed into a durable association.[15] The Chinese were very pleased.[16] The Japanese said nothing.[17] The only discordant note in the chorus of jubilation came from the pen of William Martin, who, looking at the other side of the coin, suggested that the United States must count itself lucky that the League of Nations existed. To America, having interests in the Far East and wishing to act but not alone, the League offered a handy and useful refuge in joint action.[18] This cynical comment, although written by one of the most widely read journalists in Europe, could hardly dampen the general enthusiasm.

The Council had been in session for three days before Gilbert took his seat. It was an assembly of utmost gravity and solemnity. Unlike the earlier meeting in September, at which the principal powers had been represented by their permanent delegates, the foreign ministers themselves were now in attendance—the pale, ascetic Lord Reading; burly, bewhiskered Dino Grandi; rotund, craggy Aristide Briand. They all came, as if to underline the urgency of the situation and emphasize the value placed on America's attendance. The discussions on the thirteenth had proved fruitless. The old, now familiar saws were repeated: the Japanese ready to withdraw and negotiate after the Chinese agreed to certain safeguards for Japanese life and property; the Chinese refusing to enter into any negotiations until after withdrawal.[19] Briand tried to bring the two divergent viewpoints together in the next two days in secret meetings and private conferences, but to no avail. There was no improvement in the situation in Manchuria. Fighting was in progress, the hope for a cessation dim, the Council's September 30 resolution a scrap of paper. The time for some action to bring the contestants to heel and stir them

[15] *F.R., 1931,* III, 215–17. The remarks were cabled by Gilbert; see also *New York Times,* Oct. 17, 1931.

[16] Chinese legation in Washington to State Dept., Oct. 15, 1931, D/S File 793.94/2256.

[17] Only the Japanese and Norwegian delegates on the Council abstained from making welcoming speeches. The Norwegians remained silent in order to avoid embarrassing the Japanese, who would otherwise have been the only ones silent.

[18] *Journal de Genève,* Oct. 16, 1931. The Rome *Osservatore Romano* (Oct. 18, 1931), in commenting on American participation, reflected a muted cynicism.

[19] Gilbert to State Dept., Oct. 13, 1931, *F.R., 1931,* III, 184.

into an awareness of the danger of large-scale war had come. On October 17, with Gilbert present, it was decided to invoke the Kellogg Pact. On that same evening, the foreign ministers in Geneva whose countries had signed the pact telegraphed Peking and Tokyo, reminding them of the obligations of that treaty, particularly Article II, which required them to settle their disputes by pacific means. Germany, Spain, and the United States followed promptly from Berlin, Madrid, and Washington.[20] Here was the first fruit of collaboration. America had joined in the discussions which formulated policy. The Council did not have to hold its breath, as before, while waiting to see whether Washington would follow. This was, indeed, an historic moment.

But those who looked to future solidarity were to be sadly disabused. Stimson did not plan to take part in any deliberations involving the application of purely League machinery. He envisaged American collaboration to be only temporary. In his original instructions to Gilbert authorizing him to sit with the Council on matters affecting the Kellogg Pact, he specifically ordered the consul to leave the table and resume his position of auditor and observer when those discussions came to an end.[21] When that time came, he telephoned Gilbert to withdraw from the Council table because, he said, continued attendance may be misconstrued "both here and in Japan." [22] There are the two clues to Stimson's determination to steer clear of further participation even as he authorized collaboration.

The public reaction to American connection with the League was mixed. Stimson's parallel but independent support of Geneva's action in September and early October did not arouse much disputation at home. Those people who in 1919–20 had urged ratification of the Treaty of Versailles and approval of the Covenant and who during the 1920's had fought for a closer relationship with the League were, of course, pleased. The Stimson Papers are full of congratulatory letters from societies and various individuals and groups such

[20] Gilbert to State Dept., Oct. 17, 1931, *ibid.*, 224–25. For the American note, see *ibid.*, 275.
[21] Memorandum of transatlantic conversation between Stimson and Gilbert, Oct. 16, 1931, *ibid.*, 206.
[22] Oct. 19, 1931, *ibid.*, 241–42.

as the League of Nations Association and religious and peace societies. Walter Lippmann reflected a considerable body of opinion when he called Stimson's interest in the League "a good sign for the world" and "an important step in the right direction." For ten years, he wrote, Europe was anxious to know what America would do in a crisis; how she would reconcile her obligations under the Kellogg Pact with her supposed hostility to the League of Nations. The United States had refused to answer, and the refusal had contributed to Europe's uncertainties. Now, Stimson had given the answer by his co-operation. Many of the letter-writers made the wish that co-operation would lead to direct and official consultation. Those who had from the beginning opposed membership in the League did not bother greatly to register their views. The connection thus far was nebulous and the dangers of involvement not threatening, although in some of the letters of approbation the Secretary received there were warnings against more intimate relations.[23]

The furor arose only when the move for Gilbert to take an active part came to light. Immediately, the old battle lines of 1919–20 were re-formed, the slogans and catchwords of the Great Debate were dredged up from the past, and the ancient warriors girded for the fray. Hiram Johnson, William E. Borah, and Hamilton Fish voiced their disapproval. Johnson accused "the dictators" (Hoover and Stimson) of taking the United States into the League against the wishes of the American people, who once had voted against it.[24] The Hearst press and McCormick's *Chicago Tribune* joined in the outcry, as did some other newspapers, notably two New York organs, the *Evening Post* and *Daily News*. The *Tribune* headed an editorial "Mr. Stimson Joins the League," while the *Daily News* urged "Let's Shinny On Our Side of the Street."[25] Hearst's *New York American* laid the blame on "an internationally minded Mr. Hoover and his spotlight-seeking Secretary of State [who] have done their utmost to place this nation in its present predicament."[26] The business interests

---

[23] See Stimson Papers, Box 14, Letters Received; also D/S File 793.94/2085, 1871, 1990; Walter Lippmann in New York *Herald Tribune*, Sept. 29, 1931.
[24] *New York Times*, Oct. 16, 1931, and *Outlook*, Oct. 28, 1931, p. 267.
[25] *Literary Digest*, Oct. 24, 1931, pp. 5–6.
[26] *New York American*, Oct. 15, 1931.

spoke also, through the *Commercial and Financial Chronicle,* which called Stimson's acceptance of the League invitation "improper and dangerous," [27] and individuals voiced objection in personal letters to the Secretary.[28]

Unquestionably, the dangers of arousing the passions of 1919–20 affected Stimson's policy. He was ever mindful of the political effect for the President.[29] But the vociferous opposition, however important, was not the chief cause of Stimson's withdrawal. After all, he did have a considerable amount of support in the nation, more for than against according to the *Literary Digest.* The *New York Times, Portland Oregonian, Dallas News, Philadelphia Inquirer, Christian Century, New Republic,* and other newspapers and periodicals came out warmly for the Secretary's courageous move.[30] Prominent citizens praised him in public and private.[31] The principal reason for Stimson's retreat from Geneva lay in Japan, not in America.

The Secretary was determined to give Japan no cause to believe that the United States was taking the lead in any movement to sit in judgment on her or to act as policeman or prosecutor or was even ranged against her.[32] This explains why, when he first considered the possibility of invoking the Kellogg Pact, he threw the initiative to the League and when Drummond hesitated, he told Gilbert that if the Council would not do it, no one would.[33] Then when he learned of Japan's strong objection to Gilbert's sitting with the Council, his enthusiasm for joint action faltered. Indeed, the whole picture changed and he was ready to end the brief adventure.[34] He was all the more resolved to pull out after discussions on the pact ended because a resolution was being formulated in the Council, as a sort of amendment to the September 30

[27] Oct. 17, 1931, p. 2487.
[28] See D/S File 793.94/2301, 2310, 2549.
[29] Castle, Diary, Oct. 22, 1931.
[30] *Literary Digest,* Oct. 31, 1931, pp. 3–4; *New York Times,* Oct. 18, 1931 (editorial and p. E3); *Christian Century,* Oct. 28, 1931, pp. 1337–1338; *New Republic,* Oct. 28, 1931, p. 286.
[31] Stimson Papers, Box 14, Letters Received.
[32] Stimson to Neville, Oct. 14, 1931, *F.R., 1931,* III, 194–95; Stimson to Gilbert, Oct. 17, 1931, *ibid.,* 220–21; Stimson to Peck, Oct. 16, 1931, *ibid.,* 208.
[33] Counselor of British embassy to Stimson, Oct. 19, 1931, *ibid.,* 258; telephone conversation between Gilbert and Stimson, Oct. 16, 1931, *ibid.,* 202–207.
[34] *Ibid.*

resolution, to set a time limit for Japanese evacuations, which he considered unwise and unduly tough.[35] He was not prepared to antagonize the Japanese in any way or be associated with a policy calculated to arouse Nippon's ire. He let it be known also that he did not favor any talks relative to the Nine Power Pact at that time.[36]

Both Castle and Hornbeck agreed with Stimson's decision.[37] Hornbeck was writing memoranda to the Secretary on this point almost daily.[38] From Tokyo, Neville had been urging all along no involvement with the League.[39] And President Hoover, who was worried lest the United States get progressively drawn into League affairs and enmeshed in Article XVI, approved the Secretary's action.[40] American policy was still predicated on the assumption of Shidehara's good faith and ability to master the military. Serious the situation was, undoubtedly; but given time and patience and understanding, the problem would be resolved by direct and bilateral negotiation.

Gilbert's projected withdrawal spread real consternation in Geneva. Briand, Drummond, and Reading were terribly upset. Reading himself got on the telephone on October 19 to plead with the Secretary to reconsider. Gilbert's removal, he said, would convey the impression of America's dissatisfaction with what the Council was trying to do, thereby weakening the League's prestige. It might even lead to Briand's downfall as foreign minister, and it would certainly have a bad effect on the coming disarmament conference. The next day, Gilbert talked to Stimson and reported the temper in Geneva. The letdown, he said, was very great after the high drama of American participation. More important, however, was the conviction that Japan would interpret America's move as a diplomatic victory and give her a new lease on life. The Secretary was greatly irritated. He did not want to provoke the Japanese; he did not relish facing hostile opinion at home, yet he relented in the face of the pressure from Geneva. The extent of his annoyance may be gauged by the gradual ero-

[35] Stimson, Diary, Oct. 19, 1931.
[36] Castle to Peck, Oct. 22, 1931, *F.R., 1931*, III, 292–93.
[37] Stimson, Diary, Oct. 19, 1931.
[38] See those of Oct. 17 and 18, 1931, D/S File 793.94/2227, 2233.
[39] Neville to State Dept., Oct. 16, 1931, *F.R., 1931*, III, 200.
[40] Castle, Diary, Oct. 20, 1931.

sion of his position. At first he told Gilbert to attend no more secret sessions, then he instructed him to take part in one more secret and one more public meeting at the Council table and thereafter in a seat assigned to observers in future open sessions, and finally he permitted him to continue sitting at the Council table in public meetings.[41]

Meanwhile, the Council took up the discussion of Japanese evacuation. By this time the realization was beginning to dawn among the leaders in the League that the Far Eastern crisis was not a local affair but rather that it was inextricably interwoven with every problem then before the world: disarmament, economic recovery, sanctity of treaties, security, and the general peace machinery. Briand's presence made a difference. He took the broadest view of the responsibilities of the international organization to which he was devoted and grasped the opportunity to fulfill them. His prestige was enormous, and his influence weighed heavily. Reading, too, had come to comprehend the relationship between war in Manchuria and the peace and well-being of Europe. To Sir Robert Vansittart he wrote: "A failure by the League to find some way round the difficulty would be nothing short of a calamity at the present juncture and might imperil any hopes we may have of making progress towards a solution in the more immediate field of Europe in which we are so much concerned." [42] Both he and Briand were impatient with Japan, and under their guiding hands and with Cecil's active assistance, the Council on October 24 voted to demand Japanese withdrawal by November 16, when the Council was next scheduled to meet. At the same time, China was called upon to assume responsibility for the safety of Japanese lives and property. Both powers were requested to prepare for direct negotiations to begin after evacuation for the settlement of all differences arising out of recent events and relating to the broader issues at stake.[43]

Although he voted aye, the Chinese delegate at Geneva was not completely happy with the resolution for withdrawal. The time set for evacuation was too distant, but at least set-

[41] The conversations and instructions are in *F.R.*, *1931*, III, 251–58, 259–66, 266–75, 276.
[42] *British Documents*, p. 810, n. 3.
[43] *F.R.*, *Japan*, *1931–1941*, I, 29–30.

ting a specific date gave promise of the League's willingness to move in the right direction. He pleaded with the Council to remain in session until withdrawal was completed and urged that neutral observers be appointed to be present at the subsequent negotiations, for China must not be abandoned to Japan. As if to brace the League's spine, he warned that "this is admittedly the gravest issue that has confronted the League since its foundation . . . because it may ultimately involve stretching and testing to the utmost the authority and the confidence of the League . . . and the readiness of world public opinion to support any wise and effectual action to safeguard the peace of nations." With more confidence than was warranted, the government, on November 1, appointed a commission of seven, with Wellington Koo as chairman, to conduct the negotiations for reoccupation of Manchuria.[44]

The Japanese reaction was sharp, categorical, and hostile. Yoshizawa flatly refused to accept a time limit for withdrawal. Japanese troops would not leave their areas of occupation, he said, until after negotiations had settled all the problems between the two powers. These negotiations must be between the two nations alone, without observers from other parties, and based on five principles: "mutual repudiation of aggressive policy and conduct, respect for China's territorial integrity, complete suppression of all organized movements interfering with freedom of trade and stirring up international hatred, effective protection throughout Manchuria of all peaceful pursuits undertaken by Japanese subjects, and respect for treaty rights of Japan in Manchuria." [45] Here it must be noted that Yoshizawa spoke for the Cabinet; his instructions came from Shidehara. This was not the blatant militarist speaking. On the morning of October 23, the Cabinet had decided to reject the Council's draft resolution setting a time limit, and instructions went out to Geneva at once, whereupon Yoshizawa cast the only dissenting vote in the Council on the next day. Now Foreign Office and army were in complete agreement. Did this mean the end of the schism

[44] See *F.R., 1931*, III, 264, 278, 302–303, 340, and 351 for speeches by Alfred Sze and Chiang Kai-shek.

[45] *Ibid.*, 291–92, 294, 299, 310, 336–38, 372. The third principle concerned the very effective Chinese boycott of Japanese goods on the mainland.

between the two factions? Had the civilian authorities finally capitulated to the military? [46] Not necessarily. Shidehara really had no choice. Again, as in the days immediately following the early fighting at Mukden, he had to tread warily in the face of public opinion. Except for some liberals, the Japanese public and press were united in condemning the League, called by the *Japan Times* "the Soiled Temple of International Justice." There was a powerful determination to resist any interference by a third party in Sino-Japanese affairs. Consent to withdraw before guarantees of security and respect for treaty rights would be an admission that Japan had been wrong from the beginning.[47] Shidehara also feared for his own life and for the lives of his colleagues. One week earlier, a group of young army officers had mounted a plot to assassinate the key members of the government if they would not support the army policies. Fortunately, the plot had been betrayed by a certain lieutenant colonel and the schemers were arrested, but it had been a close call.[48]

Thus had the League of Nations, for better or worse, made the first really positive move to end the fighting by imposing a definite deadline. World attention now riveted on the United States. Much of the force of the resolution for withdrawal depended upon unanimity of world opinion and agreement between Geneva and Washington. Gilbert had sat at the table during the discussions but had kept silent. Would Stimson now give his support? The French ambassador in Washington relayed to the Secretary Briand's deep concern lest the solidarity be cracked, and Drummond urged America's prompt action to scotch reports in the press of various countries that Washington and Geneva were at odds.[49] Stimson did not plan to cut the cable between Washington and Ge-

[46] *Osaka Mainichi,* Oct. 24, 1931; *Japan Advertiser,* Oct. 29, 1931; Hugh Byas in *New York Times,* Oct. 14, 1931.
[47] Neville to State Dept., *F.R., 1931,* III, 280; *Japan Times,* Oct. 26, 27, 1931; Hugh Byas in *New York Times,* Oct. 18, 1931; see the resolution by Shimbi Doshikai (a social organization of Upper House members, scholars, army and navy officers, and businessmen), *Japan Times,* Oct. 30, 1931.
[48] See Kido, Diary, Oct. 17, 1931, and IMTFE, pp. 1978–81, for the "October Incident." Nakamura, pp. 135–36, has some interesting details of this abortive plot.
[49] Briand to Claudel, Oct. 31, 1931, *F.R., 1931,* III, 344; Drummond to Gilbert, Nov. 2, 1931, *ibid.,* 353.

neva, although Yoshizawa was making every effort in Geneva to create the impression of a rift.[50] The Secretary wanted very much to uphold the League's action, but he was seriously disturbed by the time limit in the resolution. Reports from Manchuria indicated that in some places it would not be safe to withdraw Japanese troops by November 16 because of the anarchy which existed, and from Tokyo, Neville cabled his warning that Japanese public opinion would not permit evacuation by that date unless negotiations were in process. In Washington, Debuchi served noticed that Japan would not sign a blank check by withdrawing at a given time before guarantees were given by China.[51] Within the Department of State, there was unanimity on the unwisdom of setting a specific time limit. R. S. Miller, an officer in the Far Eastern Division, called it "unrealistic." Stanley Hornbeck objected because the fluidity in the Manchurian situation and the destruction of the Chinese administration did actually jeopardize Japanese safety.[52] Nor were Stimson and his advisors alone in deploring the time limit. Both the British and French governments privately repudiated the action of their representatives at Geneva. The British ambassador in Washington, reflecting the views of the new foreign secretary, Sir John Simon, who had replaced Lord Reading on October 27, labeled the action "unfortunate." [53] The career men in the Foreign Office strongly disapproved. In a lengthy memorandum,[54] Sir John Pratt, a specialist on China, urged an entirely different policy: that China be told Great Britain would not play policeman and eject Japan from Manchuria and that Japan be made to realize Great Britain had not lost sight of her case. He suggested that Japan be told that "our traditional friendship with and admiration for Japan is still one of the main-

[50] By thanking Gilbert for Stimson's better understanding of the crisis than Briand displayed, *F.R.*, *1931*, III, 260–61, 314.

[51] Debuchi to Castle, Oct. 14, 1931, *F.R.*, *Japan*, *1931–1941*, I, 24–26, and Oct. 28, 1931, *F.R.*, *1931*, III, 333; report of Hanson and Salisbury, Oct. 22, 24, 1931, *ibid.*, 288–91, 319–20, 327–28; Neville to State Dept., Nov. 4, 1931, *ibid.*, 366–67, and Oct. 26, 1931, D/S File 793.94/2230.

[52] See the memoranda by R. S. Miller, Oct. 30 and Nov. 2, 1931, D/S File 793.94/2477, 2495, and those by Hornbeck, Oct. 19, 1931, D/S File 793.94/2230, 2231.

[53] British ambassador to Castle, Nov. 2, 1931, *F.R.*, *1931*, III, 351.

[54] *British Documents*, pp. 826–29.

springs of our policy in the Far East . . . that British interests have nothing to gain from Japan's misfortunes, but that
the prosperity of Japan is one of the objects of British policy."
Similarly, C. W. Orde, counselor in the Foreign Office,
wrote: [55] "I confess to the view that Japan has a much better
case than her arbitrary action and the bad showing of her
representative at Geneva have allowed to appear. If this is
so, it is surely a mistake to allow our view of the situation to
be governed by displeasure at her tactical mistakes and to take
action which, by strengthening China's tactical position, will
tend further to obscure the question of fundamental justice.
It is surely certain that the prestige of the League will in the
long run be effected [*sic*] more by the degree in which fundamental justice is recognized by her, than by the emphasis with
which she reprobates arbitrary action by one of her members."
The French ambassador reflected the general feeling of the
Quai d'Orsay, which strongly objected to Briand's policies
at Geneva, when he told Castle of his disapproval.[56]

The task before the Secretary of State was to find a formula
which would "make clear my general support of the League
position and yet possibly leave a ladder by which Japan could
climb down in case of a deadlock." [57] The formula was found
and incorporated in an oral communication to the Japanese
government drafted by Castle on November 3 and read by
Forbes to the foreign minister two days later.[58] Stimson reiterated the League's demand for evacuation and insisted that
it should not be contingent upon the settlement of all the
broader questions not connected with the immediate Manchurian issues. He urged that Japanese forces not be used to
wring concessions from China. But no mention was made of
a time limit for withdrawal, only that it be effected as soon
as possible.

The omission of the specific date was interpreted by some
observers as a weakening of the League resolution. For the

[55] *Ibid.*, p. 822.
[56] French ambassador to Castle, Oct. 23, 1931, D/S File 793.94/2369. The
Dutch minister in Washington also regretted the League's action. Memoranda
by Castle, Nov. 11, 18, 1931, D/S File 793.94/2752, 3018.
[57] Stimson to Claudel, Oct. 29, 1931, *F.R.*, *1931*, III, 342–43; also Nov. 4,
1931, D/S File 793.94/2510.
[58] *F.R., Japan, 1931–1941*, I, 34.

United States, however, it must be viewed as a wise move. Stimson simply refused to get himself into a position which could not be enforced and from which there might be no retreat. The most awkward situation could result had he held to a specified time, only to have it ignored by the Japanese. It could have served only to arouse the Japanese, many of whom were coming around to the view that the United States refused to concede to them the position in Asia which America had traditionally claimed in the Western Hemisphere. Public opinion in Japan at that time was particularly inflamed by the publication of Herbert Yardley's *The American Black Chamber,* depicting his decoding of Japanese messages during the Washington Arms Conference.[59] The Secretary ascribed the League's blunder to a complete ignorance of the oriental mind and to Cecil's zeal.[60] The French editor Stephane Lauzanne suggested that Stimson's action stemmed from his predilection for the Japanese over the Chinese because the former represented order and the latter decadence, but the accusation cannot be substantiated.[61] It is true that the Secretary considered many of the Japanese claims in Manchuria to rest on sound basis and that "China has been nagging and inching up on Japan for a long time," but he did believe the use of force to be unwarranted and inexcusable.[62] He most certainly did not favor the Japanese over the Chinese.

Even without the time limit, his remonstrance of November 5 was strong and uncompromising. Indeed, when Neville received it in Tokyo he urged Stimson to modify it, and the American military attaché, upon reading it, made the comment "This leads directly to war."[63] But Stimson ordered him to deliver it exactly as sent, and in Washington he reinforced the message in an interview with Debuchi, to whom he spoke quite firmly.[64] To the German ambassador he advised

[59] New York *Herald Tribune,* Oct. 18, 1931; see the pamphlet issued by the Japanese Patriotic Association (Mukden), *To a Certain Nation,* translation in D/S File 793.94/3083, which called the United States "THE GREAT HYPOCRITE of the world."
[60] Stimson to Elihu Root, Dec. 14, 1931, Stimson Papers, Box 27, Letters Sent.
[61] *Le Matin,* Oct. 31 and Nov. 1, 1931.
[62] Stimson to Charles Howland, Oct. 27, 1931, Stimson Papers, Box 27, Letters Sent.
[63] Forbes, Journal, Series 2, Vol. 4, p. 15 (confidential section).
[64] Stimson to Debuchi, Nov. 4, 1931, *F.R., 1931,* III, 367–68.

discounting any reports that America's Far Eastern policy had weakened.[65]

The fat was in the fire, but the Japanese watched it sizzle with calm composure. The government made clear its intention not to retire until China accepted the five principles, and there was no possibility of a reversal of position.[66] There was no indication that the gestures by the League or by the United States made even the slightest impact on Tokyo.[67] Instead of withdrawing, the army continued operations. As a result of a fierce three-day battle on November 4–6 around Tsitsihar by the Nonni River in which artillery, aircraft, cavalry, and infantry were used, the military extended its lines farther eastward. The belief was strong in the West that the end of the battle merely signaled a lull pending the arrival of reinforcements and an attack on Chinchow, which had long been rumored as the next Japanese objective.[68] It would be ludicrous to assert that Shidehara had the support of public opinion; he was its servant. Japanese sentiment was virtually united behind the army and becoming increasingly excited in its determination that the government must stand firmly in defense of the national interest in Manchuria. The nation was in the grip of a wartime hysteria.[69] War maps appeared in shop windows, talk was of a "shifting front," "our troops," "the enemy"; soldiers were everywhere, military trucks rolled along the streets, troops embarked for the theater of operations, appeals for funds were made for the brave fighting men.[70] Although an undercurrent of opposition still existed among liberals, intellectuals, socialists, and younger business and professional men, many of the formerly bitterest antagonists of the adventure on the mainland appeared to have been bitten by the patriotic bug and became staunch apologists. A noted liberal and pacifist, Ozaki Yukio, ridiculed the Chinese claim that the treaties which granted Japanese legal

[65] Memorandum by Stimson, Nov. 5, 1931, D/S File 462.00R296A/9.
[66] Shidehara so informed Forbes, Nov. 5, 1931, and Briand, Nov. 9, 1931, *F.R., 1931*, III, 375–80, 397–98.
[67] *New York Times,* Nov. 8, 9, 1931.
[68] *Ibid.,* Nov. 3, 7, 9, 16, 1931.
[69] The Japanese ambassador in Great Britain, Matsudaira Tsuneo, mentioned this to Dawes on November 15, 1931, *F.R., 1931*, III, 450; see also *New York Times,* Nov. 6, 1931, and Takeuchi, p. 366.
[70] Elizabeth Green, "The Manchurian Disease," *Pacific Affairs,* V (January, 1932), 52–53.

rights in Manchuria were invalid because they had been negotiated under duress. If that were true, he told Castle, then the Treaty of Versailles similarly had no force. It would be far better, he added, for the Western powers to force China to live up to the treaties than to censure Japan for wishing to enforce its rights under law.[71] The Japanese League of Nations Association indicted Geneva for acting prematurely, before it had all the facts.[72] Motoyama Hikoichi, a prominent newspaper owner, spelled out the popular attitude when he said that "in the main issues regarding the Manchurian question the whole nation is in perfect accord, regardless of political parties or philosophic schools."[73] Even within Shidehara's own Minseito party a split was developing under the leadership of Adachi Kenzo, the home minister, who on November 10, without consulting the prime minister, called for the creation of a new government cleansed of timid elements, a clear indication that the political moderates were becoming less moderate.[74]

The League of Nations, now adjourned, was powerless to enforce its resolution. For one thing, there was no police power to carry it out, but that really did not matter since the League lacked juridical force anyway, the resolution not having been unanimous. More important, public opinion in Great Britain and France was so largely pro-Japanese as to deny the resolution even the minimal strength of moral pressure. Some Liberal and Socialist British newspapers, such as the *Manchester Guardian,* the *Spectator,* and the *Daily Herald,* sided with China and demanded strong action by the government. The *Spectator* warned that if Japan did not heed the League "that is an end of any pretence that war as an instrument of national policy has been renounced . . . war is re-enthroned . . . a straight road back to 1914 lies open."[75] But the majority of the press and public supported Japan.

[71] Memorandum by Castle, Nov. 13, 1931, D/S File 793.94/2721.

[72] "Declaration of League of Nations Association of Japan," *International Gleanings from Japan,* Supplement No. 1, Nov. 9, 1931, pp. 2–4.

[73] *New York Times,* Nov. 15, 1931, quoted the speech. See also "Japan Christians Call for Peace," *Christian Century,* Dec. 16, 1931, p. 1598 for a similar view.

[74] Takeuchi, p. 366.

[75] *Spectator,* Nov. 14, 1931; see also the remarks by Mr. Mander in Parliament on Nov. 11, 1931, *Parliamentary Debates,* House of Commons, Fifth Series, Vol. 259, pp. 201–202.

The powerful Beaverbrook and Rothermere chains denounced the League for involving England in futile negotiations. If London had its way, reported the *New York Times* correspondent from the British capital, the Chinese would be forced to negotiate without requiring the Japanese to withdraw troops. Many prominent Britons openly defended the Japanese action. They considered Kuomintang hotheads responsible for the crisis in provoking Japan by deliberate acts of hostility. The feeling was strong that British interests would best be served in the Far East by the closest friendship with Japan, if only because of the vast British territories within easy steaming distance from that country.[76] Shades of remorse over the abrogation of the Anglo-Japanese Alliance were apparent.

The French press was more outspoken than the British in condemning Briand and the League and sympathizing with Japan. The conservative journals berated the Council's invitation to the United States and its action of October 24. They opposed any policy calculated to create a rift between Japan and France. The similarity between Japan's insistence on upholding the Treaty of 1915 and France's insistence on maintaining intact the Treaty of Versailles was mentioned frequently. Indeed, Tokyo was hailed as the bulwark of the European *status quo*. Even the liberal and leftist organs, usually pro-League and pro-Chinese, doubted the wisdom of League policy if it meant antagonizing Japan to the point of her withdrawing from Geneva. They seemed more concerned with keeping the League intact than with settling the Far Eastern problem.[77]

Not only did Briand have to contend with a hostile public opinion at home, but even in his own foreign office he did not enjoy wholehearted support. Philippe Barthelot, the po-

[76] Charles Selden in *New York Times*, Nov. 12, 1931; also Sir Herbert Russell, *Naval and Military Record*, Nov. 11, 1931, and J. O. P. Bland in *New York Times*, Oct. 19, 1931. British textile magnates were not displeased to see Sino-Japanese relations embittered. The Chinese boycott greatly benefited British cotton sales in China, which had jumped 100 per cent since September. Mills which had been running at 40 per cent capacity in August were now up to 70 per cent. Before this, Japan had been usurping the British textile market in China. See *New York Times*, Nov. 13, 1931.

[77] See the dispatches from the American Embassy in Paris analyzing French opinion, Oct. 17, 20, 23, D/S File 793.94/2184, 2235, 2394; also *New York Times*, Nov. 18, 1931.

litical director, and his deputy, Alexis Leger, were out of sympathy with their chief.[78] Still, Briand valiantly strove to get the Japanese to acquiesce. In two notes, sent on October 26 and November 6, he urged prompt withdrawal and deletion of the fifth of the five principles which the Japanese had made conditions for negotiations as unrelated to the immediate issue. In another note on November 5, he scored Japanese seizure of the salt revenues on the ground that it was not necessary to Japanese security and violated that paragraph of the September 30 resolution which pledged the two nations against aggravating the situation.[79] There were rumors and reports that he was thinking of even more drastic action, such as a boycott or removing the diplomatic representative of the League powers from Tokyo,[80] but it was all to no avail and Briand was disheartened to the point of admitting, by inference, that setting a time limit for evacuation was an error.[81] It was a curious fact that Briand had gradually transformed his and the Council's role from arbitrator between the two powers to advocate for China.[82] But the change was not deliberate. Although he admonished both powers to cease fighting, clearly Japan called the tune in the field. China was powerless and needed special pleading, for the Nanking government could not meet its opponent on equal footing. Japan had only China to oppose; Chiang Kai-shek faced not only the enemy across the sea but also Communists, a rebellious Cantonese faction, and a half-dozen war lords fighting for fiefs in various provinces.

Briand and Drummond knew they could not look to the United States to salvage the League's position. Stimson was standing pat. He was worried over the situation but could do nothing "except to watch the thing go through to the conclusion"; [83] he had aroused enough hostility in Japan by his note. The Secretary had not expected details of the note to get out to the public. At a press conference on November 5, he had said only that a note had been sent in support of the

[78] Gilbert to State Dept., Nov. 7, 1931, *F.R., 1931*, III, 387–89.
[79] The notes, sent home by Gilbert, are in *ibid.*, 345–46, 396–97, 402.
[80] *New York Times*, Nov. 6, 1931, and *Washington Post*, Nov. 7, 1931.
[81] Charles G. Dawes, *Journal As Ambassador to Great Britain* (New York, 1939), p. 416.
[82] New York *Herald Tribune*, Nov. 6, 1931.
[83] Stimson, Diary, Nov. 16, 1931.

League position and that "we were pressing Japan." [84] Only Drummond and the French government had verbatim copies, but the *New York Times* correspondent in Tokyo pieced together enough of the material, gained from Forbes it was believed, to print a pretty accurate account of the contents.[85] Now tempers were so high in Tokyo that the embassy staff moved about the city under guard.[86] At home, the President seemed to have had enough of the League of Nations and wanted to get completely disconnected from it.[87] Hiram Johnson still raved.[88] To allay the suspicions of senatorial foes of the League and save the President political embarrassment, Stimson had to deny publicly that he had identified the United States with Geneva by the note of November 5. He claimed that he was "acting independently through diplomatic channels and reserving complete independence of judgment as to each step." [89] Army and navy spokesmen wanted no part in the Far Eastern business because they knew that Japan enjoyed an impregnable position in eastern Asia. No army could match hers, and the navies of the great powers were too distant. She controlled the Sea of Japan and the Korean Strait, and the South Manchurian posts and Korean-Manchurian rail connections guaranteed the security of troop movements. To oppose her would be folly, especially with the retirement of seventeen vessels from the United States Navy in November.[90] From everywhere the cry went out for more drastic reduction of armaments—some impelled by motives of economy, others from pacifist conviction.[91] The determination not to get involved in war rang on all sides, from Milwaukee, where

[84] *Ibid.,* Nov. 5, 1931.
[85] Hugh Byas in *New York Times,* Nov. 6, 7, 1931.
[86] Forbes, Journal, Series 2, Vol. 3, Nov. 17, 1931.
[87] Castle, Diary, Nov. 4, 1931.
[88] *Washington Post,* Oct. 31, 1931; also New York *Herald Tribune,* Oct. 28, 1931. See also the letter to Stimson from the National Patriotic League, Nov. 3, 1931, D/S File 793.94/2473.
[89] *New York Times,* Nov. 7, 1931. Harold J. T. Horan of the *Washington Post* called Stimson's denial a red herring drawn across the trail to Scotch criticism. See the edition of Nov. 7, 1931.
[90] Secretary of War Patrick J. Hurley expressed the view at a Cabinet meeting on November 13. Stimson, Diary, Nov. 13, 1931. See also the article by the military expert, Colonel F. D. Palmer, in *New York Times,* Nov. 12, 1931.
[91] See the resolution passed by the National Grange on November 18, 1931, at its sixty-fifth annual convention. National Grange, *Journal of Proceedings,* 1931, p. 27.

a state legislator informed his congressman that "what the people in China may decide to do about killing each other is NOT OUR BUSINESS," [92] to Hanover, New Hampshire, where the editor of the Dartmouth College daily wrote on Armistice Day, "We are the men who will be mangled in the next western war. And we are the men who are laughing at all the tommyrot that is being handed out this morning at 11 o'clock all over the country. We know it's all a farce." [93]

Pro-Japanese sentiment continued strong among articulate and important people. Editorials in the influential *New York Times* were very generous to Japan. Considerable sympathy and understanding were expressed for Japan's position. Hugh Byas in a long feature article in the *Times* explained Japan's actions as admittedly crude but only the product of existing conditions. In another item, he indicated that it would have been more realistic had the League coupled the demand for withdrawal with one for safeguards by China.[94] In a letter to the same newspaper, Herbert Bayard Swope condoned the Japanese desire for expansion. They need more room, he wrote. "Sixty-three million people living on rocky islands; enterprising, bold, intelligent, industrious, and honorable, have the right to exist. If existence demands expansion—as we have so often been told has been the case among nations—then why forbid Japanese expansion to follow natural lines?" It would be far better for the United States, he added, to have a controlled and directed China.[95] Herbert S. Houston, upon his return from a trip to the Orient as a member of the American Committee of the International Chamber of Commerce, told three hundred members of the New York Advertising Club that Japan wanted no war. He compared Japan's relation to Manchuria with the United States' to Latin America and stated that one could not expect Japan to arbitrate her vital interests in that part of the world any more than we would be be willing to arbitrate the Monroe Doctrine.[96] The former editor of the *Christian Science Monitor,* Willis J. Abbott, after a trip to Shanghai to attend a conference of the

[92] Otto A. Kehrein to Representative John C. Schafer, Oct. 27, 1931, copy in D/S File 793.94/2416.
[93] *The Dartmouth,* Nov. 11, 1931.
[94] Byas in *New York Times,* Nov. 1, 5, 1931.
[95] Oct. 28, 1931.
[96] *New York Times,* Nov. 5, 1931.

Institute of Pacific Relations, spoke in the same vein.[97] Elihu Root, Forbes, Neville, and Admiral Montgomery M. Taylor, commanding the Asiatic Fleet, were similarly pro-Japanese in their views. Taylor was exceedingly scornful of the one hundred thousand Chinese soldiers in Manchuria over whom ten thousand Japanese rode so easily.[98] Even some missionaries in China blamed the Chinese as much as the Japanese for the difficulties in Manchuria.[99]

Stimson did keep in close touch with the situation through Forbes and Gilbert in the hope that something salutary could be worked out gracefully and without involvement for the United States. Talk of recalling the American ambassador from Tokyo or joining a League boycott or embargoing munitions as a means of reflecting displeasure did not get far.[100] A Japanese proposal to withdraw if satisfactory policing conditions could be established received no encouragement from Washington, despite Forbes' endorsement.[101] A ray of light broke through the clouds momentarily as a result of a suggestion Stimson had made at the time he sent his note to Japan. As a compromise measure, he had proposed to Briand and Drummond that negotiations get under way before Japanese evacuation, but in the presence of neutral observers, who would prevent the Kwantung army from exerting pressure on the Chinese. If China would accept this formula, Japan would be expected to relinquish her demand for a settlement of all problems relating to the network of treaties prior to withdrawal. If only negotiations could begin, Stimson believed, progress could be made gradually toward a peaceful solution of all issues. On November 14, a headline in the *New York Times* and a news item from its Paris correspond-

[97] *Ibid.*, Nov. 20, 1931.
[98] Forbes to State Dept., Nov. 5, 1931, *F.R., 1931*, III, 378; Taylor to Admiral Pratt, Nov. 5, 1931, and Taylor to Col. J. O. Taylor, Sept. 25, 1931, Taylor Papers, Box 269; Neville's view sent by Forbes to State Dept., Nov. 7, 1931, D/S File 793.94/3161. Neville told Chester Rowell that the Manchurian situation was being taken too seriously. See Rowell Papers, Nov. 19, 1931. See Stimson, Diary, Nov. 14, 1931, for Root's view; also Stimson to Root, Dec. 14, 1931, Stimson Papers, Box 27, Letters Sent.
[99] Rev. R. W. McClure to Wynn Fairfield, Nov. 23, 1931, American Board of Commissioners for Foreign Missions Papers, 1930–1931, Foochow (Houghton Library, Harvard University).
[100] Castle, Diary, Nov. 9, 1931.
[101] Forbes to State Dept., Nov. 12, 1931, *F.R., 1931*, III, 430; State Dept. to Forbes, Nov. 13, 1931, *ibid.*, 432.

ent optimistically reported an agreement on this formula, but it was a false hope and on the following day a denial was published. China would commence no negotiations before evacuation and the Japanese would not delete the fifth point.[102] By the time the Council convened on November 16, conditions had not changed. The deadline for withdrawal had passed, and not only had no move backward been made, but fighting was still in progress.

The Council met on the appointed day in Paris, ironically, in the same room in which the Kellogg-Briand Pact had been signed three years earlier,[103] with two strikes against it. One was the defiance by Japan; the other was the absence of an American representative. As early as November 9, Briand and Drummond had urged upon Secretary Stimson the importance of American representation at the Council meeting; the session was not to be construed as a new one, but merely as a continuation of the earlier one which had been adjourned, they said. They feared that a break in the solidarity would tend to stiffen the Japanese.[104] In the United States, a considerable amount of pressure for full participation converged on the State Department. A resolution to that effect was passed unanimously on November 9 by the Interorganization Council on Disarmament, made up of 33 religious, pacifist, and study groups. On November 10, a petition signed by 198 prominent Americans—ministers, bankers, educators, and politicians—expressed the same hope, and the following day, 50 business and education leaders addressed to the President an open letter which urged the same course.[105] Within the department, Allen T. Klots strongly supported seating an American at the Council table.[106] But Capitol Hill cast its shadow over the deliberations in the White House and in the State Department. The President, Stimson, and Castle feared the reaction of senatorial foes and vetoed Klots' suggestion.[107]

---

[102] Stimson to Claudel, Nov. 4, 1931, *ibid.*, 370; Stimson to Forbes, Nov. 5, 1931, *F.R., Japan, 1931–1941*, I, 36–37; Stimson to Dawes, Nov. 10, 1931, *F.R., 1931*, III, 423–26; *New York Times*, Nov. 14, 15, 1931.

[103] China objected to the move from Geneva to Paris on the grounds that Briand would be under the eye of the French government which was pro-Japanese. Johnson to State Dept., Nov. 3, 1931, *F.R., 1931*, III, 361; also Peck to State Dept., Nov. 11, 1931, D/S File 793.94/3121.

[104] Gilbert to State Dept., Nov. 9, 1931, *F.R., 1931*, III, 399–401.

[105] *New York Times*, Nov. 12, 1931; also D/S File 793.94/2779.

[106] Castle, Diary, Nov. 10, 1931.

[107] *New York Times*, Nov. 12, 1931.

Congress was to meet soon, and a political hassel was not wel-
come. Hoover was also thinking of the effect of close collaboration upon French demands for an American guarantee of
her security.[108] It was clearly important, however, that the
United States be kept abreast of developments at Paris. The
senior men in the embassy were not available for this task.
The ambassador and James T. Marriner, one of the counse-
lors, were home; the other counselor, Norman Armour, was
on leave in Europe. Gilbert could not be sent; he was needed
at Geneva, and he had also been too closely identified with
active collaboration. Charles G. Dawes, the ambassador in
Great Britain, was the logical choice. The former Vice-President, well known in Europe for his work on the commission
which had formulated a reparations plan bearing his name,
was ideal for the job. He did not believe in too close association with the League and was a big enough man, said Stimson
to Hoover, who really preferred sending no one to Paris, for
the Council to go to him, thus making unnecessary his going
to the Council.[109] To assist Dawes, Stimson ordered G.
Howland Shaw, an experienced career Foreign Service officer
serving in Turkey, to temporary duty in Paris. Dawes was instructed to be available for consultation with League leaders
in their search for a solution. He was neither to instigate nor
initiate, neither push nor lead, and to take no sides. If anything, he was to serve as a brake on the League. "Keep your
hand on the shoulder or coat collar of Briand and not let him
go too fast," cautioned Stimson. The Secretary hoped fer-
vently that no fuss or ceremony would be made over Dawes,
as had been done with Gilbert the previous month. Too much
formality would scare too many Americans.[110] William Martin,
in the *Journal de Genève* on November 17, hailed Dawes'
presence at Paris. In view of his importance at home, Martin

[108] Hoover voiced these fears to the trustees of the World Peace Foundation
on November 17, 1931. See letter of Raymond T. Rich, executive director of
the Foundation, to Evans Clarke, Feb. 10, 1932, Twentieth Century Fund
Papers (New York City).
[109] Stimson, Diary, Nov. 9, 1931. Eugene Dooman, first secretary of the
American embassy in London, was the opinion that Dawes was more
concerned with avoiding contact with the League than with settling Sino-
Japanese problems. Furthermore, he was very decidedly pro-Japanese. See
Castle, Diary, Nov. 15, 1932.
[110] Stimson to Dawes, transatlantic conversation, Nov. 10, 1931, *F.R., 1931,*
III, 407–14; also Stimson to Dawes, Nov. 10, 1931, *F.R., Japan, 1931–1941,* I,
41–44.

wrote, he can assume responsibilities and take action on the spot, thus avoiding the frequent misunderstandings of the previous month occasioned by Gilbert's constant telephoning to Washington for instructions. Briand, however, was not happy with the "second cousin twice removed" co-operation. The League's prestige was bound to be injured, he claimed, if collaboration now were less than before. To placate him, Dawes suggested that he be asked to join the Council after the second or third meeting on the ground that questions affecting America's interest were involved. Stimson gave his approval, grudgingly and with the understanding that Dawes would take a seat only when absolutely necessary and on specific treaty matters, for "otherwise we will open ourselves to unjustified attack by foes in the Senate." [111]

Japan's failure to withdraw at the appointed time left the League in a most awkward and embarrassing position, to say the least; its injunction had been defied and nothing could be done about it. An American newspaper put it neatly in an editorial which stated: "How to confess this without pleading guilty to blunders which such exalted persons simply cannot make is the problem which supersedes that of peace." [112] The first day's session served only to emphasize the Council's helplessness. Japan insisted on acceptance of the five points as a prelude to withdrawal, while China maintained its position on evacuation before negotiations. An impasse had been reached, and the only way out lay in a course of action which would be acceptable to Japan and yet provide for a solution to the problem. Such a plan Matsudaira Tsuneo, the Japanese ambassador to Great Britain, proposed, on November 17, providing for the creation of a commission to investigate conditions in Manchuria and in China, thus enabling the League to deliberate on the basis of complete information. Briand and Drummond, with the approval of Sir John Simon, who had been thinking along the same lines independently, grasped

[111] Shaw to State Dept., Nov. 14, 1931, *F.R., 1931*, III, 444–45; also telephone conversation between Stimson and Dawes, Nov. 16, 1931, *ibid.*, 452–56. Thousands of telegrams reached Hoover urging Dawes to sit on the Council, but apparently Hoover resisted any blandishments for closer co-operation. The League of Nations Association was responsible for prompting the telegrams. See Clark Eichelberger, executive secretary, to Newton D. Baker, Dec. 1, 1931, Newton D. Baker Papers, Box 145 (Library of Congress).

[112] New York *Herald Tribune*, Nov. 17, 1931.

the opportunity and on November 22, after a few days of exploratory discussions on verbiage, issued a statement suggesting a resolution reaffirming the September 30 resolution and proposing a commission of inquiry.[113]

Two serious obstacles had to be overcome, however, before the plan could be consummated. The Chinese voiced grave objections to the proposed action: it left evacuation to Japanese discretion and provided no means for bringing the two nations together for a general settlement. They demanded that the proposed commission supervise Japanese withdrawal before the investigation, lest while they study the situation the Japanese should further entrench themselves in the area of occupation and perhaps even form a new government which would recognize Japan's paramount position.[114] The Chinese contentions were really unassailable, but Briand and Drummond could scarcely admit it. Japan had to be pleased, and they began working on Sze to withdraw his objections. Wearing him down would not be easy, but more troublesome and dangerous was the threat of a new Japanese advance, which could wreck the whole program. The army had occupied Tsitsihar on the nineteenth, and reports from trustworthy sources indicated an attack on Chinchow to be in the offing. Reinforcements of one division and three air squadrons from home and an announcement by headquarters in Mukden of a new offensive lent credence to the rumors. The government in Tokyo seemed powerless to stem the move. It was in critical condition, staggering under criticism by the press and attacks by the military. Here lay the great danger to the League. The possibility of a coup was talked of everywhere, and even the assassination of Wakatsuki, Shidehara, and others in the Cabinet appeared imminent.[115]

Support from the United States was desperately needed, not only to help convince the Chinese and bridle the Japanese, but

[113] Dawes to State Dept., Nov. 17, 18, 21, 22, 25, 1931, *F.R.*, *1931*, III, 468, 480–81, 526, 536–37, 568.

[114] Johnson to State Dept., Nov. 22, 1931, *ibid.*, 527–28, 533; Nov. 25, 1931, D/S File 793.94/2902; Dawes to State Dept., Nov. 23, 24, 25, 1931, *F.R.*, *1931*, III, 533, 551–52, 556, 563–64.

[115] Johnson reported the imminence of the Chinchow attack. See Johnson to State Dept., Nov. 22, 1931, *ibid.*, 530; also *New York Times*, Nov. 24, 1931. Forbes, on November 20, reported the assassination plot. *F.R.*, *1931*, III, 513. Japanese trade and shipping suffered greatly from the Chinese boycott, and this caused further dissatisfaction with the Cabinet, which drew the blame.

also to assent to the commission idea and give permission for an American representative to be included. Stimson was perfectly willing to give some help to the League. The idea of a commission of inquiry's ascertaining the facts which would serve as a basis for settling the whole business appealed to him.[116] Since the plan originated in Tokyo, he could accept it without disturbing relations with Japan. As soon as news of Matsudaira's proposal reached him, he set in motion the machinery for formulating policy on the question of American membership on the commission. Hornbeck categorically opposed participation, either as member or associate investigator, on the ground that it might eventually involve the United States in subsequent action which the League might take pursuant to the commission's findings. Castle agreed with Hornbeck but seemed to vacillate when he concluded that if the commission had representatives from other nations not League members, America should be included. Stimson concurred in the views of his advisers but was willing to join the commission if Briand insisted. For this move he gained President Hoover's approval on November 20, despite indications of senatorial opposition. Both Senators Borah and Joseph T. Robinson, the Democratic floor leader, decried any efforts to inject the United States into a purely oriental controversy.[117] At the same time, the Secretary was putting pressure on the Chinese, through Dawes in Paris and Johnson in Nanking, to accept. He warned them that their desire for a time limit for evacuation was bad, that the commission plan must go through because therein lay the most hopeful path to a solution of the problem. He assured the Chinese that ultimately the settlement must be between the two contestants but that the findings of the commission would greatly facilitate the negotiations. Finally, the Chinese were ready to capitulate, chiefly because what America wanted counted heavily. But much of the credit must go to Dawes. He was unrelenting in exerting pressure on Alfred Sze, and although Sze suspected his close friendship with Matsudaira and believed him to be pro-Japa-

[116] Stimson to Dawes, Nov. 21, 1931, *F.R.*, *1931*, III, 520.

[117] Memorandum by Hornbeck, Nov. 20, 1931, D/S File 793.94/2891; Castle, Diary, Nov. 20, 1931. The *Washington Post* (November 23, 1931) recorded the views of Robinson and Borah; Stimson noted Hoover's approval in his diary on November 20, 1931. He informed Dawes of the decision on the same day. *F.R.*, *1931*, III, 503–12

nese, he was willing to accept Dawes' arguments as coming from Washington.[118] Nelson T. Johnson in Nanking played his part by guaranteeing the government that Stimson's refusal to permit an American to sit with the Council meant neither a *rapprochement* with nor a concession to Japan.[119]

To the task of halting the Japanese advance, Stimson himself now moved in with the greatest vigor. It was not remarkable that he changed his approach so drastically and began to talk tough. Strong action seemed absolutely necessary in the face of the damage which might be done, by reckless military action, to the only intelligent and honest conciliation proposal now before the world. In the strongest remonstrances to Debuchi and Shidehara, he vented his displeasure over the attack on Tsitsihar. He threatened to make public the correspondence between Washington and Tokyo, which he had refrained from doing these past two months in order not to arouse public passions. He warned that an attack on Chinchow would be considered an aggressive act. Unless hostilities ceased, the proposal for a commission would be worthless. He belittled the contention that the advance was necessary to protect Japanese military lines. No Japanese garrison had anything to fear from Chinese troops, he stated.[120]

Stimson's onslaught must have struck fear and wonder in Shidehara. Neither he nor Debuchi had expected such powerful blows, and they reeled. The foreign minister, through Debuchi, urged the Secretary to keep cool. From Tokyo, Forbes reported him to be "cordial and conciliatory" and on November 24 relayed a pledge to evacuate Tsitsihar and call

[118] Stimson to Shaw, Nov. 23, and Shaw to Stimson, Nov. 22, 1931, *F.R.*, *1931*, III, 547–49, 536; also Stimson, Diary, Nov. 23, 1931. Dawes played a remarkable role in Paris. Although he attended no sessions, he was the hub of all the deliberations. All the important delegates called regularly at his hotel, where he helped iron out difficulties and compromise divergent viewpoints. Cleverly, he kept out of the limelight, maintaining no official relations with the Council. He arranged to have no invitations issued to him for social functions and did not "run around making a spectacle of myself" (Dawes to Stimson, Dec. 7, 1931, D/S File 793.94/3095–1/2). Thus he gave opponents of the League in the United States no cause for alarm, thereby saving the President from embarrassment and easing his own path to a possible nomination in 1932. See reports from P. J. Philip, *New York Times*, Nov. 16, 22, 25, 1931; also Castle, Diary, Nov. 13, 1931, and Dawes, *Journal*, p. 418.

[119] Stimson to Johnson, Nov. 17, 23, 1931, *F.R.*, *1931*, III, 464–65, 549.

[120] Stimson, Diary, Nov. 19, 1931; Stimson to Forbes, Nov. 23, 1931, *F.R.*, *Japan*, *1931–1941*, I, 48–49; Stimson to Debuchi, Nov. 19, 1931, *ibid.*, 44–46; also Nov. 22, 1931, *F.R.*, *1931*, III, 534–35.

off operations against Chinchow, which, of course, had the support of the war minister and chief of staff.[121] The Cabinet did not want the commission of inquiry plan to fail. It was the one solution satisfactory to the military in that it did not demand evacuation.

While pressuring the Chinese and bludgeoning the Japanese, Stimson had kept the public completely in the dark. He did not even let Briand know that a favorable decision on the commission had been reached in Washington. At press conferences, he refused to disclose his instructions to Dawes and denied reports of his cracking down on Tokyo.[122] When correspondents questioned him on the Far East, he displayed irritation and requested that they discuss something else.[123] Speculations abounded. Reports from Paris indicated that the League officials were puzzled. A New York magazine castigated Stimson for his silence, comparing him to the prewar statesmen Isvolski, Holstein, and Poincaré, and implied that, like them, he was practicing the old, out-of-date secret diplomacy.[124]

Stimson's reluctance to make known his moves was based on a number of factors. First, he did not want to arouse the Japanese public and jeopardize Shidehara's position, which would surely have happened had his recriminations to Tokyo been known. Second, he withheld his approval of the commission plan from Briand lest the latter use it as a club to coerce other countries. Finally, and just as important as all the foregoing, he simply did not believe in "open diplomacy." The Secretary was ever conscious of the dangers to a negotiation from public passions and pressure. Reports from Paris, however, now indicated that the draft resolution on the commission was meeting no objection from the other nations. This, plus China's capitulation and Japan's pledges, led Stimson finally to instruct Dawes, on the twenty-fourth, to inform Briand of the decision. As for the public, he never did reveal his dealings with Tokyo, even when he was accused of having encouraged Japan by assuring her of his support,[125] nor did

[121] Debuchi to Stimson, Nov. 21, and Forbes to Stimson, Nov. 24, 1931, *F.R., Japan, 1931–1941,* I, 47–48, 50.
[122] *New York Times,* Nov. 22, 1931.
[123] *Ibid.,* Nov. 17, 20, 1931.
[124] *Ibid.,* Nov. 21, 1931; New York *Herald Tribune,* Nov. 24, 1931; New York *Nation,* Nov. 25, 1931, p. 560.
[125] New York *Herald Tribune,* Nov. 17, 1931.

he make a public statement of his approval of the commission plan. This elitist Secretary of State deigned only to brief a few selected press chiefs at his home on the morning of the twenty-fourth, and this only after the President grew restless over criticism in the press of the department's silence. As a matter of fact, by this time Stimson was quite pleased with his achievements and did not mind a leakage to the press.[126] Any failure of the resolution now would be ascribed to the disputant who made trouble.[127] That afternoon, he indulged in his favorite recreation, horseback riding in Rock Creek Park.

The Secretary's satisfaction was premature. On November 28, the news that Honjo was moving on Chinchow exploded like a bombshell all over the Western world.[128] Stimson was furious—to the point of a violent outburst at a press conference at which he disclosed Shidehara's earlier pledge.[129] He ordered Forbes at once to seek an explanation.[130] Shidehara was in a delicate spot. Stimson's divulgence of his pledge embarrassed him; the army did not approve of the Foreign Office's making categoric pledges.[131] Further, a remark made by Stimson was inaccurately reported in the Tokyo press and came out as "the Japanese army is running amuck." The uproar in the press worried the foreign minister. Fortunately, the tension eased when Stimson denied having made the statement and expressed regret over the misinterpretation. Shidehara again pledged to halt operations following a promise to the Cabinet by the chief of staff and the war minister to wait until the commission had made its investigation.[132] Shidehara had acted fast, not so much because he feared Stimson's wrath or a stern warning from the British, whose vast interests in the Peking-Mukden Railroad lay athwart the army's path to Chinchow,[133] but because he could not afford to see the commission plan fall through. Once again Stimson felt relieved. On the thirtieth, he noted in his diary: "I think now the Japanese don't intend to let their army do any more solo

[126] Stimson, Diary, Nov. 24, 1931.
[127] Stimson to Dawes, Nov. 23, 24, 1931, *F.R., 1931*, III, 543–45, 559–60.
[128] *New York Times* headline, Nov. 28, 1931.
[129] *New York Times*, Nov. 28, 1931.
[130] Stimson to Forbes, Nov. 27, 1931, *F.R., Japan, 1931–1941*, I, 51.
[131] Forbes to Stimson, Nov. 28, 1931, *ibid.*, 51–53.
[132] Takeuchi, p. 369; Debuchi to Stimson, Nov. 28, 1931, D/S File 793·94/2945-1/2; *New York Times*, Nov. 29, 1931.
[133] *New York Times*, Nov. 26, 1931.

work on its own, and I think they will go ahead and make a settlement."

The way was now clear for Briand to put the resolution on the commission to a vote in the Council, and on December 1, he announced its formal approval by all the member nations, save China and Japan. Both nations were willing to accept with certain reservations. The Chinese wanted Japanese troops removed at least east of the Liao River, while Japan insisted on protection from bandits and guerrillas. During the next ten days, neither would yield. Briand grew impatient, fearful lest the Kwantung army advance on Chinchow before agreement could be reached and wreck the only prospect for a settlement of the crisis. The League had exhausted all remedies. If the commission plan fell through, no alternative action was contemplated. Stimson helped greatly to stabilize conditions during this difficult period by continuing to put pressure on Shidehara to keep the army in check. Through Forbes, Debuchi, and Dawes, he warned that an advance at this time would be considered an act of aggression and would inflame American public opinion.[134] Fortunately, on December 10, both sides gave way, the Japanese presumably because Dawes assured them that the Chinese would withdraw from Chinchow, thereby wiping out the principal base of bandit operations, and the Chinese because the Kwantung army pledged to remain east of the Liao River.[135] On that day, after twenty-five days of continuous conferences, including Sundays, the Council unanimously adopted the resolution. A commission of five was appointed to conduct the investigations, and the Council adjourned until January 25. Stimson immediately issued a statement backing the Council's action.[136]

So passed the second phase of the Manchurian crisis. Hostilities had ceased, and everybody breathed more easily. Prospects for peace and a final settlement seemed hopeful, although the odds that the Japanese would upset the apple

[134] Dec. 7, 8, 10, *F.R., 1931*, III, 629–30, 637–40; *F.R., Japan, 1931–1941*, I, 54–56, 58–59.

[135] Stimson denied that Dawes got a pledge from the Japanese. The allegation was printed in the New York *Herald Tribune* on December 11, 1931, as received from a Paris correspondent, who had it from League officials. See D/S File 793.94/30574/7, 30585/7.

[136] For details of the Sino-Japanese differences, see *F.R., 1931*, III, 617 ff. Stimson's statement is in *F.R., Japan, 1931–1941*, I, 60; also *New York Times*, Dec. 11, 1931.

cart with an attack on Chinchow were considered to be fifty-fifty.[137] Debuchi, after a talk with Stimson, told reporters in Washington he could see a silver lining in the Far Eastern clouds. The Secretary offered Briand his and the President's congratulations "on the successful termination of the difficult negotiations concerning the Manchurian question." Castle was pleased that world attention could now be directed to the "infinitely more important questions of debts and reparations." [138] An equitable solution appeared possible following the commission's report.

Many observers, however, saw a real victory for Japan already won, "a handsomely staged and impressive but virtually unconditional surrender" by the League.[139] The resolution deprived Japan of none of her gains. Her troops were left in undisturbed possession of a vast stretch of the Manchurian Railway: from Dairen in the south to Tsitsihar in the northwest to Kirin in the northeast to Antung on the Korean border in the southeast, a distance of 1,368 miles as compared with the 691 miles controlled on September 18. The Council reiterated the demand for a speedy withdrawal to the original zone, but no date was set and there was no indication that the Japanese would evacuate any time soon. The resolution did not provide for a study by the commission of the causes of the conflict, nor did it interfere with the possibility of direct negotiations between the two powers.[140] The adoption of the commission plan itself was a tacit admission of the failure to dislodge the Japanese.

Who was to blame for the League's failure? Many thoughtful persons placed the responsibility on the United States, specifically Stimson's withholding prompt and complete support for the resolution of October 24. Newspaper editors in China and William Martin in Geneva shared this view.[141] Even Norman H. Davis, the American ambassador-at-large in Europe and an ardent protagonist of co-operation with

[137] *New York Times*, Dec. 11, 1931.
[138] Stimson to Edge, Dec. 11, 1931, *F.R., 1931*, III, 676; Castle, Diary, Dec. 10, 1931.
[139] New York *Herald Tribune*, Dec. 10, 1931.
[140] *New York Times*, Dec. 11, 1931.
[141] See various issues of the Peking *Leader, Peking Times,* and *Tientsin Times* for the first half of December 1931, and William Martin in *Journal de Genève*, April 17, 1932. See also the memorandum by George H. Blakeslee, an adviser to the Department of State, Dec. 28, 1931, D/S File 793.94/4151.

Geneva, indirectly ascribed the Council's weakness to Stimson's "blowing hot and cold."[142] None of these opinions, however, has great merit. America did not enfeeble the League; it was made impotent by its own chief members. Verbal support by Stimson would have made no difference to Japan. Only force could have accomplished Japanese evacuation, and neither Britain nor France would go beyond suggestion and persuasion. Furthermore, neither power favored the deadline in the resolution and Japan knew it. Japan knew also that neither government stood completely behind its representatives at Geneva. The Quai d'Orsay considered Briand excessively zealous and impetuous, and Downing Street gave Cecil no encouragement. It was true that at two of the Council's November meetings Sir John Simon became sufficiently aroused to demand quick action under Articles XV and XVI of the Covenant and evacuation independent of the proposed commission, but it was only momentary.[143] He soon returned to his usual calm and generally pro-Japanese outlook. Neither he nor Anthony Eden cared to go beyond public opinion at home and in the Dominions, which was decidedly favorable to Nippon.[144] In France, sympathy of officials and businessmen for Japan was so great that reports of secret Franco-Japanese political and economic understandings were widely believed by veteran diplomats and newsmen.[145] Stimson would have been foolhardy, indeed, to have

[142] Norman H. Davis to Walter Lippmann, Nov. 25, 1931, Norman H. Davis Papers, Box 35, Lippmann Folder (Library of Congress).

[143] See Dawes to Stimson, Nov. 18, 23, 1931, *F.R., 1931*, III, 481, 485, 546; also "Memorandum by the Secretary of State for Foreign Affairs respecting Manchuria," Nov. 23, 1931, *British Documents*, pp. 943–47. Simon really did not understand the complexities of the Far Eastern situation. His suggestion on November 16 that China guarantee Japan's treaty rights and admit their validity was completely unrealistic. See Dawes to Stimson, Nov. 16, 1931, *F.R., 1931*, IV, 460–62. His evaluation of the situation in the Far East in the House of Commons on December 10 was quite naïve. See *Parliamentary Debates*, House of Commons, Fifth Series, Vol. 269, pp. 460–71.

[144] A leading article in the London *Times* (November 23, 1931) went so far as to question whether China fulfilled al the criteria for League membership and at the same time gave Japan virtually a clean bill of health. Australia and New Zealand were pleased to see the Japanese on the march on the grounds that her conquests in China would exhaust, if not satisfy, her. For Canadian opinion, see American consul at Montreal to State Dept., Dec. 14, 1931, D/S File 793.94/3229. Prominent Canadians did not approve the League's action. They appreciated the legal validity of the Japanese position.

[145] Castle, Diary, Dec. 15, 1931; also *New York Times*, Dec. 15, 1931. There

rushed in where the two pillars of the League did not wish to tread. Since the United States was not a member, he was able to dissociate himself from the action, which he considered unwise. By refusing to support an untenable position he was continuing a policy completely realistic and intelligent —remaining within his capabilities and avoiding needlessly antagonizing Japan. He deserves more credit than Europeans tended to give him for his stern admonitions to Japan, which helped to halt the projected move on Chinchow, and his pressure on the Chinese, which made possible the acceptance of the commission plan.

was disappointment in Geneva when the French government decorated the retiring Japanese ambassador. See New York *Herald Tribune,* Dec. 29, 1931. Rumors of Japanese support to France in Yunnan and on the question of disarmament in exchange for French support in Manchuria were most prominent. Memorandum by Castle, Dec. 15, 1931, D/S File 500A15A4/6491/2.

CHAPTER FOUR
in which
Stimson loses patience and
proclaims nonrecognition

. . . *the entire structure of the peace treaties, which have been laboriously constructed in the world since the great war, was in fair way to be irreparably damaged, if not completely overthrown, by the action of the Japanese army. That would be a loss in my opinion, which would outweigh a very large amount of estrangement between this country and Japan, serious as the latter consideration was.*

H. L. STIMSON, DECEMBER 12, 1931

O<small>N</small> DECEMBER 11, 1931, the Minseito cabinet fell. Inukai Tsuyoshi, leader of the Seiyukai party, replaced Wakatsuki as prime minister, and one month later Inukai's son-in-law, Yoshizawa Kenkichi, moved from the Paris embassy to the Foreign Office. Foreign policy had nothing to do with the change in government; the Manchurian question was not a party issue. As put aptly by the London *Times*, "Manchuria did not enter into the case against the government."[1] Home Minister Adachi Kenzo had been agitating for weeks for a new coalition cabinet consisting of nationalists from both parties who would pursue a stronger military policy, but it was a smoke screen: the real issue was fiscal policy. The Big Business interests abhorred Wakatsuki's orthodox financial views. They wanted to abandon the gold standard, which the Minseito resisted. Within twenty-four hours after gaining power, Inukai dutifully suspended the free movement of gold, which, incidentally, netted the Mitsui, Mitsubishi, and Sumitomo interests between thirty and sixty million dollars.[2]

On the same day, the Cabinet approved a large military budget to be used to pacify and occupy all of Manchuria and authorized reinforcing the Kwantung army with troops from Korea.[3] This came as no surprise to Western observers. Although the new government owed its existence to a purely domestic affair, it was widely believed that the repercussions in foreign policy would be great. Wakatsuki and Shidehara had been unable to control the military, but at least they had at times served as a brake. Neither Inukai nor Yoshizawa cared to emulate his predecessor. Indeed, the new foreign minister had shown a remarkable sympathy for the military while he represented Shidehara at Geneva and pleaded Japan's case. Furthermore, Araki Sadao, who replaced Minami at the War

[1] London *Times*, Jan. 16, 1932. Ambassador Forbes believed Stimson, by his "unwisdom," responsible in some measure for Shidehara's removal from the Foreign Office, but there is no reason to accept this view. Forbes did not observe very acutely or analyze very perspicaciously. See Journal, Series 2, Vol. 5, p. 474. The French ambassador in Tokyo considered him to be incompetent and commented "sur l'insuffiance de la representation Americaine à Tokyo," *British Documents*, p. 856.

[2] See Rodney Gilbert in New York *Herald Tribune*, May 22, 1932, and Hugh Byas in *New York Times*, Dec. 12, 1931.

[3] See "Summary of Proof of 'Japanese Military Aggression in Manchuria,'" IMTFE, p. 25; also testimony of General Araki Sadao, IMTFE, Exhibit 188c.

Office, was an unabashed firebrand, whereas Minami, outwardly, at least, had acted with restraint. The worst was expected.[4]

The worse soon turned out to be a renewed drive on Chinchow. The build-up for the attack began on the very day the government fell. That morning, the regularly scheduled Mukden–Chinchow–Peking train did not leave Mukden. Three days later, General Honjo told a *New York Times* correspondent that the Chinese must halt bandit operations around Chinchow and withdraw from the city. On the same day, in Tokyo, Premier Inukai confirmed the general's view.[5] Four days later, the War Office announced the dispatch of an ultimatum to the Chinese commander, and during the next few days cables from the capital reported active military preparations. When on the twenty-third of December no reply came from Chinchow, the army moved.[6]

Relentlessly and doggedly, the Kwantung troops pushed into southern Manchuria. The cold was severe, twenty degrees below zero frequently, but the soldiers were warmly clad in heavy olive-drab uniforms, sleeveless goatskin jackets, and overcoats with hoods. Opposite them the Chinese were ragged and nondescript, wearing many and varied uniforms and owing as many allegiances. The state of the army represented the political chaos at home. The Nationalist government had ceased to function. Public hostility, student demonstrations, and Cantonese rebels caused Chiang Kai-shek's downfall. On December 15, he resigned, along with Wellington Koo and T. V. Soong, the other prominent leaders. The Central Executive Committee ruled, but ineffectually. Pending the organization of a new government to include Cantonese elements, there was no strong hand at the helm. In Manchuria, the Young Marshal, Chang Hsueh-liang, the symbol of Chinese resistance, gave way to his uncle, Chang Tso-hsiang, as commander of Chinese troops, thus virtually guaranteeing a retreat before the Japanese.[7] Meanwhile, Honjo's forces neared

[4] *New York Times*, Dec. 14, 16, 1931; Castle, Diary, Dec. 13, 1931; Prince Saionji also feared the consequences. See Kido, Diary, Dec. 12, 1931. Ambassador Forbes believed that Araki was the dominant figure in the new cabinet. Forbes to State Dept., Jan. 29, 1932, *F.R., 1932*, IV, 673.

[5] *New York Times*, Dec. 15, 1931 (from Hallett Abend).

[6] *New York Times*, Dec. 19, 1931 (from Hugh Byas).

[7] See Peck to State Dept., Dec. 15, 1931, *F.R., 1931*, III, 701–2; Johnson to State Dept., Dec. 10, 1931, *ibid.*, 670; *New York Times*, Dec. 16, 1931.

Chinchow: Tienchwangtai on the twenty-fourth; Tawa Station on the twenty-eighth; Panshan on the twenty-ninth; on the last day of the year, they halted fifteen miles from their objective. After consolidating various elements which had been operating separately, the victorious Kwantung army occupied Chinchow, the last Chinese stronghold in Manchuria, on January 3, 1932. The Chinese had fled south of the Great Wall.[8] Organized resistance in Manchuria had come to an end.

The Western world was shocked at the Japanese advance. Diplomats had considered the Council's December 10 resolution and Tokyo's pledge to halt operations to have closed the Manchurian affair, at least until the commission of inquiry would render its report. Now the whole miserable and vexatious question was reopened. No one was more upset and chagrined than Secretary Stimson. For him, Chinchow marked a turning point. The betrayal of their promise by the Japanese destroyed completely and finally his faith in them. No longer could they be trusted; no longer could he accept the assumption that a division existed between the army and the Foreign Office; no longer could he look for an ultimate victory by the diplomats over the military and a peaceful solution to the Sino-Japanese difficulty.[9] He had been moving gradually and reluctantly to this position even before the attack on Chinchow. In late November, he had begun to realize that diplomatic pressure and persuasion, confidence and trust would never be effective. Discouraged and saddened, he saw the end of a possibility of conciliation. To a friend he wrote on November 20 of the futility of his efforts to bolster the hand of the civilian authorities.[10] The change in government and the advance on Chinchow proved to be the decisive event.

Now his thinking on the Manchurian problem underwent a radical and decided change. Toughness was to be the new

[8] See Chinese minister in Washington to State Dept., Dec. 31, 1931, *F.R., 1931*, III, 712.

[9] Stimson and Bundy, *On Active Service*, p. 231. The fact that the Japanese chose to attack during the Christmas season added to his annoyance; he considered it a deliberate effort to affront the Christian world. See Castle, Diary, Dec. 24, 1931.

[10] See Stimson, Diary, Nov. 19, 1931; the letter, to Frederic Coudert, is in the Stimson Papers, Box 27, Letters Sent. See also Stimson to Dawes, Nov. 19, 1931, *F.R., 1931*, III, 496.

line. He made one more attempt at diplomatic pressure and
persuasion—in a note to Tokyo on December 22 and in an
interview with Debuchi on the following day. In Tokyo, the
prime minister assured Forbes that Japan had no designs on
Chinese territory, but the ambassador cabled his doubts that
operations would cease in Manchuria, "where a free hand
seems to have been given the military." [11] A temporary halt
in the Japanese advance, which created a spurt of optimism,
was only temporary and operational. When it became clear
that the remonstrances in Tokyo and Washington were of no
avail, Stimson began to cast about for stronger measures to
register his country's dissatisfaction. He did not think it necessary to move slowly and quietly now. There was no Shidehara
to be given a chance to regain control, and there was no
danger of driving the military to any greater defiance. He
was prepared even to risk Japanese animosity, which would,
in his opinion, be outweighed by the damage to the peace
structure if he did not act.[12] Some one had to take the initiative. The League was making no move; not a voice was raised
in Geneva or in the capitals of the member states to convene
the Council to consider the new threat to peace.

Although Stimson determined to move ahead of the League
and to abandon, if necessary, his previously prudent and cautious policy, neither his military capabilities nor the state of
public opinion had been altered. The navy had not improved
since the fall, and should Japanese ire be aroused to the point
of war, the United States would be in no better position to
meet the enemy.[13] As for the public attitude, it had not
changed measurably. Sympathy for China had grown greater,
but not to the point of jumping to her defense. The American
press, unlike that of Britain and France, was predominantly
pro-Chinese, but of the most ardent Sinophiles, few suggested
active intervention in any form in Asia. The Hearst press,
particularly on the West Coast, damned the Japanese but
restricted itself to verbal attacks. The New York *Nation*

[11] Forbes to State Dept., Dec. 22, 1931, *F.R., Japan, 1931–1941*, I, 65. The note
is in *ibid.*, 65–66. See also *New York Times*, Dec. 24, 25, 27, 28, 1931.
[12] Stimson to Elihu Root, Dec. 14, 1931, Stimson Papers, Box 27, Letters Sent.
[13] Stanley K. Hornbeck recalled, in a conversation with the author on August
19, 1956, that early in 1932, at the time the department was deliberating sterner
measures against Japan, two admirals visited him to say that the navy was
not prepared to support a strong American policy in the Pacific.

branded Japan the outlaw but did not believe much could be done about it. Even the missionaries, in their speeches up and down the country upon their return home for their quinquennial holiday, although painting a sad picture of prostrate China, called for a policy which would keep America out of the oriental fight. The price for saving China was great, and few were prepared to pay it.[14] Of all the important newspapers, only the Scripps-Howard group demanded positive action at any cost. Their editorials pounded at the government for an aggressive policy. "The Hoover-Stimson policy," said the New York *World-Telegram,* "is . . . ineffective. . . . Millions of American citizens are waiting for the State Department to act." [15] Millions of citizens were not waiting for action, although there were some very articulate pacifists, liberals, and internationalists, such as John Dewey, Raymond L. Buell, Newton D. Baker, Abbott Lawrence Lowell, and Dorothy Detzer, who with tongue and pen supported Scripps-Howard president Roy Howard, the spearhead of the drive for strong measures.[16] The vast majority wanted to steer clear of the oriental imbroglio and would support no policy calculated to get America involved. A sizable number of people still believed Japan the injured party, or, at least, that both sides shared the blame. Editorially, the New York *Herald Tribune* continued to approve Japanese action in Manchuria.[17] On December 9, Wilbur Forrest, executive assistant to the newspaper's president, spoke before the Smith College Club in New York and in the strongest language defended

[14] See JFOD, SP 185, p. 352, for estimate of Hearst press; New York *Nation,* "Japan the Outlaw," Jan. 6, 1932; Walter Lippmann, New York *Herald Tribune,* Dec. 24, 1931; for the missionary view, see a letter from Leonard Christian, Foochow, Nov. 23, 1931, to W. C. Fairfield, secretary of the American Board of Commissioners for Foreign Missions, American Board Papers, Foochow Mission Minutes, Telegrams, Cables, Statistics, 1930–1939; see also New York *Marine Journal,* Jan. 15, 1932, for accurate appraisal of American attitude.

[15] Dec. 7, 1931; *The World-Telegram* was the most important newspaper in the chain; see also Stimson's comment on the chain, Diary, Dec. 8, 1931.

[16] R. L. Buell to Newton D. Baker, Dec. 9, 1931, Baker Papers. At a luncheon on December 12, 1931, in New York, John Dewey labeled the Administration's policy "so confused . . . that the most charitable interpretation of our State Department's and our President's action is that they do not know themselves what they are doing or what they should do." *New York Times,* Dec. 12, 1931.

[17] See editorials of Dec. 21, 27, 31, 1931.

Tokyo's seizure of the territory north of the Great Wall. Japan
brought peace to Manchuria, he said, and the best thing possible would be for Japan to annex the area and develop it.[18]
Hugh Byas was still sending home dispatches from Tokyo to
the *New York Times,* explaining sympathetically Japan's unhappy position in Asia, ringed by Russia and China and at-
tempting to gain for herself a foothold in the world after
the other great nations had got theirs.[19] Edward Price Bell,
noted European correspondent for the *Chicago Daily News,*
was getting the same point across to his chief, Colonel Frank
Knox.[20] These people certainly wanted no action by the
government to oppose Japan. Similarly, those who considered
both sides at fault called for America to assume the role of
mediator, if not to stand aloof.[21]

In casting about for possible courses of action, Stimson had
before him a number of alternatives which had been suggested from time to time by various individuals and groups.
The demand for a meeting of the nations signatory to the
Nine Power Pact arose early in the conflict,[22] but it was not
seriously considered by the Department of State. At times,
in desperation, Stimson seemed inclined to call the nations
together to discuss the threat to the territorial integrity of
China,[23] but he realized in more lucid moments that Japan
would resist on the grounds that a mere police action could
not be even remotely construed as a threat to alienate territory. Further, a conference would have been a great blow to
the League's prestige, an admission that the League machinery had failed. The Secretary never even got around to
sounding out the nations on the matter although he occasionally mentioned the idea to the foreign ambassadors in Washington. It is unlikely that the plan would have received a
favorable response. The world had a surfeit of conferences:
one on reparations was in progress and another on disarma-

[18] New York *Herald Tribune,* Dec. 10, 1931.
[19] *New York Times,* Dec. 27, 1931. See the same view in *The Congregationalist,* Nov. 26, 1931, p. 1580.
[20] Bell to Knox, Dec. 29, 1931, Edward Price Bell Papers, Box Outgoing,
1931–34 (Newberry Library).
[21] See *Advocate of Peace,* 93 (December 1931), pp. 200–201, and *World
Alliance,* 7 (December 1931), p. 7.
[22] See the open letter to President Hoover from the Women's International
League for Peace and Freedom, Dec. 4, 1931. Original in SCPC.
[23] Stimson, Diary, Dec. 8, 1931.

ment was scheduled for early in 1932.[24] More important, the French and British foreign offices did not wish to challenge the Rising Sun, either formally or openly.

To recall the American ambassador from Tokyo was another pet scheme, propelled chiefly by Roy Howard. Others advocated the idea, such as the editor of the *Nation*, Dorothy Detzer, and the League for Independent Political Action, headed by John Dewey.[25] This measure, too, the State Department did not seriously entertain. It would have been, indeed, a futile and hollow gesture, a gratuitous move which would have availed nothing. Stimson even thought Howard "a damn fool" for suggesting it.[26]

Many people considered an embargo on arms and loans, levied equally against both warring nations, to be an ideal means for registering American displeasure and shortening hostilities.[27] This plan, however, fell of its own weight. America did not furnish enough of the sinews of war to either belligerent to make a difference in the military resources. But even were this not true, the peace groups which talked loudest of embargo differed among themselves on the question of discrimination. Some, for example, wished to single out Japan as the aggressor and point the embargo at her alone.[28] Congress, too, reflected this dichotomy. In the late twenties there had been introduced in both houses a number of resolutions for prohibiting the exportation of arms to warring nations, but nothing was ever done because of disagreement on impartial *versus* discriminatory embargo.[29] When Congress met

[24] Castle, Diary, Dec. 9, 1931.

[25] See *New York Times*, Nov. 27, 1931, and New York *Nation*, Jan. 6, 1932. The board of directors of the Women's International League for Peace and Freedom refused to go along with Miss Detzer, the executive secretary. See Mrs. Hannah C. Hull, chairman of the national board, to Mme. Drevet, Dec. 20, 1931, Hull Papers, Correspondence, 1931, SCPC. The forty-one peace societies meeting as the Interorganization Council on Disarmament also vetoed the measure, *New York Times*, Nov. 24, 1931.

[26] Stimson, Diary, Dec. 3, 1931.

[27] The National Council for the Prevention of War, the Federal Council of Churches of Christ, in America, the Foreign Policy Association, the League of Nations Association, and other organizations petitioned the President. See *New York Times*, Nov. 25, 1931.

[28] The Women's International League wished to single out Japan. See the open letter to President Hoover, Jan. 7, 1936, WIL Papers, SCPC.

[29] See 70th Cong., 1st sess., HJRes. 1, SJRes. 14; 2nd sess., SJRes. 215, HJRess. 412 and 422; 71st Cong., 1st sess., HJRess. 1, 13, and 122; also *Congressional Record*, 70th Cong., 1st sess., pp. 4560 and 4646.

on December 8, 1931, new resolutions were proposed, and there began hearings, which again rotated around the two opposing views.[30]

The measure most widely debated was the economic boycott, or, to use the European term, economic sanctions. Called by some the most plausible method for coercing the aggressor and the most practical support of peace and by others the surest road to war and the least plausible method for coercing the aggressor, it had figured heavily in American thinking ever since the earliest days of the crisis. The Twentieth Century Fund, a private research organization, which in September 1921 had organized a committee to study intensively the whole question of sanctions from every angle—political, legal, diplomatic, and economic—began a serious investigation of the question in October. The various groups devoted to world peace, international organization, and disarmament held numerous meetings to consider the issue. Magazines featured articles, newspapers editorialized, legislators debated. Everybody talked about it, and with great passion.

It seems clear that, at this time, more opposed than favored sanctions. In general, the most ardent support came from the liberals, the internationalists, and the pacifists. Having accepted the fact of Japanese aggression, many of them believed the only way to humble the Island Empire was by a complete cessation of trade, by economic isolation.[31] But even in those ranks, there was hesitation and doubt. In a series of autumn meetings of the Interorganization Council on Disarmament, which consisted of representatives of the various peace groups, serious questions were raised about the danger of a boycott's leading to hostilities should Japan choose to retaliate. A motion to request the State Department to institute a boycott of Japan did not pass; agreement could be reached only on a resolution not to obstruct the League of Nations if that body

[30] See Elton Atwater, *American Regulation of Arms Exports* (Washington, D.C., 1941). Part III, chap. i contains an account of the movement to regulate arms export, 1928 to 1934.

[31] National Council for the Prevention of War *News Bulletin,* November 1931, p. 7; League of Nations Association *News,* November–December 1931; speeches by Upton Close and John Dewey at the meeting of the New York chapter of the League for Industrial Democracy as reported in the *New York Times,* Dec. 13, 1931; the views of the Foreign Policy Association in *New York Times,* Nov. 12, 1931.

invoked the sanctions article of the covenant, and few were willing to become involved in such action lest American warships be required to join an international blockading squadron.[32] The only clear and undistorted voice in support of boycott emanated from the Scripps-Howard newspaper chain, whose arguments, when distilled to their essence, reflected Roy Howard's desire for immediate, strong action.

The opposition stemmed from many diverse sources. Farmers, manufacturers, importers, exporters, and financiers all pointed out the disastrous effect on the American economy, then in the depths of the depression, of a stoppage of Japanese-American trade. Statistics told the story. More than half of America's raw cotton went to Japan; the greatest part of the raw silk to feed American factories came from Japan. Annually, America exported almost half a billion dollars in goods to Japan and imported from that country slightly over one-quarter billion. To be sure, America was Japan's best customer, absorbing 32 per cent of her total exports and receiving 97 per cent of her silk, and a boycott might well ruin Japan, but it would ruin America, too.[33] Religious groups, caring naught for economic arguments or material considerations, abhorred the idea of sanctions because of the danger of inviting reprisal, which would lead to war. A war to end a war was undesirable.[34] The majority of the nation's press echoed these sentiments and inveighed resolutely against sanctions, either in conjunction with the League or alone.[35]

The pressure on the policy-makers in Washington from proponents and opponents of sanctions was great, but the decision to reject the measure was made quite independently. All during the autumn months, Stimson flirted with the idea, now leaning toward it as the crisis and his exasperation with Japan deepened, now abandoning it as he more soberly contemplated the possible complications resulting from such action. His vacillation is revealed clearly in his diary entries

[32] NCPW *News Bulletin,* November 1931, p. 2; also Dorothy Detzer to Mrs. William Hull, Nov. 27, 1931, Papers of the WIL, SCPC.

[33] *Journal of Commerce,* Nov. 9, 1931; *New Republic,* Dec. 2, 1931, p. 59. For Japanese views on the effects of a boycott, see "Japanese-American Interdependence," *Contemporary Japan,* I (1932–33), 198–201.

[34] *Christian Century,* Dec. 23, 1931, pp. 1616–18; *World Tomorrow,* XIV (December 1931), 388.

[35] *Literary Digest,* Dec. 5, 1931, pp. 3–4.

at the time. Within the Department of State, opinion similarly fluctuated. Of the Secretary's principal advisers, Allen T. Klots, James Grafton Rogers, and Stanley K. Hornbeck from time to time inclined toward a boycott as the only means of bridling Japan, while the undersecretary, William R. Castle, consistently and adamantly opposed it. At a meeting on December 6 at Stimson's home, the whole question was examined from every angle. The staff had before it a long policy paper prepared by the Economic Affairs people in the department which urged that a boycott be instituted. After a detailed inventory of Japanese and American trade relations, the study concluded that a boycott would have little effect on the American economy in the long run but would virtually destroy textile manufacturing and silk producing in Japan and permanently injure Japan's economy. Eight to ten million people alone engaged in producing the silk crop would be thrown out of work and a $220,000,000 annual loss would be incurred in textile exports.[36] Hornbeck, Klots, and Rogers, troubled by the possibility of the failure of the League of Nations resolution on the commission of inquiry, came out in favor of the recommendation, provided the League or some nation other than the United States took the initiative. Castle vigorously dissented. He pointed to the baneful effect on world economy and the possibility of American involvement in hostilities. He warned of the opposition of southern cotton growers and of the political capital which the remnants of the "Battalion of Death" would make of it.[37] Stimson reluctantly agreed with his deputy. The Secretary felt that something should be done to bring the Japanese to their senses and boycott seemed to be a good measure, but the complications worried him—the dangers of war, the opposition of the American people, and the possible political repercussions. Soon the others came to realize the futility of the project and withdrew their support. Hornbeck returned to his usual position of advising doing less rather than more on the grounds that whatever the United States might do, short of war, would have no effect on Japan except to sharpen resentment against America. He agreed with the view of R. S. Miller, one of his assistants in the Far Eastern Division, who

[36] "Memorandum on the Manchurian Situation," D/S File 793.94/4314.
[37] Castle, Diary, Dec. 6, 7, 1931.

urged waiting until the financial pinch hit Tokyo when the bills for the Manchurian adventure would come due. In three to six months, he believed, the financial strain would solve the problem.[38] Even had Stimson and the others wished to push sanctions, the path was blocked by President Hoover's position. From the very beginning, Hoover had for a number of reasons refused to give his consent.[39] For one thing, he suspected that the United States would be alone in levying a boycott and so bear the brunt of Japan's ire. Although sanctions figured regularly in the deliberations of the League Council, the chances of action were remote in view of British and French opposition. Hoover learned of the British attitude early in October from Ogden Mills, who had made specific inquiry while in London, and Gilbert had telegraphed from Geneva that Drummond himself considered pressure through economic action out of the question while the world was in a depression.[40] Moreover, the President feared the wrath of the new Seventy-second Congress, which had convened on December 7, 1931. He needed all the support and good will he could get for his domestic program and could not afford to risk alienating the slender Republican majority in the Senate or the Republican minority in the House with a rash foreign policy. Within a few days after the opening session, Hiram Johnson, William Borah, George Moses, George Norris, and other stalwarts were voicing displeasure with the Administration's meddling in Europe and objecting to a boycott. On December 14, Johnson called for all the correspondence on the Manchurian crisis. He was going to audit the State Department account to see just how much damage had been done.[41] Finally, and as important as the foregoing reasons, Hoover, true to his Quaker faith, abhorred getting

[38] For Hornbeck's views, see memoranda, Dec. 15 and 16, 1931, D/S File 793.94/3383, 4078; Miller's memorandum is dated Dec. 19, 1931, D/S File 793.94/3164.

[39] Stimson, Diary, Nov. 14, 27, 1931.

[40] Hoover, *Memoirs, 1920–1933*, p. 367; Gilbert to State Dept., Oct. 7, 1931, *F.R., 1931*, III, 130; E. R. Perkins, "The Non-application of Sanctions Against Japan, 1931–1933," in D. E. Lee and G. McReynolds, *Essays in History and International Relations* (Worcester, Mass., 1949), p. 218.

[41] For congressional views, see *Congressional Record*, 72nd Cong., 1st sess., pp. 384, 463, 536, 818, 1160; also *Outlook*, Dec. 9, 1931, p. 458; *New York Times*, Dec. 15, 1931.

involved in any situation which might lead to violence. Of the long and intense discussions on a boycott during the autumn, the only positive outcome was Stimson's private assurance to Geneva that if the League should invoke the sanctions article, the United States would not interfere or attempt to break a blockade set on foot to enforce it.[42] He hoped, at least, that Japan would be kept guessing about American intentions and was vastly annoyed when the New York *Herald Tribune* published a statement, which he promptly denied, that he had privately promised the Japanese that he would not support a boycott.[43]

The course of action Stimson was finally to take, a milder one than any of the other alternatives, popularly called nonrecognition and embodied in the identical notes to Japan and China of January 7, 1932, had been a topic for speculation in official circles in Washington and the other world capitals since at least mid-November. In the United States, it had scarcely been discussed, either in the press or public forum—being unable to compete with the other, more dramatic programs—but the idea percolated in the minds of a few of the more sophisticated publicists and officials. Early in October, a congressman from Illinois suggested to President Hoover that he announce his government's refusal to recognize "any alienation of territory or trade privileges by Japan in Manchuria." [44] On December 1, Walter Lippmann, in his syndicated column, urged that Japan be prevented from enjoying the political fruits of her occupation of Manchuria by the withholding of recognition of any new treaties negotiated at bayonet point. Some weeks later, he wrote Stimson along the same lines.[45] In November, Hornbeck, in a number of memoranda, advanced the same plan.[46] President Hoover had it in mind, too, and Stimson thought about it frequently as a likely policy. He discussed it with his assistants on November 19, and on the same day, when he talked to Dawes over the

[42] Stimson to Dawes, Nov. 19, 1931, *F.R., 1931*, III, 489–92.
[43] New York *Herald Tribune*, Nov. 17, 1931; Stimson to Dawes, Nov. 17, 1931, D/S File 793.94/2735A, and memorandum by Castle, Nov. 18, 1931, *F.R., 1931*, III, 477.
[44] D/S File 793.94/2138 (Oct. 12, 1931).
[45] New York *Herald Tribune*, Dec. 1, 1931; Lippmann to Stimson, Dec. 22, 1931, Stimson Papers, Box 14, Letters Received.
[46] D/S File 793.94/2888, 3005.

transatlantic telephone, he mentioned the possibility of disapproval of Japanese action, taking the form of a statement on nonrecognition.[47]

So the idea was in the air. It was a reasonable solution to the problem to which no objection had been raised, and, of course, it was not a new one. Sixteen years earlier, when Japan had presented the infamous Twenty-one Demands to China, Secretary of State William Jennings Bryan had warned Japan that the United States "cannot recognize any agreement or undertaking which has been entered into or which may be entered into between the Governments of Japan and China, impairing the treaty rights of the United States and its citizens in China, or the international policy relative to China commonly known as the Open Door policy." And in 1929, Secretary of State Frank B. Kellogg, before he left the department, considered inserting nonrecognition into the Pact of Paris as a sanction against an aggressor.[48]

Stimson had nonrecognition so much in mind that on December 2 he actually drafted a statement and, the next day, laid it before Hornbeck, Klots, Castle, and George H. Blakeslee, an adviser on Far Eastern affairs in the department. They did not believe, however, that anything should be done pending the outcome of the League resolution on the commission of inquiry. They did advise issuing the statement if the resolution were defeated.[49] The resolution passed the Council and the Secretary laid the draft aside. But as the Japanese set their sights on Chinchow, Stimson began thinking again of a means for exerting pressure, and with sanctions no longer a possibility, he turned to nonrecognition. On the fourteenth, he poured out his determination in a letter to Elihu Root, his old mentor, to issue the nonrecognition statement if the Kwantung army moved on Chinchow.[50] As reports arrived in Washington describing the military's advance toward the city in the closing days of December, Stimson grew restless. The time was at hand. On January 2, 1932, he learned

---

[47] Stimson and Bundy, *On Active Service*, p. 234; Stimson, *The Far Eastern Crisis*, p. 93; *F.R., 1931*, III, 496–98.

[48] For a brief historical account of the principle of nonrecognition in American foreign policy, see R. L. Buell's article in New York *Herald Tribune*, Mar. 27, 1936, sec. 2.

[49] Stimson, Diary, Dec. 3, 1931.

[50] Stimson Papers, Box 27, Letters Sent.

of the imminence of the fall of Chinchow, and the next morning, after an uneasy night, he arose at six to write out, in longhand, a final draft. Later that day, he showed it to Klots, Blakeslee, R. S. Miller, and Hunter Miller, the department's historical adviser. They all approved. The next afternoon, Hornbeck and Castle saw it. The latter recommended deletion of a sentence which guaranteed the territorial and administrative integrity of China. Stimson consented. Hornbeck objected to the categorical and binding character of the words "will never recognize." "Never," he suggested, was an awfully long time. As a substitute, he offered "does not intend to recognize." This, too, Stimson accepted. In the evening, he sought the President's approval. Busy with the nation's and the world's economic troubles, Hoover quickly approved. During the next two days, the chief officers in the department reworded, rephrased, and polished the language, and at noon on January 7, the note was cabled to Forbes in Tokyo and to Peck in Nanking for delivery to the respective foreign offices.[51] It was a brief message and stated that the United States "cannot admit the legality of any situation *de facto* nor does it intend to recognize any treaty or agreement entered into between those Governments [China and Japan], or agents thereof, which may impair the treaty rights of the United States or its citizens in China . . . and that it does not intend to recognize any situation, treaty or agreement which may be brought about by means contrary to the . . . Pact of Paris." [52]

So the famous Stimson Non-Recognition Doctrine came into being. Although directed to both contestants, it was obviously meant only for Japan, which alone had the power and the inclination to upset the *status quo* by violence. Although Stimson maintained at the time and subsequently that the note was intended solely to protect American rights in Manchuria and to assert the general view that no good

[51] The birth pains of the note may be followed in Stimson, Diary, Jan. 3, 4, 6, 1932, and in Castle, Diary, Jan. 8, 1932. In conversation with the author on August 19, 1956, Stanley Hornbeck confirmed substantially the story as the diaries revealed it—with one exception. Stimson noted at the time that Hornbeck had fought "tenaciously" against a definite statement. Hornbeck recalled that he was "neither for nor against it."

[52] The text of the note is in *F.R., 1931,* III, 7–8.

could result from a violation of the Pact of Paris,[53] it must be construed, in the light of his increasing chagrin, as a censure of Japan and, indeed, was so interpreted widely, both at home and abroad. As the Secretary wrote many years later, it was arrived at by a "natural and almost inevitable sequence." [54] Some reproach had to be made, some displeasure and disapproval voiced. Force or even measures "short of force" were out of the question. The only alternative was a statement that refused to recognize any situation which came about by dishonorable and distasteful means and which at the same time, if only indirectly, registered disgust with a nation that was violating the norms of fair play and international morality. The ideas and the language of the doctrine came from many minds and many pens. In respect of authorship, it was no more Stimson's than the Monroe Doctrine was Monroe's. Stimson drew from the views and phrases of Lippmann, Kellogg, Bryan, Hoover, Hornbeck, Castle, and Klots, just as Monroe, a century before, had drawn on those of Jefferson, Madison, Clay, and John Quincy Adams. But inasmuch as the President's name was attached to the earlier doctrine because he was responsible for launching that message, then the later doctrine should bear the Secretary's name because he took the initiative for its launching. Had it not been for Stimson's determination to take some action after the Chinchow assault, there would have been no nonrecognition policy.

Just as the Monroe Doctrine had no effect on the plans of the nations against which it was directed, so did the Stimson doctrine do nothing to deter Japan. Just as the earlier doctrine had set forth a new principle, at least for the Western Hemisphere, the ideas of the two spheres and no further colonization, so did the Stimson Doctrine, in relation to the postwar treaty structure, state a new principle, nonrecognition of any situation resulting from a violation of the Pact of Paris. Both were viewed with distaste or treated with

[53] See report of Stimson's press conference in *New York Times*, Jan. 8, 1932; see also *On Active Service*, p. 234.

[54] *On Active Service*, p. 235. The statement was not, as the New York *Herald Tribune* claimed (January 9, 1932), influenced by the business interests of the country.

cavalier disdain or hostility in the world's capitals. The Monroe Doctrine did not win the undying affection of the Latin-Americans for whose benefit, in part, it was enunciated; neither did the Stimson Doctrine receive the undiluted approbation of the Chinese, who were supposed to gain some advantage from it. Neither doctrine contemplated implementation by force. Both were greeted at home at the time of enunciation with mixed feelings.

It was not strange that the reaction at home was generally favorable. Stimson had reflected superbly the sentiments of a majority of Americans. He had voiced their revulsion to the reports of the Japanese advance on Chinchow, yet had made no commitment to aid the victims of aggression. He represented the outraged conscience but at no expense, or so it was thought. "This is talking turkey," said one newspaper; "a great piece of diplomacy," editorialized another; little wonder Senator Borah and Admirals Mark Bristol and William Pratt gave their approval. The message required no implementation. It was a peaceful solution, which accounted for the approbation of the churches and the peace groups. At the Conference on the Cause and Cure of War, which met in Washington at the end of January, the note received enthusiastic endorsement. Many prominent publicists and scholars viewed the doctrine as a splendid means of strengthening the treaty structure and contributing a revolutionary idea to the body of international law. "A new and significant doctrine," it was called by William P. Simms, the notable Scripps-Howard foreign-news editor. Quincy Wright, the distinguished professor of international law, after analyzing the note, concluded that "no diplomatic note of recent or even more distant years is likely to go down in history as of greater significance in the development of international law." Violence and war would cease to have value in advancing the legal position of a state, he claimed, if all the nations of the world accepted the three elements implicit in the doctrine: *de facto* occupation of territory gives no title; treaties contrary to the rights of third states are void; treaties in the making of which nonpacific means are used are void.[55]

[55] *Literary Digest*, Jan. 23, 1932, pp. 5–6; W. P. Simms in New York *World-Telegram*, Jan. 8, 1932; Ellery C. Stowell in *American Journal of International Law*, 27 (1933), 103; Quincy Wright in *ibid.*, 26 (1932), 342–48; Stimson, Diary,

The chorus of approval, however, could not smother the sharp voices of disapprobation. Adverse criticism stemmed from two extremes, from those who believed the Secretary had not gone far enough and from those who felt he had gone too far. The former, whose chief exponent was Roy Howard, constituted a very small group. They deplored the weakness of the note. It had not condemned the Japanese, had not protested their action, had not accused them of breaking the Pact of Paris, and had not even mentioned the network of treaties signed by Japan at Washington in 1921–22 which had guaranteed the territorial integrity of China and the *status quo* in the Pacific. It was, said Representative Morton D. Hull, "a plausible, fine-appearing mantle to cover the poverty of a timid, fearsome policy." Howard spoke even more bluntly when he accused Stimson of encouraging the destruction of the peace machinery by his virtual acceptance of the fact of Japan's power in Manchuria while insisting only that America's rights be unimpaired.[56]

Among those who feared that Stimson had gone too far were some of the shrewdest analysts of international affairs: Walter Lippmann, Nathaniel Peffer, Tyler Dennett, Edwin M. Borchard, and James T. Shotwell. For one thing, they were concerned about the many complications raised by the protest. They wondered whether Stimson and his colleagues had thought carefully enough of the legal consequences of nonrecognition. If an independent state were to be created in Manchuria, as appeared likely and indeed imminent, how would American citizens living and trading there be represented? Would not the citizens of those states which recognized the new state then enjoy greater trade benefits than Americans? How would any commercial relations be maintained if the new country's tariffs, tax laws, and other regulations be unacknowledged? They wondered, too, about the long-term political implications of nonrecognition. Would the United States forever withhold recognition of a new state formed in violation of the Pact of Paris, even though it be-

---

Jan. 9, 1932; Federal Council of Churches of Christ in America *News Release,* Feb. 15, 1932. *Report of the Conference on the Cause and Cure of War,* Jan. 21, 1932.

[56] Morton D. Hull in *Congressional Record,* Vol. 75, p. 10291, and New York *World-Telegram,* Jan. 8, 1932.

came acceptable to the local population? Would the United States *never* accept a settlement after a war waged in defiance of the Pact, even if the settlement were a good one? Should we defend the *status quo*, even when it perpetuates an unjust situation? How could Washington refuse to recognize changes brought about by force and violence when so many of the world's boundaries have been created that way? Thoughtful people were frankly disturbed by the many unanswered questions raised by the note and especially its categorical nature.[57]

Most objectionable to these observers was the immediate consequence for Japanese-American relations and for American security which they foresaw would result from Stimson's action. The *New York Times* summed up the sentiment neatly in an editorial whose tone was gentle but firm: "Without waiting, our Secretary of State has undertaken, on his sole responsibility, to lay down doctrines, and present stipulations which can hardly fail to cause a stir in Japan," and, continued the editor, "in language which in older days would have been regarded as indelicate, unfriendly, and undiplomatic." [58] Here was the crux of the matter. America had stepped out, unilaterally and alone, way ahead of the League of Nations and unsupported by any of the other major powers, in censuring Japan. The dangers of such a position were apparent. In the eyes of the Japanese, the United States would loom as the opponent to the Island Empire's advance on the mainland, and when the day of retribution came, the United States, as foreign-news analyst Karl H. Von Wiegand noted, might be left "holding the sack." Stimson, it was believed, had alienated Japan, as he had been careful not to do earlier in the fall, and needlessly, because the protest could hardly affect Japan's plans. "Imagine Japan," wrote former Senator William Cabell Bruce, "with her frowning battleships and valorous host of fierce and splendidly disciplined soldiers . . .

[57] Walter Lippmann in New York *Herald Tribune*, Mar. 2, 1936; Nathaniel Peffer, "The Situation in Asia," address before the Eighth Conference on the Cause and Cure of War, Jan. 20, 1932; Tyler Dennett, "America's Far Eastern Diplomacy," *Current History*, 37 (October 1932), 15 ff.; A. L. Lowell's address (Jan. 7, 1933) at luncheon of Foreign Policy Association in Boston, copy in Lowell Papers, Addresses and Major Articles, 1933–34 (Harvard College Archives); Newton D. Baker to Evans Clark, April 28, 1932, Baker Papers, Box 220; James T. Shotwell in *New York Times*, Mar. 20, 1932. See also speech by Jerome O. Greene to World Affairs Institute in New York, Mar. 23, 1932, and printed in *International Conciliation*, No. 281 (June 1932), pp. 9–26.

[58] *New York Times*, Jan. 9, 1932.

relaxing her clutch upon the throat of Manchuria merely because told by the United States that her occupation of that country is not recognized by us." It was a case of "Don Quixote Stimson and the Japanese Windmill." [59]

It was true, of course, that the Secretary's lance had no effect on the Japanese windmill. Tokyo received the news of the note quite placidly. Press reaction was mild in tone and limited in quantity. The leading newspapers in the capital disclaimed Japan's intent to violate treaties, take Chinese territory, or close the Open Door in Manchuria. "We are not such a nation as would nonchalantly trample on treaties. . . . We want to be faithful to our responsibilities as a major nation," said the Tokyo *Asahi*.[60] The Foreign Office's reply to Stimson's statement, delivered on January 16, was equally calm. In the communication, described as "smooth as soy bean oil," [61] Yoshizawa thanked the American government for its support of the Pact of Paris and of the Open Door, which Japan considered the cardinal features of its own Asia policy, and pledged to maintain both principles. He gladly accepted "additional assurances" that the United States "could always be relied on to do everything in their power to support Japan's efforts to secure the full and complete fulfillment in every detail of treaties involved in the Manchurian problem . . . [and] that the American government are devoting in a friendly spirit such sedulous care to the correct appreciation of the situation." He assured the Secretary that Japan had no designs on Chinese territory and no wish to exclude the citizens of other powers from their commercial opportunities in Manchuria. The objective was only to restore order in the province, thereby creating conditions which would be to the advantage of the whole world.

But it was perfectly clear that neither government nor

[59] These views were widely held. See W. Cameron Forbes, Journal, Series 2, Vol. 4, p. 20 (confidential section); *Chicago Tribune*, Jan. 9, 1932; M. Sommers, "What Jehol Means to Main Street," *New Outlook*, 161 (February 1932), 27; New York *Herald Tribune*, Jan. 9, 1932; G. Sokolsky, "The American Monkey Wrench," *Atlantic*, December 1932, pp. 739–48; Wilson, *Diplomat Between Two Wars*, p. 280.

[60] The comment, including the quotation from *Asahi*, may be found in *Trans-Pacific*, Jan. 21, 1932, pp. 3–4; see also Hugh Byas in *New York Times*, Jan. 9 and 10, 1932, and Neville to State Dept., Jan. 7, 1932, D/S File 793.94/ 3545.

[61] The phrase was used by Edwin L. James in the *New York Times* on January 17, 1932.

people intended to be diverted from their course on the mainland. Manchuria, they made plain, lay in Japan's sphere of special rights, its welfare and safety were of "quite extraordinary importance to the Japanese people." They were not going to permit Washington's attitude to stampede or frighten them. Whatever military operations were necessary to safeguard those rights would be taken and would be pursued until brought to a successful conclusion. Tokyo carefully pointed out that the operations were only "police actions" and not war as defined by the Pact of Paris, but at the same time the nation's press talked openly of battle areas. Captured battle trophies were exhibited everywhere and were viewed with satisfaction by millions of Japanese.[62] Viewed superficially, the Japanese reaction contained no censure of the United States, but behind the honeyed words were the unmistakable tones of irony and hostility.

Unquestionably, Japan's determination to ignore the implications of Stimson's note was stiffened by the attitude of the European powers, chiefly England. The British wanted no part in the American protest. They refused to become embroiled with Japan by identification with the "Grave United States Step Against Japan's Manchurian Policy." They refused to join in putting "Japan on trial" or in launching "America's bombshell."[63] For them, the Manchurian affair had "died a natural death." Japan controlled the province. All they wanted was assurance that British subjects would enjoy equal commercial rights in the area, and these assurances Tokyo had continuously proclaimed since September. To follow Stimson's lead was, therefore, unnecessary as well as unwise. In a communiqué handed to the press on January 9, the Foreign Office expressed satisfaction with Japan's statements championing the Open Door in Manchuria and announced that no protest from London would be issued. Two days later, the British ambassador in Washington informed Stimson of his government's decision.[64] The

[62] The Japanese reply is in *F.R., Japan, 1931–1941*, I, 76–77; in the same dispatch in which Forbes cabled the reply, he summarized Japanese reaction to the note.

[63] The quotations are from headlines in the London press (*Daily Express, Daily Herald, News Chronicle*) cited in the *New York Times* on January 8 and 9, 1932.

[64] *F.R., 1932*, III, 19, 22–23.

Japanese reply to the American protest, which the London
Times called "reassuring and informative," [65] and a message
containing a guarantee of the Open Door, which Tokyo sent
to London four days earlier, closed the issue for the British.[66]

The Continental nations followed Britain's lead. From
the embassies in Washington and the foreign offices in the
capitals came evasive replies. None of the powers would
commit themselves. The French government, more concerned
with Hindenburg than with Hirohito and involved in a
cabinet crisis at home, assured Stimson of complete accord
on the principles of the note—nothing more. This policy
reflected the admiration by the militarists of the Japanese
army's exploits in China. Even more so, it mirrored the views
of the key officials in the Foreign Office, who hoped that Japan
would support in the League of Nations the French position
on the necessity for a general security treaty as a prelude to
disarmament. Similarly, French imperialists expected that
Japan, satiated by a Chinese dinner, would not care for Indo-
China for dessert. Even those Frenchmen who looked upon
America's refusal to acknowledge changes in the *status quo*
in the Far East as a harbinger of support against any German
plans to alter the situation in Europe were unwilling to aid
in collaring the treaty violator in Asia. The Italian government also informed Washington that no protest would come
from Rome, and the Dutch and Belgians followed suit.[67]

The United States was out on a limb. It had stepped far
out in front, the solitary knight advancing to give battle to
the Japanese and left alone to face an embittered nation. The
position was not an enviable one, and the Secretary of State
must bear the responsibility for it. He should not have as-

[65] London *Times*, Jan. 18, 1932.
[66] Unfortunately, there is no available information on the background of
the British government's decision to withdraw support from Stimson. There
is evidence that the decision was not reached without a struggle. The line-up
probably was as follows: Lord Cecil, the delegate to the League, and Alexander Cadogan in support of the United States; Sir John Pratt, Sir Robert
Vansittart, C. W. Orde, and Sir John Simon, the foreign secretary, against.
[67] French embassy to Stimson, Jan. 19, 1932, *F.R., 1932*, III, 35–36. Leland
Stowe reported from Paris in New York *Herald Tribune*, Mar. 8, 1932; see
also *Journal des Débats*, quoted in *New York Times*, Jan. 9, 1932; also
American ambassador in Rome to State Dept., Jan. 13, 1932, D/S File 793.94/
3504; Dutch minister to Stimson, Jan. 12, 1932, *ibid.*, 793.94/3681, and Belgian
embassy to State Dept., Jan. 15, 1932, *F.R., 1932*, III, 31.

sumed the position of defiance without the collaboration of
the other great powers. It was dangerous enough to have
risked Japanese ire without the means for military implementation, but to do it alone was double jeopardy. It is true
that Stimson had confided his plan to the British and French
ambassadors in Washington before sending the note and that
their reactions had given him hope of their support, but he
should have made certain of their governments' concurrence
before dispatching the protest and if it had not been forthcoming, should have held his hand. Years later he justified
his unilateral action on the ground that to have attempted to
discuss the matter with other nations with a view to joint
action would have produced "hesitation, delays, and leaks to
the press. These would have impaired, if they had not destroyed, the psychological effect of the note." He had gone
ahead on his own with the expectation that the note would
serve as a "standard to which the wise and honest may repair." [68] Great Britain, particularly, he had thought, would
"repair to the standard." He had pinned his hope on the
British because of the long history of Anglo-American co-
operation on Far Eastern questions. Only ten years earlier the
two nations had joined in stabilizing the situation in the
western Pacific, and as recently as 1929, the prime minister,
during his visit to the United States, had pledged solidarity
on Asian matters. The British, Stimson had believed, as signatories of the Pact of Paris and of the 1921–22 treaties guaranteeing China's territorial integrity and with vast interests on
the mainland, would surely have seen the wisdom of issuing
a warning to Tokyo. To him, English and American interests
in the western Pacific were identical.

But the British did not see the situation as Stimson did.
London's stated reason for withholding support was that as
a member of the League of Nations it would be improper
to act outside the organization. It was pointed out also that
the nature of the American note did not require or merit
collaboration by the other powers since it merely reaffirmed
America's rights.[69] The real motive, however, was the disin-
clination of the foreign minister, Sir John Simon, and the

[68] *The Far Eastern Crisis,* pp. 97–98.
[69] *Daily Telegraph,* Jan. 9, 1932; Bassett, *Democracy and Foreign Policy,*
pp. 70 ff.

Tory leaders in the government and in the nation to act against Japan out of the conviction that British interests in the Far East would best be served not by Anglo-American but by Anglo-Japanese co-operation. Japan was the stabilizing factor in Asia, as Sir John said at a private press luncheon at the time, and stability was what the British needed to make secure their vast holdings and huge investments. Japan was the policeman in Asia, and good sense dictated friendship for the representative of law and order as the means for safeguarding property. Japan represented the great imperial tradition which the Tories so admired. Japan alone had the navy in the western Pacific which could threaten the communications lines of the British Empire.[70] Japan alone could act as the bulwark against the extension of communism in China and in India. That was why the Conservative press fondly recalled the old Anglo-Japanese Alliance, which had been foolishly "sacrificed on the altar of Anglo-American friendship." That was why the London *Times* and other journals in leading articles applauded the government's handling of the situation. As the *Saturday Review* noted, "the policy of playing second fiddle to the United States has not done this country much good anywhere." [71] England, it was believed, had at last broken free of American tutelage and had set out on an independent Asian policy and closer co-operation with Japan, which marked a return to the wiser policy of pre–Washington Conference days. What the Tories apparently did not realize was that Japan's political and military hegemony might soon destroy Britain's trade in the Far East or that her incursions in China might tend to enhance the appeal of communism to the disillusioned and defeated Chinese.

Not all Britons approved of their government's position. Many Liberals lamented the "rot in political circles" which led to choosing Japan over the United States. They scorned the failure of any responsible official to recognize the great questions of sovereignty, of Chinese independence, of the

---

[70] P. A. Reynolds, *British Foreign Policy in the Inter-war Years* (London, 1953), p. 85. See also J. M. Kenworthy in *New Outlook*, 160 (March 1932), 172 ff.

[71] Quoted in Quincy Howe, *A World History of Our Own Times* (2 vols.; New York, 1949–53), II, 435.

sanctity of treaties involved in the situation. Sir John Simon, said the *Manchester Guardian,* acted the part, not of "a statesman honoring solemn treaty obligations and pinning his faith to a new world order . . . but that of a lawyer picking holes in a contract in the interests of a shady client." [72] To *The Economist,* Great Britain had abdicated the leadership of the English-speaking world in the Far East to the United States by refusing to join in action considered by the eminent international-law authority A. D. MacNair to be "a minimum which considerations of international decency require." [73] Particularly objectionable was the unhappy language of the British communiqué, which, taken together with its blatant and brazen exploitation by the press, read like a rebuff to the United States. Even among those people who viewed the statement as a wise one suited to the national interest there were some who labeled its form and phraseology and its treatment by the press a "capital blunder." Writing some years later, Sir John Pratt, an adviser on Far Eastern affairs to the Foreign Office at the time and a principal architect of policy in that area, decried the role of the London *Times,* which showed an "uncanny skill in publishing its more unfortunate leading articles at the moment when they would be calculated to do the maximum amount of damage." [74]

Whatever the motives for British policy, whatever its wisdom, it "rubbed Japanese fur in such a way as to bring forth purrs." [75] It had also isolated Stimson. Even the Chinese turned away from the Secretary. They considered the protest too late and too weak; a grandiose scheme and an idealistic principle having the "head of a dragon and the tail of a rat"; a mere scrap of paper unlikely to be followed by a string of battleships and hardly calculated to halt Japanese aggres-

[72] *Manchester Guardian,* Oct. 1, 1932. See also Wickham Steed, "British Policy in the Pacific," *Nineteenth Century and After,* III (1932), 396–409; Toynbee, *Survey of International Affairs, 1932,* p. 542; *Spectator,* Jan. 16, 1932; and the speeches by Lord Lothian of Dec. 12, 1934, and by Lord Lytton of May 17, 1934, quoted in Bassett, *Democracy and Foreign Policy,* pp. 131–32.

[73] *The Economist,* Jan. 16, 1932; A. D. McNair, "The Stimson Doctrine of Non-Recognition," *British Yearbook of International Law, 1933* (London, 1933), p. 65.

[74] *War and Politics in China* (London, 1943), p. 227; see also his letter to the London *Times,* Nov. 30, 1938; also Reynolds, *British Foreign Policy,* p. 89.

[75] Clarence K. Streit's words in *New York Times,* Jan. 24, 1936.

sion.[76] Stimson, however, was not daunted. He had done what he believed had to be done and not once did he regret it. He was satisfied that his action had achieved at least two objectives. Immediately, it had headed off a break in Sino-Japanese relations which China had contemplated before the note had been sent. In a larger sense, it served as a milestone in international relations by demonstrating that a war and a violation of the Pact of Paris, even in far-off Manchuria, would not go unnoticed. That the United States may have played its hand rashly did not seem to trouble him.[77]

[76] For reaction of the Peking press, see *The Leader*, Jan. 10, 1932; *Shih Chieh Jih Pao*, Jan. 9, 1932; *Ching Pao*, Jan. 11, 1932; also *China Weekly Review*, Jan. 16, 1932, and *China Critic* quoted in *International Digest*, 2 (1932), 29–32. The *New York Times* and New York *Herald Tribune*, Jan. 11, 1932, summarized Chinese opinion.

[77] Stimson, Diary, Jan. 7, 1932. Stanley Hornbeck was deeply troubled that Stimson was playing a lone hand. In a memorandum dated January 12, 1932, he warned the Secretary: "If we do not intend to back up our insistence [that the principles of the peace treaties be observed], we should avoid going very far ahead of the other powers in our enunciation of it." D/S File 793.94/3610–3/5. The *New York Times*, some weeks later (January 29, 1932), wistfully regretted that Great Britain had shrewdly surrendered to the United States "the privilege, or peril, of being *fortitor*, while itself remaining *suavitor*" but did praise Stimson for taking the initiative in a situation which demanded some censure.

CHAPTER FIVE
in which
**Stimson becomes angry and
warns Japan**

*If our military win, the whole Pacific is ours;
if they lose, Communist revolution must follow and we become part of the Soviet Union.
That perhaps is the ultimate solution to our
economic isolation. All the loss in blood and
treasure considered, either eventually is better than the present strangulation.*
STATEMENT BY A JAPANESE RAILWAY EXECUTIVE, 1932

*The open door policy in China was an excel-
lent thing, and I hope it will be a good thing in
the future, so far as it can be maintained by
general diplomatic agreement; but as has been
proved by the whole history of Manchuria,
alike under Russia and under Japan, the open
door policy, as a matter of fact, completely dis-
appears as soon as a powerful nation deter-
mines to disregard it and is willing to run the
risk of war rather than forego its intention.*
THEODORE ROOSEVELT, 1910

Tʜᴇ ꜰᴀʟʟ of Chinchow placed southern Manchuria solidly under the control of Japan. The conquest of the territory was a quite remarkable achievement. Sixty thousand troops had secured domination over 200,000 square miles of territory and 20,000,000 people in four months against a force of 400,000 men. Except for mopping-up operations, the military task had ended. It remained only to tighten the economic and political grip.

The first steps in fastening the hold on Manchuria had been taken almost simultaneously with the beginning of military operations back in September. Although the Foreign Office in Tokyo invited foreign nations to participate in the development of the province and continually pledged support for the principle of the Open Door, the Kwantung army's economic brigades took immediate measures to discriminate against non-Japanese business, financial, and commercial interests. While the world fastened its attention on the battlefield, the foundations for the financial and economic domination of the area by Japan were being laid.[1] Slowly, gradually, but inexorably, the Open Door was being closed. As one American observer noted, the door was open "facing a long corridor, Japan, through which trade must pass before it enters Manchuria."[2]

The devices used to achieve this purpose were varied and numerous: closing banks, mines, and industries in which foreigners had interests and reopening them under Japanese management; passing new laws regulating trade and monetary exchange; preventing local government bureaus from purchasing from foreign firms supplies and equipment which could be bought from Japanese manufacturers; and diverting business from foreign to Japanese companies. By December, gigantic strides had been taken. Banking, light and power, and transportation had become virtual Japanese monopolies. The Bank of the Three Eastern Provinces and the Frontier Bank, which had been closed in September, reopened on October 15 in Japanese hands. Immediately upon securing Mukden, the two municipal electric power plants had been

[1] American consul general at Mukden to State Dept., Oct. 20, 1931, D/S File 793.94/2727.
[2] Tyler Dennett, *Current History*, 37 (October 1932), 18.

107

taken over; one began to operate again very soon under Kwantung-army auspices, supplying half the city's power, the other half was brought from the long-established Japanese plant of the South Manchurian Electric Light Company at Fushun thirty miles away. By the end of the year, all light and power from Dairen on the south to Changchun on the north was provided by Japanese-owned plants. Similarly, all the railways in southern Manchuria, with one exception, had come under army management by December.[3]

American interests, which were greater than those of the British and second only to Japanese and Korean, suffered greatly under the impact of the Kwantung army's economic policy. Anderson, Meyer and Company, which had for years supplied the local electric plants with machinery, lost all of its business. Frazer, Federal Incorporated had its interest in the bus company in Newchwang seized; the oil companies, Standard of New York, Texas, Socony Vacuum, and Asiatic Petroleum, found many of their customers for kerosene, gasoline, and other petroleum products looking elsewhere. Radio Corporation of America, American Harvester, Ford, and General Motors all, in one way or another, were affected. Hardest hit of any American enterprise was the National City Bank of New York in whose path the Japanese placed the most onerous and hamstringing obstacles. Remittance fees for sending money by the main office to branches in Dairen, Mukden, and Harbin were raised, long-distance calls were delayed until the markets closed, and, above all, the bank could no longer accept real estate as security for loans, thus being cutoff from the most important source of loans.[4]

The United States government lodged regular and frequent protests in Tokyo, but to no avail.[5] The Foreign Office kept assuring Forbes that the door would remain open, while across the narrow sea the army was pushing it shut. Soon

[3] American consul general at Mukden to State Dept., Oct. 20, 1931, D/S File 793.94/2727.

[4] Carnegie Endowment for International Peace, *Manchuria: A Survey of Its Economic Development* (New York [1931]), pp. 206–207; memorandum by Stanley K. Hornbeck, Jan. 1, 1932, D/S File 793.94/36101/5; Victor Keen in New York *Herald Tribune*, Dec. 26, 1931; American consul general at Mukden to Nelson T. Johnson, Oct. 5, 1931, *F.R., 1931*, III, 119–24.

[5] See, for example, Forbes to vice-minister for foreign affairs, Jan. 27, 1932, D/S File 793.94/4207, and JFOD, S5.1.1.0–33, pp. 15, 17, 47–48.

the American companies began to adopt a more realistic attitude than Washington and accepted the fact of Japanese hegemony either by removing the control of their Manchurian agencies from Shanghai to Tokyo, as General Motors and Ford did, by combining branches in the area with those in Japan, as the National City Bank did, or by transferring distributorships from Chinese to Japanese agents, as the oil companies did.[6]

At the outset, the Kwantung army exercised economic control by manipulating the existing political structure. Japanese advisers were placed in the provincial bureau of finance and industry, and sympathetic Chinese who could be depended upon to enforce the new regulations replaced recalcitrant officials in the various government bureaus, local and provincial. Thus the new governor of Manchuria, Yuan Chin-kai, dutifully carried out the army's orders, as did Mukden's new mayor, Chao Ching-pao. In some smaller cities, Japanese were installed as mayors and the principal municipal departments staffed jointly by Chinese and Japanese. Before long, however, it became clear that permanent control could not be maintained so long as any link remained between China and Manchuria, however tender and tenuous it may have been. Japan could not forever rule a Chinese province. The military leaders, therefore, inevitably turned their attention to severing the link by the formation of an independent government which would be tied to the Island Empire by treaty. Because of the obvious international complications, the army abandoned any idea of annexation.[7]

Reports of a separatist movement in Manchuria reached Washington from many sources in Asia and Europe. As early as September 30, 1931, Nelson T. Johnson sent home from Peking an item, which had appeared in a Japanese-owned newspaper in Mukden, suggesting the creation of a new nation.[8] Thereafter, Prentiss Gilbert from Geneva, Myers and Vincent from Manchuria, Chinese officials from Nanking,

---

[6] John Carter Vincent to State Dept. (undated), D/S File 893.5034 Manch/2.
[7] IMTFE, *Proceedings*, p. 1969; also Nakamura, p. 176.
[8] *F.R., 1931*, III, 93. Immediately after the September 18 attack, the Kwantung army took steps to organize a separatist movement in Manchuria. Two elaborate plans, one on September 22 and the other on October 2, were drawn up to effect an independent state. See Nakamura, sec. 2, chap. ii.

and others warned the State Department of the schemes which were afoot.[9] Debuchi, when confronted by Castle with the reports, denied Japanese complicity in any separatist movement. He answered the undersecretary that the Foreign Office had instructed all consuls in Manchuria not to "interfere either for or against any kind of political movement." [10] What he did not say was that neither the consular nor the Foreign Office officials could deter the military leaders from their course. Not even the war minister or the chief of the General Staff could influence them. On November 15, Minami telegraphed Honjo and warned him of the dangers of setting up an independent government. World opinion would be aroused, he said, and intervention by the Nine Power Pact signatories might well follow. He urged the general at least to await developments at Geneva, where the Japanese government's position seemed strong enough to expect a favorable solution to the whole question. But his entreaties went unheeded.[11]

The ringleaders in the plot were Major General Itagaki Seishiro and Colonel Doihara Kenji, both fanatical nationalists and, it will be recalled, ringleaders of the assault the previous September. At first they tried to get one of their Chinese puppets to head the new state, but no one was willing, not even Yuan Chin-kai. It is to the credit of Yuan and the other Chinese that they refused to be accomplices in the dismemberment of China despite the fact that they had no love for the Nanking regime. Doihara then hit upon a quite brilliant idea. Why not clothe the new government in imperial vestments? Why not invest it with the prestige and glamor of the Manchus? Why not restore the last Manchu emperor to his throne in Manchuria? He lost no time in going to Tientsin, where Hsuan-tsung, the last emperor of China, who had been dethroned in 1912, was living quietly and in seclusion as Henry Pu Yi. The negotiations between the two, although conducted in secrecy, soon became public knowl-

[9] *F.R., 1931*, III, 106, 144–45, 348, 393, 451–52. From Tokyo, the British ambassador reported similar information. See Lindley to Reading, Sept. 28, 1931, *British Documents*, p. 688.

[10] *F.R., 1931*, III, 102.

[11] IMTFE, Exhibit 299; see also Exhibit 2435 and *Proceedings*, pp. 4354 and 18974; also Nakamura, p. 110.

edge. The Japanese consul general in Tientsin, under instructions from the Foreign Office, urged Doihara to drop the whole business. He begged Pu Yi to resist the blandishments of the Kwantung army's emissary, but Doihara warned the consul to stay away from the emperor and doggedly persisted in his campaign to win Pu Yi over.[12] He made all kinds of promises of military support and a guaranteed future if the Manchu would go to Mukden and head the new state. He even assured Pu Yi that the Imperial Household looked upon the project with favor, which was not true.[13] Whether Doihara succeeded in convincing him or whether he abducted him is not clear. In any event, the two left Tientsin on November 8 and after a fast journey by automobile, train, and boat, arrived in Manchuria five days later. At the War Crimes Trials in 1946, Pu Yi testified that Doihara had forced him to go, that he had gone to save his own life. But at the same trials, Mr. H. G. W. Woodhead, a British subject and a friend of the emperor, claimed that Pu Yi had told him in September 1932 that he had made the trip on his own accord.[14] The important fact, however, is only that the Kwantung army, with the chosen instrument safely under its protection, was prepared to move ahead with the plan to establish an independent state in the conquered territory, regardless of the opposition at home. Happily for the militarists, but not crucially important, the opposition at home virtually disappeared within the next two months. The fall of the Wakatsuki ministry in December removed Cabinet resistance, and after a lecture on January 11, 1932, by General Itagaki before the Imperial Household on the need for setting up a new state under Japanese auspices, the emperor's advisers, except for the old Marquis Kido,[15] apparently gave way. For the successful elimination of obstructionist views in the capital, the efforts of the volatile jingo head of the Foreign Office's press bureau, Shiratori Toshio, must be recorded. His constant and blatant support of the Kwantung army from the very begin-

[12] The story of the consul's efforts to foil Doihara's plot is in the correspondence between the consul, Kuwashima Kazue, and Shidehara, IMTFE, Exhibits 285, 286, 289, 290, 299, 300.
[13] IMTFE, Exhibits 291 and 295.
[14] IMTFE, *Proceedings*, pp. 3956 ff. and Exhibit 3158.
[15] Kido, Diary, Jan. 11, 1932.

ning, in defiance of his superiors, played a vital part in keeping the military's torch burning brightly in Tokyo.[16]

As the Kwantung army fastened its hold on southern Manchuria and moved to create a new nation, the world watched and wondered. Where would it stop? Would the military be satisfied with one Chinese province? Indeed, would they be satisfied with all of China? Was India on the timetable? Would any part of Asia escape the gargantuan appetite of the Island Empire? Late in January, one of these questions was answered by events in Shanghai which indicated that the Japanese were interested in extending control immediately over at least one other Chinese area. On the eighteenth, a mob of Chinese attacked some Japanese Buddhist priests, resulting in one priest's death. Two days later, fifty members of the Japanese Youth Protection Society set fire to a factory in front of which the assault had taken place. On the same day, the Japanese Residents Association in Shanghai adopted a resolution calling on the government in Tokyo for protection.

The Foreign Office hastened to comply, if only to relieve the pressure from the business interests and the nationalists at home, who had been clamoring for some time that the Chinese be chastised for a whole series of anti-Japanese activities, such as frequent attacks on Japanese children moving between school and home, a constant barrage of hostile press copy,[17] and, above all, a powerful and comprehensive boycott of everything Japanese. The Chinese refused to buy from them, sell to them, use their currency, patronize their banks, or enter their employ. They even sabotaged the transportation of their goods.[18] Japanese business was hit hard. Next to the United States, China was Japan's best customer, normally

---

[16] Shiratori had powerful connections, which made it virtually impossible for the foreign minister to drop him. He was a nephew of Viscount Ishii and had the support of the president of the Privy Council and of the chief of the Asiatic Bureau of the Foreign Office. He was very close to Baron Hiranuma, president of the powerful Kokuhonsha (National Foundation Society). The British ambassador in Tokyo called him an irresponsible official and liable to drink too much. See Lindley to Reading, Oct. 30, 1931, *British Documents*, p. 862.

[17] The Japanese were particularly incensed by an item in *Min Kuo Daily News* (Shanghai), January 9, 1932, which regretted that a bomb hurled at the emperor in Tokyo by a Korean inflicted no injuries.

[18] See IMTFE statements by Vice Admiral Samejima T. (Exhibit 2420) and Captain Kitaura T. (Exhibit 2421).

absorbing about 20 per cent of her exports, chiefly textiles. On the twenty-third, the Japanese consul general in Shanghai demanded an apology from the mayor of Shanghai for the attack on the priests, punishment of the assailants, and suppression of anti-Japanese propaganda. On the same day, the commander of the Yangtze Naval Patrol, Admiral Shiozawa Koichi, issued an independent statement, a warning that he might find it necessary to protect Japanese life and property with force. Four days later, the consul general issued an ultimatum to the Chinese mayor, giving him twenty-two hours to accede to the demands. The following day, the twenty-eighth, well within the time limit, the mayor signified his intention to comply; nevertheless, Shiozawa ordered an attack.

At midnight, naval planes commenced an aerial bombardment of Chapei, one of the three boroughs in the native city,[19] and were followed by a force of two thousand marines, who swarmed over the district. The scurrying of the diminutive and dogged troops in the streets of Shanghai against the backdrop of the glare of burning buildings soon appeared on films in theaters and in descriptions in the press all over the Western world. Searching for an explanation of the attack, some observers viewed it as a smoke screen to conceal the exploitation of Manchuria. Others considered it merely a bid by the navy to regain prestige lost at the London Naval Conference of 1930 and by the army's glorious exploits in Manchuria in 1931.[20] Most people, however, agreed with a Chinese estimate that Japan, having conquered Manchuria, was entering the second phase of an expansionist program with North China the objective and the navy the instrument. A remark passed by the Japanese minister to China on January 27 as he departed Tokyo for the mainland made clear that the attack

[19] Shanghai consisted of the native city, the French concession, and the International Settlement. The Settlement was governed by a municipal council, popularly elected, consisting of one American, two Japanese, five Chinese, and six Britons. The Consular Corps acted as an advisory body. The Settlement was policed by a mixed corps of British, Japanese, Chinese, and White Russians and defended by the Shanghai Defense Force, which included British, American, French, and Japanese military and naval units.

[20] The shock of the attack was heightened by the fact that the Japanese navy had always been considered less nationalist and more moderate, liberal, and internationally minded than the army. It was reliably reported to have opposed the army's move in Manchuria. See Count Kabayama to Stimson in Stimson, Diary, Jan. 8, 1932.

was not just a navy show. He said that "no other means are left but drastic action to stop the boycotts." [21]

The reaction in the United States to the assault was sharp and the shock severe. Americans had just about become reconciled to a *fait accompli* in Manchuria and, in the calmer days of early January, were even ready to believe that the Japanese would soon come to their senses.[22] When the rotten business started again, they were outraged. Even the doleful accounts of the depression, of seven million unemployed, and of bank failures lost their morbid attractiveness in the face of the onslaught in Shanghai. Pictures in the American press of homeless and abandoned children in the city virtually obliterated the pinched faces of the starving people in the United States.[23] Many who had once been sympathetic to the Japanese now turned against them. The *New York Times,* which earlier had found its "indignation against the Japanese way of doing things . . . considerably dampened by the sordid history of a dozen years of Chinese civil strife," [24] lamented the butchery in Shanghai, which generated apprehension, not confidence, and impaired Japan's standing as a nation.[25] Willis J. Abbott, the editor of the *Christian Science Monitor,* who, in the fall of 1931 had sought to justify the move in Manchuria, was now bitterly critical of Shanghai.

But it was not only that hostilities had broken out again which troubled Americans. It was that the theater of operations had shifted south of the Great Wall, where material and sentimental attachments were much greater than in Manchuria. The attack struck much closer to the pocketbook and to the heart. Missionary and educational activities in North China were very considerable, and the sight of thousands of Chinese being mauled by Japanese shells pained the numerous denominations and sects to whom the mission of saving the souls and training the minds of heathens was the principal feature of the earthly life. No wonder the distinguished preacher S. Parkes Cadman, speaking for the Federal Council

[21] Quoted in *New York Times,* Jan. 28, 1932.

[22] See the editorial in the *Boston Globe,* Jan. 12, 1932.

[23] For some reactions, see Stimson, Diary, Jan. 23, 1932; statement in Women's International League for Peace and Freedom *Bulletin,* Jan. 21, 1932, SCPC; *New York Times,* Jan. 29, 1932.

[24] *New York Times,* Jan. 27, 1932.

[25] *Ibid.,* Jan. 30, 1932.

of Churches of Christ in America, and other prominent clergymen inveighed heavily against Japan's actions.[26] The economic stake consisted of financial investments, trade, and property. The latter, calculated at $115,000,000 and distributed among oil installations, tobacco warehouses, and business and manufacturing establishments, faced destruction. Financial interests, such as the American and Foreign Power Company, which owned the Shanghai Power Company, and the International Telephone and Telegraph Company, which controlled the Shanghai Telephone Company, could expect confiscation. Exporters and importers, who did an annual business of slightly over $150,000,000 could anticipate a sharp drop in trade, if not complete cessation, should the Japanese close the door. No wonder Wall Street, which had sided with the Japanese during the Manchurian crisis, did not conceal its deep concern.[27] Another factor in the American attitude was that 3,614 United States citizens lived in Shanghai, many more than ever resided north of the Great Wall.

Washington's reaction matched the nation's. The capital was tense. Secretary Stimson, who after the dispatch of his January 7 note had turned his attention to preparing for the forthcoming disarmament conference at Geneva, now shifted the focus back to the Far East. He was deeply concerned over the trouble in Shanghai, fearful lest the violence ultimately lead to war between China and Japan with all kinds of dangerous consequences for the United States. Monday, January 25, was a hectic day for him. He had followed closely the events of the preceding week and had gradually formulated a course of action, which he laid before the President, his departmental colleagues, and other members of the Administration upon returning to his office after the week end. He proposed a twofold plan: to send the Asiatic Fleet to Shanghai from Manila if the British would send ships at the same time and to serve notice on the Japanese that American interests in the area were too large to be ignored by his government. The fleet, he hoped, would serve three purposes: protect American life and property; strengthen Chiang Kai-shek, who was staving off demands that he declare war on Japan immedi-

[26] *Ibid.*, Feb. 1, 1932.
[27] Oswald G. Villard to Jane Addams, Jan. 25, 1932, in Jane Addams Papers, SCPC.

ately, by demonstrating that the powers were sufficiently concerned to send ships; and, above all, show the Japanese he meant business. This last was to be a trump card. He wanted the fleet to act as a sword suspended over the Japanese. If they could be kept guessing and worried about whether the navy would intervene, the effect might well be sobering. Stimson put great reliance upon "the unconscious element of our great size and military strength. . . . Japan was afraid of that, and I was willing to let her be afraid of that without telling her that we were not going to use it against her." [28]

The reception of the Secretary's plan was distinctly cool. Neither Secretary of the Navy Charles F. Adams, Jr., nor Admiral William V. Pratt, the chief of naval operations, could get enthusiastic about a large-scale operation for the Asiatic Fleet. It had suffered from the effects of an economy-minded Congress and a "small navy" Administration and was far from its peak of efficiency. It was undermanned, inadequately trained, and, except for the flagship, the vessels were overage. Another factor in the attitude of the naval chiefs was undoubtedly the view of the commander of the fleet, Admiral Montgomery M. Taylor, whose dispatches reflected disgust with the Chinese for their disunity, brutality toward the peasant, venality, and admiration for the Japanese.[29] In the Department of State, the principal advisers urged caution. Hornbeck thought it premature to do anything until American rights were actually impaired. He was not thinking along the lines of broad policy but, rather, in terms of specific responses to immediate threats to American interests. Joseph E. Jacobs opposed any objection to Japanese use of Chinese territory as a base of operations for protecting nationals. Castle worried lest the presence of the fleet in the Shanghai area lead to an accidental clash with the Japanese. "War! It is not beyond the bounds of possibility," he noted in his diary.[30]

It was from the President that Stimson got encouragement

[28] Stimson, Diary, Jan. 26, 1932.
[29] See Taylor to Pratt, Jan. 23, 1932, Taylor Papers, Box 269. It was significant that Admiral Pratt entertained Ambassador and Mrs. Debuchi in his home on January 30.
[30] Hornbeck Memorandum, Jan. 25, 1932, D/S File 793.94/3643; Jacobs Memorandum, Jan. 29, 1932, D/S File 793.94/4479. Castle, Diary, Jan. 29, 1932.

and approval for his twin plan. Hoover sanctioned a strong protest to Japan and the dispatch of naval forces to protect American interests. He was determined, however, that there would be no Japanese-American war. He believed the Chinese would eventually throw the invader off, but if they did not, the United States would not do it for them. Foreshadowing his "Fortress America" stand twenty years later during the Korean War, he vowed to fight for the defense of the continental United States but never for Asia.[31] He refused even to use the veiled threat of implied force, which caused Stimson to complain bitterly in his diary, "He is too likely to let the other fellow know the element against ourselves which the other fellow might not guess. I am a thorough believer in the policy of not drawing until you are ready to shoot, but when you have a case where the chances are a thousand to one that you will not be drawn into a fight, I am willing to let our size and strength speak for itself and not to disclaim publicly our willingness to fight if it becomes essential."[32]

Armed with presidential permission, the Secretary moved to put his plan into effect. On the twenty-seventh, he instructed Forbes to inform the foreign minister that the United States could not "regard with indifference" a situation in which a foreign government authorized a naval commander to use force to support the demands of a local consul and to urge the Japanese to practice self-restraint in Shanghai. On the same day, he called the consul general in Shanghai, Edwin S. Cunningham, to request the Japanese naval authorities to take no action endangering American property. Two days later, after the attack had begun, he lodged a second protest to Tokyo. On the following day, he called Debuchi in to tell him flatly the whole thing was Japan's fault. On the thirty-first, he directed Forbes to remonstrate again if Japan continued to advance.[33]

As for naval forces to protect American interests, Stimson preferred not to go in without Great Britain. He soon discovered, however, that the British were not interested in a naval demonstration, or anything else, for that matter, except

[31] Stimson, Diary, Jan. 26, 1932.
[32] *Ibid.*
[33] *F.R., Japan, 1931–1941,* I, 161–62, 165–67, 171; *F.R., 1932,* III, 81.

verbal protest. Although experts in the Japanese Foreign Office predicted a change in the British attitude as the area of operations drew close to the British sphere of influence in the Yangtze Valley,[34] London remained unperturbed by the events in Shanghai, except for a very momentary revulsion at the conduct of the Japanese. As during the Manchurian crisis, sympathy was with Japan, which continued to be viewed as the bulwark of order in the Far East, the guarantor of stability, and the obstacle to the communization of China. Many Britons recalled that in 1927 a British force had found it necessary to protect nationals and end a boycott in Shanghai, precisely as Japan was now doing. Others privately condoned Sino-Japanese tension because the Chinese boycott cleared a rival from the sharply competitive textile market in China.[35] No one wished to offend the United States needlessly, but if it came to a choice between Japan and America, the ultra-nationalist, imperialist London press had no trouble coming to a decision. The *Daily Mail, Daily Express, Morning Post, Times,* and *Daily Telegraph,* with one voice, warned the government to keep hands off, except, perhaps, for a word of caution to Tokyo.[36] Only a few warnings were raised by the Socialist *Daily Herald,* the Liberal *Manchester Guardian,* and by men like Wickham Steed and Lord Cecil that the failure of Great Britain and the United States to take immediate and strong joint action would mean "good-bye for many a year to Anglo-American co-operation on disarmament or anything else" and "still worse trouble would develop." [37] The net result of the British position was a compromise: a warning to Tokyo to stay out of the International Settlement, and an invitation to Washington to follow suit with a warning of its own (so the United States was to be assuaged), but no movement of ships from the Singapore base (thus no offense to Japan).

Disappointed but undaunted, Stimson prepared to go in

[34] "Review of British Foreign Policy in the Far East," March 1940, prepared by the Second Section of the Survey Department of the Japanese Foreign Office, JFOD, 120010–542.

[35] See *New York Times,* Jan. 28, 29, 1932.

[36] See *ibid.,* Jan. 31, 1932; New York *Herald Tribune,* Jan. 30, 1932; Atherton to State Dept., Jan. 29, 1932, D/S File 793.94/4107.

[37] *New York Times,* Jan. 28, 1932; Gilbert to State Dept., Jan. 29, 1932, *F.R., 1932,* III, 94–95.

without the British. He was determined to let Japan and the world know that America meant to protect her citizens in their lawful pursuits wherever they might be. On January 30, Cunningham informed the department that conditions justified an increase in the force then in Shanghai, which consisted of about twelve hundred marines and one destroyer.[38] The next day, at a conference, called by the President, of the secretaries of state, war, and navy, the army chief of staff, the chief of naval operations, Castle, and Hornbeck, the decision was approved to dispatch at once elements of the Asiatic Fleet (the cruiser *Houston* and six destroyers) under the commander, Admiral Taylor, the Thirty-first Infantry Regiment (one thousand men), and four hundred marines of the Fourth Marine Regiment.[39]

Stimson's program was now completed. Protests had been sent; the fleet was on the move. The Japanese could draw whatever conclusions they wished. His purpose was to keep them guessing. To that end, he urged the members of the Cabinet to say or do nothing to indicate that the United States would not use any and every weapon at its command.[40] At the same time, he acceded to the call by the Senate for the Japanese-American diplomatic correspondence since September 1931. The request had been made back in December, but Stimson had delayed the transmittal to avoid exciting the American public and aggravating the situation. Now, however, it suited his purpose perfectly to throw open the correspondence and let the Japanese worry that their stubbornness and aggressiveness during the Manchurian crisis would be revealed in the exchange and arouse American ire.[41]

His plan was further abetted by the treatment in the press of the Shanghai trouble. The newspapers featured the crisis on their front pages in large headlines, speculated on the possibility of action by the powers, and hinted darkly at a joint

[38] Cunningham to State Dept., Jan. 30, 1932, *F.R.*, *1932*, III, 133.

[39] Stimson, Diary, Jan. 31, 1932. J. E. Jacobs opposed the decision on the ground that in the event of trouble, the Asiatic Fleet would be bottled up far from its base. If the fleet were to be sent, he hoped that at least Taylor would not be in command because as senior in rank to the other foreign commanders, he would be forced to assume a leading position, which might compromise the United States. See his memorandum, Jan. 30, 1932, D/S File 793.94/4437.

[40] Stimson, Diary, Jan. 29, 1932.

[41] The correspondence was printed as S. Doc. 55, 72nd Cong., 1st sess.

Anglo-American naval demonstration.[42] They called the meeting at which high Administration officials approved the dispatch of the Asiatic Fleet "a war conference" and noted that the President had thought the situation serious enough to convene his advisers on Sunday. When the battle force, including nine superdreadnoughts, two aircraft carriers, six fleet submarines, and thirty destroyers, and the scouting force of the United States Fleet steamed to a rendezvous off Hawaii to begin the long-planned annual maneuvers early in February, editors made it appear as more than a coincidence that two hundred war vessels assembled in the Pacific. When nine hundred troops departed from San Francisco to take part in the exercise, the *Detroit Free Press* noted, "there were many who insisted that this task would not end there." [43] Helpful, too, was a statement by Admiral Richard H. Leigh, commander of the battle force, that his fleet was fully prepared for any contingency.[44]

Debate in Congress and agitation by various special-interest groups on a boycott and on an embargo of war material against Japan also supported the Secretary's cause. In both House and Senate, resolutions were introduced to halt the flow of munitions to violators of the Kellogg-Briand Pact and to boycott their products.[45] Numerous peace organizations issued statements, held meetings, and made pleas to the President and to prominent Senators to halt intercourse with Japan.[46] All these activities received wide publicity in the press and added to the atmosphere of the implied threat and the imminent danger which Stimson was trying to create. So sharp was the public concern over Shanghai that even Hornbeck, who abhorred threat and bluff, seemed willing to admit that a policy involving the mere intimation of the use of force might not be bad.[47] He contributed to the atmosphere by proposing "a fine economic weapon in the diplomatic contest," namely, that

---

[42] See, for example, *New York Times,* Jan. 28, 1932.
[43] *Detroit Free Press,* Feb. 1, 1932.
[44] *New York Times,* Jan. 30, 1932.
[45] HJRess. 132, 137, 153, 72nd Cong., 1st sess.
[46] Resolution of American Friends of China Association calling on American women to boycott Japanese products, *New York Times,* Jan. 31, 1932; letter to President Hoover from Women's International League for Peace and Freedom, Jan. 18, 1932, D/S File 793.94PC/46; speech by Mrs. Ben Hooper at League of Nations Association annual convention (1932) in Philadelphia.
[47] Memorandum by Hornbeck, Jan. 27, 1932, D/S File 793.94/3754.

American bankers refuse to make loans to Japan pending the "development of evidence regarding Japan's methods in handling the Manchurian problem."[48]

The only trouble with Stimson's plan was that it did not work. The Japanese simply refused to be frightened by the bogy the Secretary had raised. Their cockiness and self-assurance were greater than ever. They had the largest naval force in the area, were determined to use it against any power which stood in the way, and were confident of victory.[49] Their war machine was constantly being strengthened by the stockpiling of trucks, iron, steel, gasoline, and raw cotton which in view of the reduced level of the textile industry could have been meant only for the manufacture of explosives. Public support, while not as unanimous as during the Manchurian phase, was strong, loyal, and articulate.[50]

Tokyo had only to look across the Pacific to realize that any bellicosity displayed by the Secretary of State was a mere façade, that any positive action from that quarter was extremely unlikely. Disturbed, the people undoubtedly were; disquietude, they certainly felt; toughness and resoluteness, Stimson had definitely exhibited. But supporting a strong policy was something different, and the evidence of true intentions appeared on every hand. The New York *Herald Tribune* announced that the Foreign Affairs Committee of the House had suspended consideration of legislation to grant the President power to impose an economic embargo on violators of the Kellogg-Briand Pact because the State Department feared antagonizing Japan.[51] The various suggestions for a boycott met violent opposition from such prominent senators as Borah of Idaho, King of Utah, Reed of Pennsylvania, Walsh of Massachusetts, and Capper of Kansas.[52]

Important journals like the *Nation* urged that warships and marines be withdrawn from Shanghai lest a clash occur and that nothing in the Far East was worth shedding blood for.[53]

[48] Memorandum by Hornbeck, Jan. 21, 1932, D/S File 793.94/3607.

[49] Forbes to State Dept., Jan. 18, 1932, D/S File 793.94/3546; Captain Parker Tenney to Adjutant General, War Dept., Jan. 29, 1932, *F.R., 1932*, III, 108–109. The Japanese naval force in Chinese waters consisted of four 10,000-ton cruisers, 21 destroyers, one aircraft carrier, and three 6,000-ton cruisers.

[50] *New York Times*, Jan. 30, 1932.

[51] New York *Herald Tribune*, Jan. 30, 1932.

[52] *Ibid.*, Jan. 31, 1932.

[53] *Nation*, Feb. 10, 1932.

From the placid and calm conduct of the Asiatic Fleet, Tokyo
might well have deduced that Washington did not want to
get involved or risk a clash. And it was true, of course, that
instructions from State and Navy were clear and emphatic
on this point.[54] From the public discussions on the state of the
navy, Tokyo again could draw the correct conclusion. While
Senator Hale of Maine and other "big navy" people were talking of building the fleet up to treaty limits in view of the
trouble in the Far East, hearings before the House Naval
Affairs Committee on the Vinson bill reflected the refusal
by the Congress and by representatives of numerous organizations even to consider appropriations to increase the fleet.
It was well known, too, that the President himself opposed a
building program. Furthermore, the Democratic-controlled
House Appropriations Subcommittee on the War Department
voted on January 29 a drastic cut in military strength for
1933.[55] Such indications hardly made creditable Stimson's
bold front.

Most revealing to the Japanese was the American attitude
toward Philippine independence. There was no lack of understanding in the United States of the relationship between the
islands and American Far Eastern policy. Although arguments for and against freedom frequently revolved about economic issues, the importance of a base in eastern Asia for
defending American interests there and checking Japan was
constantly held in view. Senator Hiram Bingham, whose Committee on Insular Affairs conducted hearings on the Philippine Independence bill, warned that to give up the islands
would indicate lack of interest in Asian problems, while various officials of the State, Navy, War, and Commerce departments testified that hauling down the flag over the archipelago
would be interpreted as the final step in the retreat before
Japan in the Far East.[56] The American Asiatic Association,

[54] See Stimson to consul general at Shanghai, Jan. 30, 1932, D/S File
793.94/3724; *idem*, Jan. 31, 1932, *F.R.*, *1932*, III, 136; OPNAV (Chief of Naval
Operations) to CINC Asiatic (Commander, Asiatic Fleet), Jan. 30, 1932, Navy
File EF16 Shanghai (secret and confidential).

[55] *Baltimore Sun*, Jan. 30, 1932; *New York Times*, Jan. 29, 1932; New York
Herald Tribune, Jan. 30, 1932.

[56] *New York Times*, Jan. 31, 1932, and New York *Herald Tribune*, Jan. 31,
1932. The secretaries of war and navy reflected a Joint Board study on the
retention of the Philippines and its relation to Far Eastern policy. No. 305
(Serial No. 499), dated Oct. 27, 1931, and approved by the secretary of war

made up of firms engaged in Far Eastern trade and commerce, admitted that independence would bring relief to certain business interests but believed that economic consideration should be subordinated to strategic necessities, which dictated retaining the islands.[57] Stimson, more than anyone else, emphasized the connection by ascribing the intransigence of the Japanese to their conviction that America was moving out of the western Pacific.[58] Yet an examination of public opinion indicated clearly that it was precisely the effect of keeping sovereignty over the Philippine Islands on American commitments in Asia which underlay the majority view to let them go. The burden of argument was that holding the Philippines would lead to involvement with Japan.[59] Thirty-five of sixty-seven members of the Commonwealth Club of California, an organization representing the leading figures in business and the professions in the San Francisco Bay area, voted yes to the question "Would granting independence jeopardize the political equilibrium in the Far East?" whereupon fifty-four of seventy-five voted in the negative to the question. "Should independence be withheld on this account?"[60] No wonder the Japanese viewed Stimson's threat as a hollow gesture. His lack of support was all too apparent. No wonder the Secretary considered the passage of the independence bill as playing "ducks and drakes" with American Far Eastern policy by lending encouragement to Japanese aggressiveness. "It is like having your own people at home take off your pants when you are going out on a parade," he remarked.[61]

The Japanese had ample reason to feel rather satisfied and to believe that nothing beyond gestures, fulminations, and admonitions need be expected from the United States, or, for that matter, from any other power. The French, consistent with their earlier view, showed no alarm over the course of events in Shanghai. The chief metropolitan newspapers, plac-

---

(10/24/31) and the Secretary of the Navy (10/26/31), Navy Files EG52 (secret and confidential).

[57] See Nelson T. Johnson Papers, 1932, for a copy of the association's resolution, April 20, 1932.

[58] Stimson, Diary, Oct. 29, 1931, and Feb. 3, 1932.

[59] For the opinion of various segments of the population, see House of Representatives, Committee on Insular Affairs, Hearings on a Bill to Provide for the Independence of the Philippine Islands, 72nd Cong., 1st sess.

[60] *The Commonwealth*, Part II, Jan. 20, 1931, p. 380.

[61] Stimson, Diary, April 6, 1932.

ing all the blame for the trouble squarely on China, urged that the problem be treated as a purely local affair to be resolved by the contestants without outside interference. Prominent publicists scored the United States for abandoning the passiveness it had shown in the autumn and the League of Nations for its continued "clumsy intervention." [62] Sympathy for Japan was so pronounced that the rumors which had been circulating since September of Franco-Japanese collusion blossomed into a firm belief in the existence of an official accord or agreement. French support for the Japanese in Asia was reported to have been exchanged for the latter's defense of the French position on disarmament matters in the coming conference at Geneva. [63]

Documentary evidence of an understanding between the two nations has never been uncovered, but its shadow always hovered over the deliberations of the League. The January meeting of the Council, called to discuss Shanghai, was no exception. France's delegate continued to co-operate with the other members, but the Quai d'Orsay's attitude inevitably dampened his enthusiasm and inhibited his resolve. At least in earlier sessions, Briand had the stature to neutralize the Foreign Office's position and strike out boldly and independently; Joseph Paul-Boncour, who replaced him in Geneva in January, could not be counted on to buck Paris. But at least there was a French representative; there was none from the United States. Eight days before the scheduled meeting, Prentiss Gilbert received instructions to disassociate himself from any League machinery. He was to maintain cordial relations with the Council but not sit in its sessions. [64]

Weakened by France's coolness and America's absence, the Council convened on January 29 in the Crystal Chamber, before a large crowd of curious onlookers, to hear China's case against Japan. Fortunately for the League and contrary to the

[62] The phrase is by Pertinax in the *Echo de Paris,* Jan. 30, 1932; see also *New York Times,* Jan. 4, Feb. 1, 1932, and London *Times,* Jan. 29, 1932.
[63] Memorandum of a conversation between the counselor of the French embassy and the undersecretary of state, Feb. 1, 1932, *F.R., 1932,* III, 157–58; also London *Times,* Jan. 28, 1932. On February 3, a French deputy asked Premier Laval whether there was any truth to the reports of a Franco-Japanese agreement. Laval refused to answer and quickly left the chamber. See C. Brown, "French Policy in the Far East," *Asia,* 32 (May 1932), 284 ff.
[64] State Dept. to Prentiss Gilbert, Jan. 21, 1932, *F.R., 1932,* III, 43.

general expectation, China did not invoke Article XVI, which would have demanded a recognition of a state of war and the application of sanctions against Japan. Such action France and Great Britain would never have taken, and, of course, its effectiveness would have been nil with the United States outside the system. That China did not take that course can be ascribed to Chiang Kai-shek's reluctance to engage in legal war against Japan while America remained outside the ranks of co-belligerents. He needed Washington's support. His prime minister, Sun Fo, and foreign minister, Eugene Chen, both opposed the president's passive policy, preferring instead to sever diplomatic relations with the enemy and fight, but the generalissimo replaced them on January 28 with Wang Ching-wei and Lo Wen-kan, who were willing to support action under the less serious Article XV of the Covenant.[65] That article required only the recognition of a dispute likely to lead to a rupture, an examination of the facts, and a report and recommendation for a settlement. The order was not a large one, and the Council accomplished it easily. The members, Japan excepted, voted to create a commission of the foreign representatives in Shanghai to conduct an investigation and present a report. Although the Japanese delegate resisted China's invocation of Article XV and warned of the serious consequences to peace if the Council interfered, he knew his government would be satisfied that nothing would come of it. Japan's position would not be affected. He drew additional assurance from the refusal by the United States to permit the consul general in Shanghai to sit with the commission. It pleased Tokyo, too, that China's request to Washington to call a conference under the Nine Power Pact met with a polite but firm refusal.[66]

Japan's position was strong and secure. The only apparent danger would come from the Soviet Union, and ever since the earliest days of the conflict, Tokyo had kept a sharp and watchful eye on Moscow. Russia then was no less of an enigma

[65] See Hornbeck's memorandum, Jan. 20, 1932, D/S File 793.94/3649; Nelson T. Johnson to State Dept., Jan. 25, 1932, D/S File 793.94/3629; also *F.R.*, *1932*, III, 37–38, 76–77.

[66] State Dept. to Gilbert, Jan. 30, 1932, *F.R.*, *1932*, III, 124; Gilbert to State Dept., Jan. 30, 1932, *ibid.*, 129; Stimson to Gilbert, Jan. 30, 1932, *ibid.*, 121; Chinese minister for foreign affairs to Nelson T. Johnson, Jan. 30, 1932, D/S File 793.94/4729.

than ten years later when Winston Churchill coined the phrase, and Western experts differed sharply in evaluating her intentions and reactions. Some believed that she was not displeased by the Japanese advance into Manchuria—indeed, that she stood to benefit politically and economically by the order and stability which the Nipponese would bring to that province. Reports circulated of the existence of a secret understanding between the two powers: Russian neutrality for a division of the spoils in the area. It seemed plausible that Japan would not have moved without first securing her western flank on the mainland and that Russia would have traded neutrality for enough of northern Manchuria to provide direct access to Vladivostok. On the other hand, many observers viewed the Japanese thrust as a menace to Soviet interests in eastern Asia and predicted an imminent attack by the Red Army.[67] Nelson T. Johnson from Nanking reported the mobilizing of Soviet troops on the eastern Siberian frontier, and Naval Intelligence in Washington received similar advice from the attaché in Peking.[68]

There is no documentary proof of the existence of any agreement between the two powers. All available evidence indicates that the leaders in Moscow were greatly alarmed by the Manchurian incident. They viewed it as an element in the master-plan of the capitalist powers for the encirclement of communism, with Japan the tool and the spearhead of the perennial Western drive to destroy bolshevism. Most distressing was the threat by Japan to the Soviet maritime provinces, which were considered an objective of the Kwantung army. The Moscow press also feared the consequences of Japanese support to the White Russians in northern Manchuria. It was clear, however, that the Soviets were in no position to take any strong measures to halt the enemy, preoccupied as they were with affairs at home.[69] Indeed, they

[67] Walter Duranty in *New York Times,* Sept. 25, 1931; State Dept. to Nelson T. Johnson, Sept. 24, 1931, D/S File 793.94/1864.

[68] Nelson T. Johnson to State Dept., Sept. 27, 1931, D/S File 793.94/1858; Naval attaché in Peking to Office of Naval Intelligence, Oct. 27, 1931, D/S File 793.94/2464.

[69] *Pravda,* Nov. 2, 1931, and *Izvestia,* cited in *International Digest,* 2 (May 1932), 28–30; Nelson T. Johnson to State Dept., Jan. 22, 1932, D/S File 793.94/3600; V. M. Dean, "The Soviet Union and Japan in the Far East," *Foreign Policy Reports,* VIII (August 17, 1932); Hallett Abend in *New York Times,* Dec. 27, 1931, and Ralph W. Barnes in New York *Herald Tribune,* Oct. 16, 1931.

sought to neutralize the danger by means of a nonaggression pact with Japan, which Tokyo confidently and promptly rejected.[70]

In view of the unassailable position, it is curious that on January 31 the Japanese foreign minister requested the French, British, and American ambassadors in Tokyo to use their "good offices" to end hostilities in Shanghai. The world's capitals were taken by surprise, and speculation on Japan's motives was rife. In a letter to Sir John Simon, Stimson accurately summed up the general view that "the Japanese are turning a corner in their madness." They "have a bear by the tail and can't let go," he noted in his diary, and now want the powers "to get them out without losing face." He and others predicated their conclusions on two principal factors: the strain on Japan's economy of four months of war and the effective Chinese boycott, which resulted in a fifteen-million-dollar deficit in Japan's foreign-trade balance; the disenchantment of the public with the Shanghai adventure. The latter was most significant. The Manchurian incident had evoked a pleasant dream of empire. The imperial troops had moved from victory to victory, heavily outnumbered yet never defeated. Conquest had been easy and pride in the forces had submerged all doubts. Everybody loves a winner, but Shanghai was different. There the stubborn and unexpected resistance by Chinese soldiers had actually brought the Japanese assault to a halt. For the first time, the emperor's army had been stopped, and doubts of its invincibility dampened enthusiasm and generated war-weariness.[71] A number of other factors lent credence to the optimistic view of the Western statesmen, such as the assumption of command of Japanese naval forces in the Yangtze area by Vice Admiral Nomura Kichisaburo, considered to be a liberal and opposed to rash imperialist ventures, and the reports from Tokyo that many prominent statesmen believed the Japanese position in Manchuria would be jeopardized by the hostility of the great powers to the move in Shanghai.[72] If it occurred to anybody that the Japanese merely sought a breather for regrouping and

[70] *Trans-Pacific*, Jan. 21, 1932, p. 7.

[71] Stimson, Diary, Feb. 1, 1932; Stimson to Simon, Feb. 2, 1932, *F.R., 1932*, III, 180; Forbes to State Dept., Feb. 13, 1932, *ibid.*, 326; Kido, Diary, Feb. 3, 1932

[72] Kido, Diary, Feb. 3, 1932.

reinforcing the forces on the mainland, it was not mentioned presumably because the alternative to accepting the move on face value invited a continuation of strife and tension.

Stimson lost no time in acceding to Tokyo's wishes. Immediately, he telephoned London and, with the President at his elbow, worked out truce terms with Sir John Simon on the basis of five points: cessation of violence, no further mobilization or preparation, withdrawal of both belligerents from points of mutual contact, establishment of a neutral zone to be patrolled by neutrals, and settlement of *all* outstanding differences between the two powers in the presence of neutral observers. Sir John agreed to a joint representation with the United States and on the same day, February 1, France and Italy were included. Instructions were telegraphed to Tokyo and Nanking at once.[73] Just as quickly, it became apparent that the Japanese would not accept the terms. The fifth point was objectionable. Manchuria could not be considered an "outstanding difference" to be settled in the presence of neutrals. It was a purely Sino-Japanese affair. Japan would not permit third parties to interfere. Only Shanghai concerned the other powers because of its international character.[74]

Fearful of a breakdown in the negotiations and the end to hopes for peace, Sir John suggested the possibility of substituting in the fifth point a League commission for neutral observers or, if necessary, removing the point completely from the terms. Stimson, however, was adamant, if not belligerent, in refusing to change or eliminate any of the points. The powers must not weaken; they must not back down. The Japanese must not dictate the terms; they had had their way too much already. He would not even accept Castle's plan to make peace on the first four points if Japan were willing to "consider" the fifth at some future date. Under Stimson's insistence, Sir John capitulated and withdrew his modifications. On February 4, the Japanese officially rejected the mediation proposal. So had the faint glimmer of hope been extinguished after briefly flickering.[75]

The Japanese, however, were not yet ready for a complete

---

[73] *F.R., Japan, 1931–1941*, I, 194; also *F.R., 1932*, III, 162–65.

[74] *F.R., Japan, 1931–1941*, I, 175–82; *F.R., 1932*, III, 179.

[75] Atherton to State Dept., Feb. 4, 5, *F.R., 1932*, III, 216, 228–29; Castle, Diary, Feb. 23, 1932.

breakdown in the negotiations. The truth of the matter was that they needed time to regroup and to bring in reinforcements. They had badly underestimated the Chinese capabilities. This fact accounted for the mild tone of the note rejecting the peace proposals and the request that the Western powers suspend efforts for a truce while the Japanese themselves explored the possibilities for a cessation of hostilities with the Chinese in Shanghai. Unwilling to back down but eager to exploit every avenue to peace, Stimson agreed to leave the initiative to the Japanese; the British concurred. He was still willing to place a generous interpretation on Tokyo's actions and to accept the arrangement as clear proof that Japan had finally realized the impossibility of continuing her wayward course in the face of hostile world opinion. The desire that the details be worked out in Shanghai was viewed by the Secretary as a face-saving device lest it appear that Japan was capitulating to outside pressure. When informed that Tokyo planned to send one and one-third divisions to Shanghai to replace sailors on shore duty, he did not look upon the move as a prelude to a renewal of hostilities. When Japanese naval guns shelled the Woosung forts in the harbor on February 7, he accepted the explanation that it was done to facilitate the landing of the troops.[76] The overriding factor in his assessment of the situation was the return of the Japanese to their senses, their re-entry into the circle of decent, law-abiding nations. He had believed, ever since September, that Japan, no less than the United States or Great Britain, or France, or any other civilized state in the modern world, wished to conduct affairs with due regard for law and morality, that eventually those values in the Island Empire would triumph, and that the rash action by the army had been only an aberration and a nightmare. He stood vindicated, he believed.[77] He instructed Cunningham, the consul general at Shanghai, to sit tight and await the Japanese proposals.

Cunningham waited four days, then on the tenth of February he wrote Stimson that no word had yet been received from the Japanese. He suspected there were no peace plans.

[76] *F.R., Japan, 1931–1941,* I, 184–85, 186–88, 189–90; *F.R., 1932,* III, 234–41.
[77] He had apparently cooled off considerably since December, when the advance on Chinchow had caused him to conclude that there was no hope of Japan's ever behaving decently.

As a matter of fact, Tokyo did have peace plans, reports of which were being circulated by correspondents and reporters following a press release by the Foreign Office, and they were not very reassuring. Japan, it appeared, was suggesting that the Chinese troops remove themselves some twenty miles away from Shanghai and other principal commercial cities, Hankow, Canton, and Tientsin, thus creating a number of demilitarized zones. Such a solution as a prelude to a cease-fire was no solution at all, but rather a Japanese victory in that it would lead to a fulfillment of the Japanese plan to detach from Chinese sovereignty the chief littoral regions, thereby facilitating Japanese control. The scheme, of course, was clearly a violation of the Nine Power Pact guaranteeing the territorial integrity of China, which fact Japan readily admitted, but she defended the plan on the grounds that the pact had, after ten years' trial, proved ineffective.[78] Reports further indicated that if the Chinese refused to accede to the demands, they would be expelled by force. In one way or another, Japan was determined to achieve mastery over China, and her resolve was unmistakable. The powerful patriotic and nationalistic societies were determined to add China to Manchuria. They would brook no interference from weak elements at home. On February 9, Inouye Junnosuke, a former minister of finance and the Minseito party whip, considered too weak by the nationalists, was assassinated. The public, having recovered from the first shock of the Shanghai setback, appeared ready once again for the taste of blood. Celebration on February 11 of Kigensetsu, the anniversary of the founding of the empire, found frenzied paraders singing (the "Manchuria March" was a favorite) and shouting and swearing to defend the fatherland. The spectacle of reinforcements leaving for China with school children marching beside them to the depots reassured those who wavered.[79] All Japan had needed was time, and on February 18, she was ready. On that day, at nine in the morning, representatives of both sides met in Shanghai to arrange for a cessation of

    [78] Cunningham to State Dept., Feb. 10, 1932, *F.R., 1932*, III, 271; Nelson T. Johnson to State Dept., Feb. 9, 1932, D/S File 793.94/4080; *New York Times*, Feb. 8, 1932.
    [79] Hugh Byas in *New York Times*, Feb. 12, 1932; Forbes, Journal, Series 2, Vol. 4, p. 38 (confidential section).

hostilities. Two hours later, the conference ended in failure. The Japanese had utilized the conference to present an ultimatum, the dismantling of the Woosung forts and the withdrawal of all Chinese forces to a distance twenty miles from Shanghai, demands which the Chinese promptly rejected. Two days later, at dawn, the Japanese threw twenty thousand troops into battle and a great offensive was under way.

The Chinese were helpless. They fought doggedly and tenaciously but knew that without help defeat was inevitable. Since early February, when the truce proposals were first made, they had frantically cast about for assistance from any source, but above all from the United States. Stimson's leadership in the truce negotiations, plus the arrival at the same time of elements of the Thirty-first United States Infantry Regiment had raised hopes and buoyed spirits. The desperate plight of the Chinese was no better revealed than by the scene of Chinese civilians cheering a regiment of foreign soldiers marching on Chinese soil in battle dress. Shades of the Boxers! But when Japan refused Stimson's terms and the soldiers retired quietly to their barracks, the Chinese were frustrated. The Secretary's apparent reliance on Japan's good intentions disappointed and alarmed the Chinese. Washington seemed a useless ally indeed.[80]

Wearily and without enthusiasm, China had turned to Geneva. From the Council, little could be expected. It had already demonstrated a capacity only for establishing commissions, a poor substitute for action and a sure sign of weakness. But even had it wished to do something more significant, America's absence would have meant, at best, a repetition of the November debacle, when Washington's failure to accede to the deadline set for withdrawal emasculated the effort. The Council's pathetic position was underscored on February 2 when it met at Britain's call to hear a report on the truce negotiations. Meekly, the delegates listened to the steps being taken outside the Council by the four great powers to halt the fighting, steps which everyone present knew rightfully belonged in the Council's province. No wonder China

[80] For Chinese appeals to the United States, see the report of Mme. Chiang Kai-shek to American women in *New York Times*, Feb. 5, 1932; for Wellington Koo's appeal, see Nelson T. Johnson to State Dept., Feb. 14, 1932, *F.R., 1932*, III, 328.

had moved on February 12 to throw its case into the Assembly, where the smaller states, each of which saw itself as a potential China at the hands of one of the great European nations, could exert their will. But it was precisely this fact which caused the big powers at Geneva and the League's permanent officials to view the prospect with alarm. Aware that the breakdown in collective security in Asia endangered their position in Europe, the smaller nations stood prepared to tighten the machinery and make it effective at any cost, a cost which France, Britain, and Italy realized would have to be borne by the major powers. The rashest action was expected of the Assembly, everything from the wildest recriminations to sanctions and a naval blockade. Drummond deplored the loose talk by Assembly members, fearful lest it be translated into action, which would give Japan a pretext for war against the League.[81] There was another reason why the prominent statesmen at Geneva regretted the transfer to the Assembly. If that body were to take only a moral stand and Japan defied it as she had defied the Council, the last moral card would have been played by the League and the prestige of the organization would be destroyed, a prelude to its demise.[82]

Yet the Council really had no alternative but to accede to China's wish. On February 19, it voted to call the Assembly into extraordinary session on March 3. Before deciding to relinquish the stage, however, the delegates conformed to the usual pattern of the actor who before bowing out makes one last effort to impress his audience. With a final burst of strength and with Japan and China not participating, they drafted a firm but friendly note to Japan on the sixteenth calling attention to her obligations under Article X and urging her to take no measures calculated to impair the territorial integrity of China.[83] Three days later, the Council asked the Japanese to delay the ultimatum and on the twenty-ninth, partly to head off drastic Assembly action, proposed a truce and round-table conference at Shanghai. Japan accepted, as did China, but the former's acquiescence, which was quite unexpected, cannot be ascribed to the Council's action but

[81] Wilson to State Dept., Feb. 27, 1932, *F.R.*, *1932*, III, 456–57.
[82] Clarence Streit in *New York Times*, Feb. 12, 1932.
[83] The text is in *F.R.*, *1932*, III, 363–64.

rather, in part, to the vigorous stand taken five days earlier by the American Secretary of State in Washington.

Sometime before February 10, when Cunningham reported his suspicions that the Japanese had no peace plans, Stimson began to get the uneasy feeling that he had been taken in when he had relinquished the initiative for a truce to Japan. The same slow process of mounting anger, much as had happened at the end of the previous year over Chinchow, got under way. The realization was crystallizing that the Japanese were only stalling for time to prepare an assault to redeem the initial defeat. His frustration had been increased by the reports of the demilitarization scheme and soon it was transformed into the conviction that he had been deceived. This he refused to brook, not only because his personal pride suffered, but because he wished to preserve international law, morality, and order.[84] Some strong stand must be taken, he believed. He was not "in a very pacific frame of mind" and his thoughts he could "hardly breathe aloud" when he decided to act. His idea was to warn Japan in the strongest language that the Nine Power Treaty had not proved ineffective and that no one signatory could proclaim unilaterally its abrogation, and to reiterate the nonrecognition doctrine of the January 7 note.[85]

Stimson's plan had the full approval of his advisers in the department and of the President. He was satisfied, too, that the American people were behind him. Anti-Japanese feeling had been increasing steadily during February, and public disenchantment kept pace with his own disillusionment. Willing at the beginning of the month to attribute the best motives to Japanese actions, the attack on the Woosung forts and the ultimatum, followed by the assault, hardened the public attitude. "By her own stupidity Japan has put herself in an impossible situation," editorialized the New York *Herald Tribune*. The *Christian Century*, after labeling Japan the most menacing nation in the world, one whose cynicism knew no

[84] Stimson to Forbes, Feb. 10, 1932, *F.R., Japan, 1931–1941*, I, 191–92; Stimson to Atherton, Feb. 10, 1932, *F.R., 1932*, III, 273; Stimson, Diary, Feb. 6 and 8.

[85] The proposed text, drafted in consultation with Klots and Rogers, is in *F.R., Japan, 1931–1941*, I, 80–82.

parallel, stated bluntly: "She is an outlaw . . . her hands reek with blood."[86]

Such views must not be interpreted as an invitation to any action leading to war. An examination of contemporary opinion leads to the opposite conclusion—no one wanted to fight. The *Washington Evening Star* accurately reflected the prevailing sentiment when it said, "For the United States to go to war with Japan to prevent the seizure of China or to compel its release if seizure were already effected, would be a monstrous injustice to the American people, a sacrifice of American lives and treasure, for which there would be no justification." Most people did not think even the protection of citizens or their property in China worth war. Many called for removal of American ships and troops from Asia lest another *"Maine* incident" result.[87] There is evidence that some business people would have welcomed a small war to ease the depression by stimulating production and reducing unemployment, but such sentiments were restricted to a relatively few desperate men. Generally, the business community did not believe economic recovery warranted a war.[88] Similarly, the statement put out by the Concord, New Hampshire, chapter of the Veterans of Foreign Wars, "Everyone of us went through the Hell of the late World War and stand ready to go through it again if necessary," may be ascribed to the nostalgic desire of aging men to recapture their youth.[89] The ardent wish to avoid war did not, however, blunt the moral sensibilities of the American people. They may not have given

[86] *Christian Century,* Feb. 10, 1932, p. 182; New York *Herald Tribune,* Feb. 20, 1932; the changed attitude can be followed in the pages of the *New York Times,* Feb. 8 and 19, 1932.

[87] The *Evening Star* editorial is in *Literary Digest,* Feb. 13, 1932, p. 7; see also *Nation,* Feb. 10, 1932, p. 156, and *San Francisco Examiner,* Feb. 4, 1932; resolution of National Student Federation of America in *New York Times,* Feb. 21, 1932; Representative James V. McClintic of Oklahoma to Henry L. Stimson, Feb. 17, 1932, D/S File 793.94/4280; Emergency Peace Committee (consisting of such organizations as the Women's International League, Peoples' Lobby, War Resisters League, Fellowship of Reconciliation) to President Hoover in *New York Times,* Feb. 17, 1932.

[88] Oswald G. Villard to Jane Addams, Feb. 4, 1932, Addams Papers, SCPC; memorandum by Stanley K. Hornbeck of a conversation with a New York businessman, Feb. 4, 1932, D/S File 793.94/4059; *Magazine of Wall Street,* Feb. 20, 1932, p. 510.

[89] The statement is in a letter to President Hoover, Feb. 6, 1932, D/S File 793.94PC/51.

"a hoot in a rain barrel who controls North China," [90] but neither did they wish the wanton Japanese conduct to go uncensured. The feeling generally was that some protest under the Nine Power Pact in conjunction with the other signatories should be made and that some moral pressure should be exerted on Japan.[91]

More important to Stimson than the support of the American people, however, was the backing of the British. He did not wish to repeat the unilateral action of January 7. He did not want to bear alone the brunt of a challenge to Japan as he had a month earlier. For effective and impressive action, England and America had to move together. On February 12, immediately upon completing the draft of a protest, Stimson sent it to Sir John Simon for his approval. The foreign secretary, however, felt uneasy. The language was too strong; Manchuria ought not to be included. On the morning of the fifteenth, he told Stimson of his objections by telephone from London and said he would send along a revised draft. Eager for cooperation, Stimson was willing to wait but hoped "that your draft won't be too damn friendly." That same afternoon, Simon called again, this time expressing concern about acting outside the League. Stimson tried to convince him that Japan was not afraid of the League but would heed joint action by England and the United States. He pointed out, further, that Britain had no less an obligation as a signatory of the Nine Power Treaty than as a member of the League and joining in a protest under that treaty need not preclude action under the Covenant.[92]

Sir John sent his suggestions for revision to Washington, and though they weakened his language, Stimson, determined not to act alone, accepted them. Still the foreign secretary hesitated. Ray Atherton, the counselor of embassy in London, called Stimson on the sixteenth to say that the chances of Great Britain's co-operating were slim indeed. The only possibility, he remarked, was if all nine signatories to the treaty

[90] The words are those of the *Philadelphia Record* in *Literary Digest*, Feb. 13, 1932, p. 7.

[91] See resolution by Parents Association of Public School 26 (New York City), Feb. 9, 1932, in American Boycott Association Papers (in the possession of Mrs. Corliss Lamont); also various resolutions and memorials in D/S File 793.94/4162 and 4230 and D/S File 393.1163/549.

[92] The conversations are in *F.R., 1932*, III, 336–45.

signed the protest.[93] This, Stimson knew, was very unlikely. France was not willing to protest. The French attitude was more pro-Japanese than ever. The policy was "hands off": "Let Washington and London manage for themselves."[94] Rightly, he suspected that Simon's talk of all nine signatories participating was a dodge because the foreign secretary, who constantly had the feeling that a Franco-Japanese understanding existed, knew France would not join. Stimson was not deluded. To Atherton he replied, "I think she has let us down."[95]

The British decision to reject Stimson's plan was made the next day at a Cabinet meeting, and on the eighteenth Sir John made the announcement in the House of Commons while Lord Hailsham, secretary of state for war, did the honors before the Lords. Given the situation in Britain, no other course could have been possible. The Tories dominated the coalition Cabinet and they were determined, as they had been ever since September 1931, to cause Japan no distress. Simon, Hailsham, and Neville Chamberlain, the chancellor of the exchequer, spoke for the manufacturers, exporters, traders, financiers, and for all those who regretted the end of the alliance with Japan.[96] The Liberals and the Labourites, Lord Cecil, Gilbert Murray, Wickham Steed, and George Lansbury, who called for defending the sanctity of treaties, were deemed reckless visionaries.

Stimson was remarkably calm and magnanimous in the face of the British rebuff. He did not blame Simon, whose true inclination, he believed, was to co-operate with the United States. He had apparently forgotten a report from Hugh Wilson in Geneva only one week earlier of a speech Sir John had delivered to the Anglo-American Press Association in that city in which he had talked of China as a geographical expression and of the necessity of a nation's expanding its

[93] Atherton to Stimson, Feb. 16, 1932, *ibid.*, 356.

[94] Quoted by Norman Armour to State Dept., Feb. 8, 1932, from Paris *L'Intransigéant*, D/S File 793.94/4074. The rumors of an agreement between Japan and France continued thick and fast, especially in mid-February, when French munitions shares shot up on the Bourse.

[95] *F.R., 1932*, III, 356.

[96] See Atherton to State Dept., Feb. 18, 1932, *ibid.*, 390–92; *idem,* Feb. 23, 1932, D/S File 793.94/4547; *New York Times,* Feb. 18, 1932; Bassett. *Democracy and Foreign Policy,* p. 148, n. 1.

boundaries.[97] The onus Stimson placed on the Tories, but even then he was willing to hope that popular feeling in England would mount to the point of sweeping away Tory influence and right British policy.[98]

The problem now confronting the Secretary of State was deciding on an alternative course. Something had to be done. He refused to give up. Briefly, he scouted the possibility of a unilateral protest, but after consulting Castle and Senator David Reed, a trusted adviser, he abandoned it. Reed considered any protest futile. Perhaps he recalled Will Rogers' quip after the January 7 note: "We had better quit writing notes to Japan or she will have all of China. Every time they get a note they take another town that they hadn't thought of till our note give 'em the idea." [99] Reed's suggestion that the United States add to its fleet at Pearl Harbor and get the British to send six battleships to Singapore was considered interesting by Castle on the ground that it might appeal to the Tory imagination. Attractive as the plan was, however, Stimson did not believe the British would act.[100] For a moment, the Secretary thought of going over the head of the British government to the Dominions for support for a joint note, but he realized that little help could be expected from them. Australia and New Zealand were not displeased with Japan's progress in China. The Chinese morsel would take a long time to digest, and meanwhile the people down under would be safe. As for Canada, although opinion was revolted by the Japanese excesses in Shanghai, calm judgment swung support to Japan—in terms of benefits to Canadian commerce from a stable Far Eastern situation.[101]

One possible course of action was to encourage the League of Nations Assembly to invoke economic sanctions against Japan under Article XVI at its March 3 meeting by pledging American co-operation in advance. Such a policy was being widely discussed in the United States in late January and early February and had considerable support in influential

[97] Wilson to Stimson, Feb. 12, 1932, *F.R., 1932*, III, 301.
[98] Stimson, Diary, Feb. 21, 1932.
[99] *Cleveland Plain Dealer*, Jan. 21, 1932.
[100] Stimson, Diary, Feb. 19, 1932; Castle, Diary, Feb. 20 and 21, 1932.
[101] Jack Shepherd, *Australia's Interests and Policies in the Far East* (New York, 1940), pp. 36 ff.; American minister in Ottawa to State Dept., Feb. 12, 1932, D/S File 793.94/4225.

circles in the academic and business communities.[102] By mid-
February, a movement, led by President Lowell of Harvard
and Newton D. Baker, Wilson's secretary of war, and man-
aged by Raymond Rich of the World Peace Foundation, had
gained much momentum. On the seventeenth, Lowell spoke
over a nation-wide radio hookup, urging public support for
joining a League boycott of Japan. Events in Manchuria and
Shanghai, he said, had proved that protests and world opinion could not restrain the use of armed force by a nation. The
only effective weapon, short of war, was economic pressure.[103]
As an immediate follow-up to the address, there was circulated a petition "to the President and Congress to signify
to the League of Nations that the United States will concur
in any economic measures the League may take to restore
peace." The petition, popularly called the Lowell-Baker Petition, quickly gathered adherents. Heading the list of twelve
thousand signers, which included professors, clergymen, lawyers, judges, and businessmen, were such notables as Boston
merchant Edward Filene, publicist Chester Rowell, college
presidents Harry A. Garfield, Livingston Farrand, Kenneth
Sills, and Alexander Ruthven, historian Guy Stanton Ford,
and economist Frank Taussig. Simultaneously, other petitions were being drawn up: one by eighty-five University of
Texas professors; another by the faculties of Princeton and
Johns Hopkins; a third by five thousand civic leaders drawn
from every corner of the nation.[104] To co-ordinate the campaign and the petitions, Rich organized the American Committee on the Far Eastern Crisis, which set up headquarters
in New York in the office of the Twentieth Century Fund, a
private research organization which had recently created a
Committee on Economic Sanctions under Nicholas Murray
Butler to study the possibility of adding an economic-sanctions
protocol to the Kellogg-Briand Pact.[105] Both the committee

[102] See *New York Times*, Feb. 2, 1932, and *Magazine of Wall Street*, Feb. 6,
1932, p. 448.
[103] *New York Times*, Feb. 18, 1932.
[104] Copies of all the petitions are in *Congressional Record*, Vol. 75, pp.
4586–88.
[105] An account of the Butler Committee may be found in "Memorandum on
Economic Sanctions," a typescript in the Twentieth Century Fund Papers.
In the Newton D. Baker Papers (Boxes 220 and 240) is material relating to
the Lowell-Baker Petition and to the American Committee on the Far Eastern
Crisis. In the office of the American Association for the United Nations are the

and the Fund worked assiduously and marshaled much backing for the plan.

Despite widespread popular support, co-operation with the League on sanctions never was a real alternative for Stimson. For one thing, the President was categorically opposed.[106] In the Cabinet there was not one sympathizer and in the Senate, according to an informal poll, there were only two. Most importantly, among the opponents was Senator Borah, the single most influential congressional voice on foreign affairs, who deplored a boycott as an instrument of war. Other prominent voices raised against sanctions as the course most likely to lead to war were those of Senators George Moses, Thomas J. Walsh, and David Reed, Walter Lippmann, Professor Edwin M. Borchard, and the editors of the *Chicago Tribune,* the New York *Herald Tribune, Nation, New Republic,* and the Hearst and Gannet chains.[107] Even the pacifist groups, who generally were attracted to a boycott as a pacific instrument of coercion and as "a real advance in peace thinking," gradually and after much vacillation and soul-searching became aware of the danger that a boycott, while in itself not a warlike measure, could easily lead to hostilities in its enforcement.[108] Most of the religious organizations shared this view.[109] The Department of Commerce pitched in by warning of the evil consequences for American business.[110]

Stimson himself did not favor economic sanctions. The con-

---

records of the League of Nations Association, which contain additional material on the economic-sanctions problem, particularly in Minute Book #3. The Lowell Papers in Harvard College and the Butler Papers in Columbia College also contain material on the subject.

[106] See Stimson to Walter Lippmann, Feb. 22, 1932, copy in Baker Papers, Box 149; also Stimson, Diary, Feb. 20, 1932.

[107] *New York Times,* Feb. 14, 21, 24, 1932; Walter Lippmann in New York *Herald Tribune,* Feb. 26, 1932; *Chicago Tribune,* Feb. 25, 1932; George Soulé, "The Fallacy of the Boycott," *Harper's Magazine,* May 1932, pp. 702–709; *Congressional Record,* Vol. 75, pp. 4654 ff.

[108] See Dorothy Detzer to Emily Balch, Feb. 18, 1932, in Balch Papers, SCPC; Emily Balch to Jane Addams, Feb. 16, 1932, in Addams Papers, SCPC; the articles by Miss Detzer in the "News of the U.S." section of the Women's International League for Peace and Freedom *Bulletin,* February 1932; National Council for the Prevention of War *News Bulletin,* XI (February 1932), 2.

[109] *The Congregationalist,* Feb. 11, 1932, pp. 172–73; *New York Times,* Feb. 29, 1932.

[110] A Department of Commerce report, summarized in the *New York Times* of February 29, 1932, pointed out that more than 300,000 workers in 1,684

sequences might indeed have led to war. All advices from
Tokyo indicated that Japan would sooner fight the whole
world than die of economic strangulation.[111] Furthermore,
he knew full well that the Assembly would never invoke Article XVI, thus making the whole question of American co-
operation purely theoretical. Neither Britain nor France
would permit the smaller nations, who had no economic stake
in the Far East and who would not bear the brunt of a war,
to stampede the Assembly into so foolish and dangerous a
course as sanctions. Sir John Simon informed the House of
Commons categorically on February 21 that under no circumstances would England participate in a boycott or blockade. The Liberals and Labourites constituted a small minority
in favor of sanctions.[112]

What course, then, was open to the Secretary of State? The
problem was how unilaterally to register American repug-
nance to Japan's action without a direct protest to that nation. The solution lay in a time-worn diplomatic device frequently utilized in American history and most notably by
President Monroe in 1823: to express the government's views
and enunciate its policy, not directly in a note to the nation
concerned, but, rather, by means of a speech or a letter to a
group or person in the United States. The first suggestion for

silk mills and allied industries would be thrown out of employment as a
result of the effect of a boycott. Further dislocation would be felt among the
cotton growers, who annually marketed 40 per cent of their crop in Japan.

[111] See dispatch from Wilfred Fleisher from Tokyo in New York *Herald
Tribune,* Feb. 28, 1932; Forbes, Journal, Series 2, Vol. 4, Feb. 24, 1932; and
Stimson to Debuchi, Feb. 27, 1932, *F.R., Japan, 1931–1941,* I, 202. In his
Memoirs, 1920–33, p. 375, President Hoover maintains that Stimson favored
an official boycott but that he scotched the plan. William Starr Myers, in
Foreign Policies of Herbert Hoover, p. 162, echoes the view. All the evidence
indicates, however, that the Secretary was opposed. Some confusion over his
real position did arise, which led Raymond Rich to conclude that he favored
a boycott. Rich went so far as to inform the League of Nations Secretariat
that Stimson would bring the reluctant Hoover into line and swing American
support to Geneva. The confusion probably resulted from Stimson's encouragement of a boycott by individual Americans, which he hoped would hurt
Japan's economy and keep them guessing about the government's intentions.
See Rich to Norman Davis, Feb. 17 and 24, 1932, Norman H. Davis Papers,
Box 17, Confidential Memorandum Folder; Evans Clark to N. M. Butler,
Feb. 20, 1932, Twentieth Century Fund Papers; memorandum of a telephone
conversation between Stimson and Hugh Wilson, Feb. 20, 1932, D/S File
793.94/4458½; Stimson, Diary, Feb. 26, 1932.

[112] Charles Selden from London in *New York Times,* Feb. 24, 1932; *Manchester Guardian,* Feb. 6, 1932; *Chicago Daily News,* Feb. 24, 1932.

its use in this instance came from James Grafton Rogers, who advised a letter to some important national figure. The most obvious recipient was the man who held the key position outside the Administration in the realm of foreign affairs—the chairman of the Senate Foreign Relations Committee—William E. Borah. Stimson snapped up the idea immediately and on February 22, after a refreshing game of deck tennis, he, Allen Klots, and Rogers worked on a draft until midnight. It was laid before the President the next day, was approved at once, and sent to Borah on the twenty-fourth. The following morning, the press in every country of the civilized world brought it to readers over the breakfast table.[113]

The letter was, in many ways, a diplomatic masterpiece. It indicted no nation, castigated no power, singled out no culprit. It was moderate and measured in tone and lacked the sharpness of the January 7 note. It affirmed American belief in the wisdom and efficacy of the Open Door agreements at the turn of the century and of the network of treaties concluded at Washington in 1922 which guaranteed equality of commercial opportunity in China and the territorial integrity of that nation. It reminded both Great Britain and Japan of their solemn pledges, given on both occasions, to abide by the agreements. It appealed to all governments to withhold recognition of any situation arising from a violation of the treaties. Finally, it gave fair warning that the modification or abrogation of any part of the treaty structure released the United States from any or all of its obligations under the treaties. Stimson made it quite plain that his government would feel free to build capital ships beyond the treaty limitations and to strengthen the fortifications of the Pacific islands, which an article of one of the treaties forbade. The letter's purposes were unmistakable: to clarify for the American people their government's unalterable position; to arouse the British to accept their responsibilities; to encourage China; to suggest to the League of Nations Assembly a possible course of action at its forthcoming meeting; and to let the Japanese know the risks they invited by violating their pledge.[114]

---

[113] The text may be found in *F.R., Japan, 1931–1941*, I, 83–87.

[114] "Memorandum for the Conference at Woodley," MS in Stimson's handwriting, undated, Stimson Papers, Box 15, Letters Received; also *The Far Eastern Crisis*, p. 175.

At home, Stimson's statement received almost universal acclaim. Called "one of the most significant state papers which have been contributed to the history of the present day," "a masterstroke," "an epitome of statesmanship," "worthy to be compared with the Monroe Doctrine," [115] it was hailed by senators, both Democratic and Republican, peace groups, church organizations, educators, the business community, and newspapers from every part of the country.[116] They viewed it as forthright, lucid, and courageous. That the various treaties were interdependent appeared perfectly logical. The warning to increase capital-ship tonnage and fortify the islands was not considered, not even by the peace and church groups, to be a threatening gesture or saber-rattling but instead a duty incumbent upon the government to announce its resolve to safeguard its rights in the absence of legal guarantees. Only the barest minority took issue with the Secretary's position. The *Nation* worried about the war spirit which might be aroused by the promise of rearmament, while the *Detroit Free Press* considered it folly to continue to play wet nurse to four hundred million people in Asia, a folly which "will not set well with posterity, which may have a bill to foot." [117]

In England, the reception was not so enthusiastic. Most observers readily recognized the letter's direct appeal for Britain's support.[118] Few people, except for Liberals and Labourites,[119] were willing to give support if it meant antagonizing the Japanese. Even the possibility of the United States' build-

[115] The words are those of Harold J. T. Horan in the *Washington Post*, Feb. 25, 1932; General Douglas MacArthur to Stimson, Feb. 25, 1932, Stimson Papers, Box 15, Letters Received; Roy Howard in a telegram to Stimson, Feb. 24, 1932, Stimson Papers, Box 15, Letters Received; James T. Shotwell in a speech reported in *New York Times*, Feb. 27, 1932.

[116] See the statement by Hiram Johnson, David Reed, Thomas Walsh, and Joseph T. Robinson in New York *Herald Tribune*, Feb. 25, 1932; Dorothy Detzer in "News of the U.S.," Women's International League *Bulletin*, February 1932; Denys P. Myers of World Peace Foundation to Stimson, April 2, 1932, D/S File 793.94/4979; Federal Council of Churches *Bulletin*, XV (March 1932), 4; *Financial Chronicle*, Feb. 27, 1932, p. 1428; *Chicago Daily News*, Feb. 26, 1932; New York *Herald Tribune*, Feb. 25, 1932; *Christian Science Monitor* and *St. Paul Daily News* in *Literary Digest*, March 12, 1932, p. 12.

[117] *Nation*, March 9, 1932, p. 272; *Detroit Free Press*, Feb. 26, 1932.

[118] See London *Times*, Feb. 26, 1932, and Stimson's memorandum of his conversation with the British ambassador on Feb. 25, 1932, *F.R., 1932*, III, 440.

[119] *The Economist*, Feb. 27, 1932, p. 455.

ing a great capital-ship navy did not alter British determination to placate Tokyo, although such a prospect had, ever since the end of World War I, been one of the Admiralty's nightmares. Not even the probability that the dominions bordering the Pacific would look to a rearmed and powerful United States, not to the mother country, for protection against predatory neighbors could change the Tory government's policy. In the House of Commons, Anthony Eden stated quite emphatically, in reply to questioning by a Labor party member, Seymour Cocks, that the government was perfectly willing to accept Japan's assurance regarding her pacific intentions.[120] And so the matter rested. The analysis by the distinguished Swiss journalist William Martin of the British position made some weeks earlier, "Having failed to stop Japan at Shanghai, they will have to stop them at Singapore," [121] was not shared by the government or the majority of the people. In the words of Newton D. Baker, Britain was making it appear that the United States was "trying to play billiards on a table with a high fence down the middle." [122]

The most significant and telling effect of the letter was in Japan. There the warning of rearmament and refortification created deep concern. Tokyo knew full well that its preponderant power in eastern Asia was rooted in the nonfortification clause. Additional American capital-ship tonnage and the erection of bastions in Guam and the Philippines would constitute the gravest threat to Japanese hegemony in the western Pacific. Nor were Stimson's words viewed as hollow threats, for on the day of the publication of the Borah letter, the press carried the news that the Senate Naval Affairs Committee had approved a one-billion-dollar ship-construction bill. American intent seemed clear enough, sufficiently so that Tokyo accepted the League of Nations call on February 29 for a truce and round-table conference.[123]

---

[120] *Parliamentary Debates,* House of Commons, Fifth Series, Vol. 262, pp. 360–61. See also Wickham Steed in *Nineteenth Century and After,* 111 (April 1932), 406, and Wilson, *Diplomat Between Two Wars,* p. 277.

[121] *Journal de Genève,* Jan. 31, 1932.

[122] Baker to Roy Howard, Feb. 26, 1932, Baker Papers, Box 122 (Library of Congress).

[123] Stimson succeeded in preventing President Hoover from watering down the effect of his warning with a public statement telling the world America would not fight in Asia. See Stimson, Diary, Feb. 25, 1932.

It appeared that Stimson, at last, had found the proper formula for halting Japan's onward march, one easily as effective as joint Anglo-American remonstrances but, as it turned out, much more dangerous for the United States. The Japanese, to be sure, had backed down, but not without bitterness. Once again, Washington loomed as the sole obstacle to the fulfillment of Japan's destiny. Britain, France, the League, all seemed willing to give Tokyo *carte blanche*— only the United States stood in the way. Newspapers in the Island Empire talked of a preventive war before America could become too strong; the British ambassador in the capital even thought it possible that Japanese submarines might attack the United States Fleet in Hawaii; Forbes reported himself and the embassy under heavy guard by the Japanese secret service to prevent recrimination by an aroused public.[124] The ambassador himself thought Stimson's policy very unwise. He had constantly urged the Secretary to put no pressure on Japan, to let her finish the fighting, bring the troops home, count the losses, face the bills, and see the futility of the whole adventure.[125]

Once again Stimson found himself isolated diplomatically as after the January 7 note. The British had turned their backs on him; Japan was sore; the French reacted to the letter only by denying the existence of an understanding with Japan.[126] But, this time, China found occasion to rejoice. Here was something really substantial, not just a woolly promise "not to recognize." The prospect of a rearmed United States was viewed by Nanking as the prelude to armed intervention.[127] It was apparent that the Chinese were being carried away by their own wishful thinking. It was one thing to talk, quite another to act.

---

[124] Forbes to State Dept., Feb. 27, 1932, *F.R., 1932*, III, 457–58; Forbes, Journal, Feb. 24, 1932, Series 2, Vol. 4, pp. 48–51 (confidential section).

[125] Forbes to State Dept., Feb. 14, 1932, D/S File 793.94/1025.

[126] Elihu Root approved of the Borah letter but feared that it involved too great a risk. Stimson, Diary, March 21, 1932.

[127] Cunningham to State Dept., Feb. 27, 1932, *F.R., 1932*, III, 454, and March 3, 1932, D/S File 793.94/4897, in which Cunningham reported that the Chinese expected Japan to become impoverished trying to maintain a naval race with the United States; also Johnson to State Dept., Feb. 26, 1932, D/S File 793.94/4418.

CHAPTER SIX
in which
Stimson becomes exasperated and
threatens Japan

In our relations with Japan, the thing most to be desired is avoidance of war. . . . But neither the fact nor the appearance of weakness either in allegiance to our ideals or in equipment for defense would contribute to the averting of that test. The one hope of averting it lies in delay—giving time the opportunity to bring about changes in Japan's ideals and aspirations; but to insure delay we should give conclusive evidence of possession by us of physical force sufficient to insure our superiority in any armed conflict, if and when, between the two nations.

STANLEY K. HORNBECK, MARCH 28, 1932

Tʜᴇ ᴊᴀᴘᴀɴᴇsᴇ had heeded the Council's call for a cessation of hostilities and a truce only partly from fear of Secretary Stimson's implied threat in the letter to Borah. Another reason, crucially important, related to their plan to sever Manchuria officially and formally from China, to organize it as an independent state, to tie it by diplomatic arrangement to Japan, and to integrate its economy into the empire. To achieve this aim, they had to free themselves from the Shanghai imbroglio for two reasons: [1] first, because their energies were being greatly taxed by the unexpected Chinese resistance; second, because the success of the Manchurian venture depended in large measure upon its acceptance by the major powers in the form of recognition of the new dispensation. Hence, to risk arousing British concern by penetration of the Shanghai area, long the focus of English exploitation, appeared unwise. As for the United States, while no one expected Stimson to reverse his nonrecognition policy, withdrawal from Shanghai might serve to diminish American hostility and, given time and peace, soften Washington's intransigence over Manchuria.

Tokyo was not unmindful of the continued high level of ill-feeling in the United States,[2] particularly as it was reflected in an intensification of the demands for exerting strong economic pressure on Japan. Late in February, Nicholas Murray Butler's Committee on Economic Sanctions, which the Twentieth Century Fund had created in September of the previous year, completed its work and on March 1 rendered a report which recommended putting teeth into the Pact of Paris by adding a sanctions article to be invoked against an aggressor.[3] The committee consisted of some of the most important leaders of opinion in the country: John Foster Dulles of Sullivan and Cromwell, a prominent law firm; Lucius B. Eastman, president of Hills Brothers Company; Alanson B. Houghton, former ambassador to Great Britain; Edward N. Hurley, former chairman of the Federal Trade Commission; James

[1] Nelson T. Johnson to State Dept., March 18, 1932, *F.R.*, *1932*, III, 596.
[2] *Trans-Pacific*, March 3, 1932, p. 5.
[3] The report may be found in *Boycott and Peace* (New York, 1932); also in letter of Butler to Simson, March 5, 1932, D/S File 711.0012 anti-war/1228. See also New York *Herald Tribune*, March 8, 1932.

147

D. Mooney, president of General Motors Export Corporation; Harold Moulton of the Brookings Institution; Silas Strawn, president of the United States Chamber of Commerce. Publicity was widespread, including radio addresses by Butler, coverage in the press, discussions at luncheons, and meetings sponsored by the Foreign Policy Association and the American Academy of Political and Social Science. Its impact was great, and support was considerable.[4] On the same day, the Emergency Peace Committee, consisting of the American Friends Service Committee, the World Peace Commission of the Methodist Episcopal church, the Women's International League for Peace and Freedom, and the League for Independent Political Action, came out for joint action with other interested governments to place an embargo on arms, loans, and goods to Japan.[5] Also on March 1, William Loeb, Jr., and Mrs. Corliss Lamont organized the American Boycott Association, which sponsored an individual (nongovernmental) consumer boycott of Japanese goods. The association sent out thousands of appeals listing specific items of Japanese origin.[6] At the same time, the Federal Council of Churches supported an embargo as a "valid instrument of social discipline and vastly preferable to allowing the war to take its course."[7] In addition to the campaigns by the various organizations, numerous prominent persons, such as Raymond L. Buell, Roy Howard, Reinhold Niebuhr, Nathaniel Peffer, and George Sokolsky, suggested one or another form of economic pressure.

There is no doubt that the Japanese were disturbed by the widespread movement for their punishment. It was not that they expected the United States government to succumb to public pressure although that possibility was considered.[8] They knew too well Hoover's repeated assurances that em-

[4] For a résumé of the publicity, see Evans Clark to Nicholas M. Butler, March 24, 1932, Twentieth Century Fund Papers. The Committee on Educational Publicity in the Interests of World Peace heartily endorsed the report. See George Gordon Battle to Evans Clark, March 28, 1932, *ibid.*

[5] For the committee's activities, see Emily Balch to Jane Addams, March 11, 1932, Addams Papers, SCPC. Representatives of the committee presented a resolution to the Department of State. D/S File 793.94/4802.

[6] The records of the American Boycott Association are in the possession of Mrs. Lamont, who generously placed them at the author's disposal.

[7] See *Literary Digest,* March 19, 1932, p. 21.

[8] Editorial in Tokyo *Asahi,* printed in *Trans-Pacific,* March 3, 1932, p. 5.

bargoes and boycotts and sanctions were undesirable.[9] They were well aware that many powerful industrialists feared the unfavorable effect of a cessation of trade upon the already depressed American economy. The *Financial Chronicle* warned that sanctions may be "invoking remedies more to be dreaded than the disease," while the *Magazine of Wall Street* printed pregnant statistics revealing the dire consequences for silk manufacturers; exporters of iron, steel, cotton, petroleum, lumber, wheat, and autos; and importers of silk, tea, pottery, crab meat, and camphor.[10] They saw in the American press numerous statements by prominent educators, lawyers, and legislators—Edwin M. Borchard, Ellery Sedgwick, William E. Borah—and others voicing opposition to the idea.[11] They noted important newspapers and magazines, particularly the *Nation, New Republic,* and New York *Herald Tribune,* devoting much space to castigating the proponents of economic pressure as "zealots," "utopians," and "generators of war psychology." [12] They observed organizations as disparate as the American Peace Society and the Veterans of Foreign Wars joining hands in excoriating sanctions.[13] What worried them was that the animosity against Japan, unable to find an outlet in boycott or embargo, might be channelized into a stiffer attitude toward the Manchurian scheme which might well be shared by the opponents of economic pressure. They realized, too, that there was still a reservoir of sympathetic understanding in some circles in America which could easily be alienated by continued aggression in Shanghai. In an article appearing

[9] There is reason to believe that the Japanese knew Stimson's growing concern over the growth of the boycott movements. Stimson made no secret of it. See his conversation with the Italian ambassador, March 1, 1932, D/S File 793.94/4582. The State Department discouraged citizens from undertaking a personal boycott lest it aggravate Japanese-American relations. See Maxwell Hamilton, Far Eastern Division, to Mrs. A. H. Davis of Square Butte, Montana, March 3, 1932, D/S File 611.9412/1D.

[10] *Financial Chronicle,* Feb. 27, 1932, p. 1429; *Magazine of Wall Street,* March 5, 1932, p. 591.

[11] Borchard, "No Economic Boycott," *Nation,* March 23, 1932, p. 332, and *New York Times,* March 7, 1932. Sedgwick to Nelson T. Johnson, March 15, 1932, Johnson Papers. Borah in *New York Times,* March 12, 1932.

[12] *Nation,* March 2, 1932, p. 245; *New Republic,* March 2, 1932, pp. 58–59; New York *Herald Tribune,* March 1, 9, 1932.

[13] *Advocate of Peace,* 94 (March 1932), 13, and *Foreign Service,* March 1932, p. 4. The basis for this position stemmed, of course, from vastly different considerations. The peace people feared the danger of war; the veterans loathed the prospect of participation with the League in levying sanctions.

in March, John F. Stevens, a prominent engineer, wrote that any country which could establish a sound government in Manchuria would be a blessing to the whole world. The Chinese, he added, cannot do it; the Japanese can.[14] The noted traveler and author Herbert A. Gibbons urged his audience at a Foreign Policy Association luncheon in New York to leave Japan alone. Japan had ample provocation and had responded to it much as the United States had on many occasions.[15] Even many clergymen maintained that Japan had real grievances and that sympathy must not blind Americans to the chaotic conditions and the ruthless war lords in China.[16]

It was in great measure this reason and not because of a change of heart, as the New York *Herald Tribune* suggested,[17] that the Japanese were set to end hostilities in Shanghai. To withdraw, however, was easier said than done. The Big Business interests were all for pulling out, but the militarists and nationalists violently opposed hauling down the flag on the mainland. Shanghai was important to them, an integral part of the whole outward thrust into China. One of the most vocal and influential spokesmen, the fiery war minister, General Araki Sadao, was to bracket Shanghai with Manchuria some weeks later in a speech in the Japanese Diet in which he claimed that those two campaigns not only surpassed the Siberian expedition in importance but "when seen from certain angles, they become even more significant than the Russo-Japanese war." [18] A clear indication of the military's displeasure occurred on March 5 when members of the Blood Brotherhood assassinated Baron Dan Takuma, chairman of the board of the great Mitsui banking house and a symbol of the Zaibatsu's unwarlike policy and pernicious influence on the government. To mollify the militarists, Tokyo

[14] *Engineers and Engineering*, 49 (March 1932), 37–42.
[15] *New York Times*, March 6, 1932.
[16] Federal Council of Churches *Bulletin*, XV (March 1932), 4. Privately, many notable Americans were voicing the same views. See Forbes to State Dept., March 10, 1932, *F.R.*, *1932*, IV, 681; memorandum by J. E. J[acobs], Far Eastern Division, March 11, 1932, D/S File 793.94/4869; Edward Price Bell to Clifford W. Barnes, March 31, 1932, Bell Papers, Box "Outgoing, 1931–34"; Wayne C. Fairfield, secretary, American Board of Commissioners for Foreign Missions, to Rev. D. Downs, a missionary in Japan, American Board Papers, Letters "Japan, 1930–39."
[17] March 5, 1939.
[18] Quoted by Takeuchi, p. 375.

made one last thrust at Shanghai. On the second of March a major offensive was launched, culminating in the occupation of the Woosung forts. The Mikado's might was amply demonstrated; the withdrawal could not be construed a defeat. The following day, hostilities were suspended pending truce terms, and all eyes turned to Manchuria.

There, some two weeks earlier, the secessionist Chinese element had proclaimed the independence of the new state of Ankuo ("Land of Peace"), consisting of the four northeastern provinces: Jehol, Fengtien, Kirin, and Heilunkiang. The Japanese denied complicity in the movement, but General Honjo and other prominent Japanese acted as midwives at the birth. At every step of the way they were in the forefront, however unostentatiously. Chinese held all the executive positions, but at each official's elbow was a Japanese adviser. On March 1, the Cabinet in Tokyo approved the basic document regulating the relations with the new state, which on the same day changed its name to Manchukuo. The "Outline for Management of Foreign Relations with the Foundation of the New Manchuria-Mongol State" [19] covered a plethora of details, all of which in effect gave Manchukuo to Japan. To keep close watch over the implementation of the arrangement, the Japanese consul general at Harbin took over the directorship of the General Affairs Department of the Foreign Office. As a daily reminder of the relationship, the new state emblem consisted of the five bars of the old Chinese flag emblazoned with a rising sun. On the ninth, Henry Pu Yi was inaugurated as regent, and thus the first stage of the process of empire-building, begun on September 18, 1931, came to a close.

On March 12, the foreign minister of the new state, Hsieh Chieh-shih, informed the world powers of Manchukuo's existence. He pledged to respect all foreign rights, guaranteed the obligations of the former government, and requested diplomatic recognition.[20] That the United States would not extend recognition was anticipated, but that France and England, which had been sympathetic during the winter of 1931–32, should refuse to recognize came as a sharp blow. All indications from London at the end of February and early March

[19] IMTFE, Exhibit 222.
[20] See *F.R., 1932*, III, 579–80, for the request to the United States.

had led the Japanese to expect a favorable response. On February 24, Anthony Eden, the undersecretary of state for foreign affairs, reported to the House of Commons the establishment of the new state by *Chinese* authorities, implying thereby that China's territorial integrity had not been impaired by any signatories to the Nine Power Pact, and on the twenty-ninth stated, in reply to questions in the House, that it was not the first time since the signing of the pact that independent governments had been created in China. He further announced his Government's satisfaction with Japanese assurances that Chinese sovereignty had not been affected.[21] It seemed clear that the "little bunch of Tories," as Wilmot Lewis, the Washington correspondent of the London *Times,* labeled the group running the government, was firmly in the saddle and prepared to accept the new nation.[22] No wonder the *New York Times* reported from London on March 2: "It is expected that Great Britain will recognize Manchukuo." [23] Yet on March 11, Great Britain joined the other powers in the League of Nations Assembly in unanimously (Japan and China abstaining) endorsing Stimson's nonrecognition policy.

The action of the British government can be understood only in light of the conflict in the Assembly between Great Britain and France on one hand and the smaller nations on the other. The latter, led by Beneš of Czechoslovakia and Hymans of Belgium, were determined that the Assembly would not repeat the supine course of the Council.[24] They were determined that the larger powers would not be permitted to soft-pedal Japan's acts and carry out what one dele-

[21] *Parliamentary Debates, House of Commons,* Fifth Series, Vol. 262, pp. 359–62 and 913–20.

[22] Stimson, Diary, March 3, 1932. The Tory viewpoint was incorporated in an article by Thomas Baty, a well-known writer on international law, in the *Japan Advertiser,* August 18, 1932. Baty pointed out that recognition of Manchukuo would not violate the Nine Power Treaty because (1) the treaty does not prohibit changes in China's unity; (2) China never really controlled Manchuria; (3) Japanese troops were not in Manchuria originally to foment revolution; and (4) Manchukuoan independence was organized by local people.

[23] *New York Times,* March 3, 1932

[24] See, for example, speech by Polish Foreign Minister Zaleski, March 7, 1932, printed in *L'Echo de Varsovie,* March 9, 1932; speech by Julius Feldmans, permanent Latvian delegate to the League, March 23, 1932, reported in D/S File 793.94/4978; remarks by Swedish minister to Washington to Stimson, March 5, 1932, D/S File 858.00 PR/110; Wilson to State Dept., March 8, 1932, *F.R., 1932,* III, 532–33.

gate of a minor state referred to as the "Sato-Simon plan supported by France's Danube Union." [25] They stood prepared to push through drastic action: invocation of Article XVI. If the League could not stop aggression in Asia, no one in Europe would be safe. Such a strong policy England and France dreaded, and they knew that in the fifty-nation Assembly they could and would be outvoted. Compromise was in order, and so Sir John Simon himself proposed nonrecognition as a viable substitute.

The Foreign Secretary's capitulation did not come easily. Bucking the Tory element at home was difficult, and the struggle was reflected in his diplomatic contortions between March 3, when the Assembly convened, and the eleventh, when the resolution passed. Privately, he maintained his support of a nonrecognition statement and told Hugh Gibson, "I am going to put us squarely in line with America"; [26] publicly, he was vague and indeterminate and avoided reference to Stimson's doctrine. The American minister in Switzerland scarcely knew what to make of it and could only tell Stimson, "His attitude is a little suspicious to us." [27] Sir John's vote for the Assembly resolution on the eleventh did not mark the end of the struggle. The Tories had not been reconciled. The Foreign Secretary simply had to get off the fence at Geneva or risk a greater evil. The French assent similarly reflected a choice by that government between the lesser of two evils. The rightists in Paris were singing Japan's praises even while the vote was being taken.

So the stalwart resolution of the small powers had culminated in a victory for the rule of law, and Henry L. Stimson stood vindicated. The Secretary of State was greatly pleased. He alone had had the courage to blaze the trail. The others saw the light and followed his leadership. The end of the whole affair was in sight, he believed. Nonrecognition deprived the Japanese of the fruit of their victory in Manchuria, while in Shanghai they were retreating. All the trepidation he had felt earlier in the month over the possibility of Britain

[25] *Washington Herald,* March 8, 1932.
[26] Gilbert to State Dept., March 7, 1932, *F.R., 1932,* III, 524–25, and Wilson to State Dept., March 4, 1932, *ibid.,* 508–509.
[27] Telephone conversation between Wilson and Stimson, March 3, 1932, *F.R., 1932,* III, 502.

and France recognizing the new state and over the Japanese thrust in Shanghai vanished. At that time he had fearfully scouted the possibility of an imminent clash between the two powers as they "travelled parallel roads—America interested in keeping the door open; Japan in closing it." [28] So fearful was he for the safety of the American fleet in the Pacific that on March 2 he had warned Admiral Pratt, the chief of naval operations, to guard against a surprise attack and Pratt, in turn, had requested the commander of the regiment of marines in Shanghai for order-of-battle information on the Japanese and Chinese in the area.[29] All that was now passed. The fighting was over and the Committee of Nineteen, appointed by the Assembly on the day the nonrecognition resolution passed to supervise an armistice and a withdrawal of troops, was already operating. With real satisfaction, Stimson could reply to a reporter's question with regard to conditions in the Far East: "Over there, all is as peaceful as a young mother on a May evening." [30] He seemed unwilling to recognize certain forebodings which did not augur well for peace in Asia: the grave political and financial difficulties and the constant factional struggle in China, and the Japanese displeasure with the Assembly's resolution, which manifested itself in threats to withdraw from the League of Nations. He seemed able, too, to ignore reports from Tokyo that Japan was tightening its hold on Manchukuo. A few days later, he left Washington for a short rest.

Stimson seemed convinced that the maintenance of peace in China depended on two factors: a show of American strength in the area to let Japan know that the United States meant business and Anglo-American co-operation. To accomplish the former he opposed any move to remove the Thirty-first Infantry and elements of the Asiatic Fleet from the Shanghai region. He successfully headed off, with the help of Douglas MacArthur, the army chief of staff, a recommendation by Admiral Taylor, Consul General Cunningham, and Minister Nelson T. Johnson, to withdraw all American forces from

[28] Stimson, Diary, March 9, 1932.
[29] Stimson, Diary, March 2, 1932; CNO to CINC Asiatic, March 4, 1932, Navy Department Records, Q W17/A16-3 (320.304).
[30] *New York Times*, March 16, 1932.

Shanghai.[31] Unhappily, he could not influence the House of Representatives, which on April 4 passed overwhelmingly (306–47) a bill granting the Philippine Islands complete independence eight years after the inauguration of a Philippine president. Hard as he tried, he could not convince the congressmen that chaotic conditions in the Far East demanded American retention of the islands and that abandonment of them would be an irreparable blow to American influence in the area. He could not make them understand that their action would lead Japan to believe that the United States was ready to give up eastern Asia, thereby encouraging the Nipponese to move into the vacuum. Secretary of War Patrick Hurley, testifying in the same vein before the House Committee on Insular Affairs, was equally unsuccessful. Congress was responding not to broad strategic considerations but to the demands of certain economic groups who wanted surcease from Philippine competition.[32] And while the Senate adjourned before acting on the House measure, the report of the Senate Committee on Territories and Insular Affairs was unreservedly in favor of following the House's lead.[33]

To achieve co-operation with Great Britain, Stimson prepared to go to Europe for some face-to-face diplomacy. He knew, by reports from the embassy in London, that the March 11 resolution was well received by all shades of opinion in Britain. The Tories were relieved that sanctions which would have involved England in direct conflict with Japan had been avoided, while the nonrecognition vote, they believed, could be construed as a recommendation only. Liberals were pleased that at least some censure had been leveled at Japan. Stimson learned also that Sir John Simon was eager to continue harmonizing the approach to the Far East by the two nations. He seemed eager to convince Stimson of his good intentions,

---

[31] See Stimson to Cunningham, March 9, 1932, *F.R., 1932*, III, 543; Stimson to Nelson T. Johnson, March 11, 1932, *ibid.*, 572; CINC Asiatic to OPNAV, March 7, 1932, Navy File E T-16 Shanghai (secret and confidential); "Outline of Action—14 March 1932," by Admiral Taylor, Taylor Papers, Box 269; Stimson, Diary, March 10, 1932.

[32] Memorandum by S. K. H[ornbeck], April 13, 1932, *F.R., 1932*, III, 691; *New York Times* and New York *Herald Tribune*, Feb. 12, 1932; also *National Butter and Cheese Journal*, Feb. 10, 1932, p. 11.

[33] See the committee report, S. Rept. 354, 72nd Cong., 1st sess.

even seeking from the Secretary of State some written recognition of his services in pushing the Assembly resolution, which the Secretary graciously supplied.[34] What worried Stimson was the possibility that Sir John might backslide should his Tory masters begin to reassert their Japanese sympathies. There was some evidence already that he may have been weakening. On March 22, he told the House of Commons that Britain's role in the Far East was mediatory, not coercive, and although he said there would be no recognition of Manchukuo, he added the words "without the fullest inquiry" (meaning recognition could occur after an inquiry). He also implied that it was not unusual for a part of China to declare its administrative independence. On the following day, the principal Tory journals, the *Times* and the *Daily Telegraph,* reported Simon's words with approval. It was to stiffen the foreign secretary's spine that Stimson left the United States on April 8 for Europe.[35]

His destination was Geneva, where he was going to head the American delegation to the World Disarmament Conference, but he did not expect to accomplish anything in the way of disarmament. No one did. The conference had opened on February 1, deliberated, debated, wrangled, and finally, on March 16, recessed until April 11. Agreement was impossible. The French would not consider reducing armaments unless their security was guaranteed by multilateral treaty or by an international police force. The United States, without whose adhesion no guarantee was worth the paper it was written on and no police force was possible, would not subscribe to the French position. Its delegation operated under specific instructions to sign nothing, and it was confined within the general limitations of public opinion, so aptly expressed by Representative Britton: "Let Europe hold its own conference. We belong on this side of the Atlantic and let's stay here." [36] To

[34] Simon to Stimson, March 15, 1932, Stimson Papers, Box 15, Letters Received; Wilson to State Dept., March 11, 1932, *F.R., 1932,* III, 568, 577; Atherton to State Dept., March 15, 1932, D/S File 793.94/4858. The Tory position that the Assembly vote was only a recommendation was summarized by Thomas Baty, "Abuse of Terms: 'Recognition'; 'War,'" *American Journal of International Law,* 30 (1933), 380 ff. The French rightists took the same view in E. de Vèvre, *La Reconnaissance de Jure de la Régence de Manchourie et la Traité des Neuf Puissances* (Paris, 1932).
[35] Stimson, Diary, March 29, 1932.
[36] *New York Times,* Jan. 19, 1932.

the smaller nations of Europe, a disarmament conference held in the shadow of the Manchurian crisis was sheer sophistry. How could any nation disarm if the League could not protect it against oppression? Poland, Sweden, Czechoslovakia, and other weak countries saw China's fate as theirs unless they armed to the teeth in their own defense. A Swedish journalist predicted before the conference opened: "If the League of Nations cannot stop Japan, the Disarmament Conference will fail." [37] No, Henry L. Stimson did not go to Europe to aid the movement for the limitation of armaments, but, rather, to rally the British prime minister and foreign secretary, both of whom, along with the leaders of most of the European nations, were scheduled to appear at Geneva when the conference reopened.

He left Washington secure in the belief that there would be no weakening of the will at home during his absence. He got the President to promise to say nothing during his absence which might lead Japan to think the United States was not able or willing to stand firm against encroachments on the mainland of Asia.[38] He also went out of his way to tell the Japanese ambassador very firmly before he left that he was no less convinced that Japan had been in the wrong from the outset. He refused to be hoodwinked by Debuchi when the shrewd ambassador artfully tried to maneuver Stimson into admitting Japan's special political interests in Asia [39] (hoping to duplicate Viscount Ishii's success against Robert Lansing fifteen years earlier).

The Secretary arrived in European waters on April 14, touched briefly at Plymouth, where he conferred with Ray Atherton on board ship, and proceeded to Le Havre the next day to disembark. On the fifteenth, he arrived in Geneva and at once fell into discussions with Ramsay MacDonald and Sir John Simon. Frank and intimate talks with both of them left him encouraged. Simon pledged that the Tories in the Foreign Office would not affect government policy and that the resolution of the Assembly would be binding. Unity seemed assured.[40] An added dividend for Stimson was the

[37] Stockholm *Svenska Morgenbladet*, Jan. 30, 1932; Warsaw *Gazeta Polska*, Feb. 3, 1932; also Walter Lippmann, New York *Herald Tribune*, Feb. 3, 1932.
[38] Stimson, Diary, April 3, 5, 1932.
[39] Memorandum by Stimson, April 4, 1932, *F.R., Japan, 1931–1941*, I, 87–89.
[40] Stimson, Diary, April 16, 18, 28, 1932.

unexpected cordiality of the French. Conversations with Philippe Berthelot, the political director of the Foreign Ministry (and a principal formulator of policy), convinced him of the sincerity of the Quai d'Orsay in supporting the Assembly resolution and of the fallaciousness of the rumors of a Franco-Japanese understanding.[41] He was even successful in his relations with Matsudaira Tsuneo, the Japanese ambassador to Great Britain and delegate to the League, with whom he spoke on a number of occasions. It was Stimson who helped persuade Matsudaira to accept the resolution of the Committee of Nineteen—that a commission of neutrals set the time for the evacuation of Japanese troops following the armistice.[42]

By the time the Secretary was ready to leave Geneva on May 4, he was quite pleased with his work. To Castle he wrote: "If I had done nothing in regard to the Disarmament Conference I should feel that my conversations in regard to Japan and China had made the trip worthwhile." [43] What he meant was that he had assured continued solidarity among the powers on the Assembly's resolution for nonrecognition; and unity now was more important than ever as the Japanese moved relentlessly to tighten their hold on Manchuria and incorporate the area absolutely into the Japanese political and economic sphere. On April 11, the Cabinet had approved a plan for a single self-sufficient economic unit of Japan and Manchukuo and on the twenty-third had made four major appointments of Japanese to positions in key ministries in Manchukuo. By the end of April, there were more than six hundred Japanese advisers in the government, and the Home, Finance, and Foreign offices were completely dominated by them.[44] On the twenty-second, General Araki delivered in Osaka a notable speech, sponsored by the powerful patriotic society Kokuhonsha and heard by a large crowd of busi-

[41] *Ibid.*, April 15, 1932. Reports of French backing of Japan were still being widely circulated. See W. Colepepper, "Is France Backing Japan?" *Living Age*, 342 (April 1932), 113–16, translated from *Weltbühne*, a Berlin weekly.
[42] Stimson, Diary, April 18, 1932.
[43] Wilson to Castle, April 30, 1932, *F.R.*, *1932*, III, 735.
[44] See IMTFE, Exhibit 188B; also "Empire's Practical Assistance and Guidance Toward the New State of Manchuria and Mongolia," IMTFE, Exhibit 223. For a list of Japanese who occupied important positions in the new state, see *F.R.*, *1932*, IV, 282 ff.

nessmen, educators, veterans, and government officials, in which he pledged categorically the determination of the government to continue its policy in Manchuria: "Let the League of Nations say whatever it pleases, let America offer whatever interference [she may]. . . . Japan must adhere to her course unwaveringly." [45] All of this meant that trade between Manchuria and Europe would be at Japan's mercy. Stimson had to make sure that the bait of trade concessions would not lure the powers into the trap of recognition.

Stimson knew very well from his Geneva conversations that neither Britain nor France would do any more than refuse to recognize, nor would they permit the smaller nations in the Assembly to go beyond that point. He knew just as surely that the Hoover Administration would take no more drastic action. Indeed, it was rather embarrassing to Ray Atherton to be asked by the prime minister in London when Atherton was urging MacDonald to stand firm and step out boldly against Japan, "How far does the United States want to go; is it willing to go beyond what it has already done?" [46] What Stimson hoped, however, was that Japan should not be permitted to know that neither the United States nor the other powers would not do more. The Japanese must be kept guessing and wondering and fearing. The uncertainty, particularly about America's course, would, in the Secretary's opinion, serve as a very real check and bridle on Japan. He was therefore quite pleased that the agitation in America for a boycott was still strong. The American Boycott Association and the Twentieth Century Fund were continuing their campaigns. Most gratifying was the introduction of a resolution in the Senate by Arthur Capper of Kansas calling for the addition of a sanctions article to the Pact of Paris.[47]

Stimson's satisfaction, however, soon turned sour, for while en route home, his undersecretary made two speeches which cut the ground from under his chief's feet cleanly and neatly. Castle said quite plainly on May 4 to the American Conference on International Justice, meeting in New York, that the

[45] Quoted in part in Takeuchi, pp. 381–82, n. 172.
[46] Atherton to State Dept., April 4, 1932, *F.R., 1932*, III, 664–66.
[47] SJRes. 140, 72nd Cong., 1st sess. (April 7, 1932); see also N. M. Butler to Evans Clark, April 8, 1932, Twentieth Century Fund Papers; *International Disarmament Notes*, April 11, 25, 1932; Memorandum by Mrs. Corliss Lamont, April 20, 1932, American Boycott Association Papers.

United States government opposed any official boycott because it would surely lead to war and that nonrecognition was the Administration's firm policy. Two days later at Atlantic City, he reiterated the stand.[48] Stimson was quite furious upon his return. His whole policy, which he summed up in a letter to Walter Lippmann as "A word unspoken is a sword in your scabbard, while a word spoken is a sword in the hands of your adversary," [49] was now exposed. He never forgave Castle for the speeches, although he knew very well that the idea was Hoover's. He felt that his principal lieutenant need not have been the instrument for the betrayal.[50] His vanity also may have been touched by Castle's reference to the nonrecognition policy as the Hoover Doctrine, although since January 7 it had been known as the Stimson Doctrine.

After returning home, Stimson lost no time seeking to repair the damage Castle had caused. Some substitute for a boycott threat had to be found to keep Japan in check—and it had to be found fast because the Japanese domestic scene was exploding and the consequences for world peace could be devastating. On May 15, the aged prime minister, Inukai Tsuyoshi, was assassinated by some military and naval personnel, members of the "Young Officers of the Army and Navy" and the "Farmers' Death Band" in protest against the government's foreign and domestic policies. The truce which Inukai had negotiated at Shanghai on May 5 was considered by the patriots an impairment of honor and a show of weakness. Although it was well known that the truce had been necessary to liquidate an unsuccessful adventure and release troops for operation against Chinese forces in northwestern Manchuria, they blamed it on the Big Business interests, whose trade in the area had suffered while hostilities were in

[48] *New York Times,* May 5 and 7, 1932. Less than a week earlier Hornbeck had said much the same thing, although it was somewhat enmeshed in legal language, in an address to the American Society of International Law. See the society's *Proceedings* (1930), p. 70. Castle recalls that he cleared the speeches with Stimson by telephone to London and all Stimson asked was that he defer making the address until he, Stimson, had had time to inform the British government. Castle to the author in a conversation on June 4, 1956.

[49] Stimson to Lippmann, May 19, 1932, copy in Newton D. Baker Papers, Box 149.

[50] Castle, Diary, Dec. 31, 1932.

progress. The nationalists revolted, too, against the government's economic and social programs, which favored the rich and depressed the peasants and farmers. They wanted relief for the farmers, abolition of large fortunes, compulsory unemployment and sickness insurance, equal distribution of wealth, and destruction of the power of the great industrial families like Mitsui, Mitsubishi, and Sumitomo. They sought to end the parliamentary system, controlled by the capitalists and politicians for their own selfish interests and unsuited for orientals anyway, and substitute for it state socialism run by a military dictatorship, much like the shogunate, dedicated to patriotism and imperial glory, with equality for all of the emperor's subjects.[51]

These men were no ordinary lawless gunmen but, rather, in their own view, selfless and high-minded patriots performing a noble task in ridding the nation of selfish, unpatriotic profit-seekers. Immediately upon completing their task, they surrendered voluntarily to the police.[52] It was these same men who were ready to defy the rest of the world, who spoke disparagingly of American strength,[53] who were threatening to walk out of the League of Nations should it "persist in radically disappointing Japan's expectations and confidence in that body," [54] and who were ready even to take on Russia and extend operations into Siberia.[55]

Happily for him, the Secretary found at hand a most suitable weapon in the United States Navy. Since January, the major elements of the fleet, both the battle force and the scouting force, had been in the Pacific playing the annual war games. The maneuvers were scheduled to end in May, at which time the scouting force was to return to Atlantic Ocean ports, its normal bases. For Stimson, the opportunity

[51] See Grew to Hugh Wilson, July 21, 1932, Joseph C. Grew Papers, Letters 1932 (Houghton Library, Harvard University).

[52] See the able analysis by Edwin Neville to State Dept., May 20, 1932, *F.R., 1932*, IV, 684–88. He points to the rumors that the conspirators were pupils of an extraordinary institution, the Aikyojuku (Patriotic School) at Mito (north of Tokyo), a town whose reputation was for fanatical patriotism. See also Hirosa Kurataro, "Japan's Militarist and Fascist Revolt," *Christian Century*, April 20, 1932, pp. 506–8.

[53] Lieutenant Commander Hirata Shinsaku in *Kaizo (Reconstruction)*, reprinted in *Japan Advertiser*, April 20, 1932.

[54] *Osaka Mainichi*, April 27, 1932.

[55] *Christian Century*, May 18, 1932, pp. 632–33.

was superb. Simply keep the scouting force in the Pacific, geographically poised to strike a blow if necessary, and let the Japanese draw what implications they might. To convince the President of the wisdom of such a move was difficult. Hoover's instincts and inclinations recoiled at the prospect of so bellicose a gesture. He was even opposed to a threatening move. Stimson had to buck Castle, too, who feared the consequences of irritating the Japanese. But Stimson persisted and, with the aid of Admiral Pratt, who worked out a scheme whereby the cost of keeping the fleet in the Pacific was not as great as expected, gained Hoover's consent to keep the scouting force in the Pacific until the 1933 games. Also helpful was the argument that his hand would be immeasureably strengthened in dealing with Japan, especially toward the end of the summer, when a crisis was bound to develop over the report the League of Nations investigating commission was expected to present.[56]

The Secretary could claim still another victory for his policy of firmness and strength: the replacement of Cameron Forbes by Joseph C. Grew as ambassador to Tokyo. For some time Stimson had found Forbes quite unsatisfactory and even annoying. The ambassador had differed sharply with his chief when after the turn of the year Stimson adopted a tough line, and soon he found himself at odds with Stimson's repeated protests and threatening gestures. He believed that all Stimson had accomplished was to goad the Japanese into a frenzy of excitement, rally popular support behind the militarists, weaken the moderates, and set the United States up as the chief adversary. He had made no attempt to veil his distaste for his chief's position and was continually urging a "hands off" policy. By mid-February, relations between the two had become very strained, and Forbes had no choice but to resign.[57] Grew was an excellent replacement. A career diplomat of twenty-seven years' experience with service in numerous posts, he could be expected to appraise and report affairs in Japan with a cool and analytical detachment. Six feet tall, slender, straight, of aristocratic bearing, a product of Groton and Harvard, he instilled confidence throughout the nation.

---

[56] Stimson, Diary, May 18 and 20, 1932; Castle, Diary, Nov. 8, 1932.
[57] Forbes, Journal, Series 2, Vol. 4, pp. 245–47. The entry for March 14, 1932, is indicative of his disgust with Stimson's policy.

The press received word of his appointment with unanimous acclaim and predicted that his skill, suavity, calm judgment, and smoothness would make him an ideal representative in the troubled capital.[58] Stimson felt relieved that he would have a man in Tokyo who agreed with his views. He knew that although Grew realized the validity of Japan's aspirations, he "had no sympathy at all with the illegitimate way in which Japan has been carrying them out." [59] Grew himself was not so sure of his mission. His instructions were confusing. Hoover had told him that the Japanese must get out of Manchuria but not at the risk of war; Stimson had said simply but emphatically that Manchuria must be evacuated.[60]

Grew arrived in Tokyo on June 6 and found the state of affairs remarkably calm. Fears that the Inukai assassination would be followed by the overthrow of the parliamentary system and the seizure of power by the military had proved groundless. Normal practice was followed. The Emperor, on the advice of Prince Saionji, appointed a prime minister, who formed a new government on May 22. The new premier, seventy-three-year-old Admiral Viscount Saito Makoto, had a long and distinguished career of public service, having served as minister of the navy, Korea's best governor general, and chief of the delegation to the Geneva Naval Conference in 1927. He was a liberal, civilian in attitude, and an independent. His cabinet consisted of moderates from both major parties and included four independents. The militarists accepted the situation in return for the retention of General Araki Sadao as war minister. They fully expected that the firebrand Araki would set the tone and policy for the new government, and they were correct. They were pleased, too, with the new foreign minister, Count Uchida Yasuya, former president of the South Manchurian Railway and one of the prime exponents of a vigorous exploitation of Manchuria. As a matter of fact, observers in Tokyo were saying that the civilians were being given their last chance by the military.

[58] *Rockford* (Illinois) *Star, Detroit Free Press, Wall Street Journal,* Feb. 11, 1932. The Japanese welcomed Grew warmly. They were particularly pleased because his wife was a granddaughter of Matthew Perry, who had "opened" Japan, and the daughter of a long-time professor in a Japanese university.

[59] Entry for May 14–18, 1932, in Grew's diary, printed in *Ten Years in Japan* (New York, 1944), pp. 3–4.

[60] Joseph C. Grew, *Turbulent Years* (Boston, 1952), p. 931, n. 5.

If they proved weak and pusillanimous, did not pursue a strident policy in China, knuckled under to the capitalists, failed to effect social and economic reforms, they would be replaced by the military.[61]

Very soon it became clear that the old premier was not knuckling under to the capitalists but being led by the military. There is every reason to believe that he would have preferred to follow a liberal policy abroad and real cooperation with the League of Nations, but it was too late for that. The calendar could never be turned back to pre-1931. The road to Southeast Asia and Pearl Harbor lay dead ahead. As Grew reported shortly after his arrival, the Japanese people were self-confident and assured that the course in Asia was necessary, just, and reasonable. They supported the army and did not fear reprisals.[62] Even old-line, long-term liberals were swinging over to back an aggressive policy. There was a good deal of shock around the world when Viscount Ishii Kikujiro, long a leading figure in Japan, a former foreign minister, the negotiator of the Lansing-Ishii Agreement of 1917, a privy councilor, and the president of the League of Nations Association of Japan, delivered a rousing speech at a luncheon given June 21 by the American-Japan Society honoring the new American ambassador. In blunt language, he warned the United States not to stand in the way of Japan's "pacific and natural expansion" unless it wished to "create a grave situation." [63] Equally disturbing was the press conference held by Nitobe Inazo—one of the most internationalist-minded Japanese, a Christian and a Quaker, a leader in the effort to link Japan with the West—while on a visit to New York, in which he gave approval to all of Japan's acts in Manchuria and Shanghai.[64] The Japanese press was unanimous in endorsing Ishii's sentiments and in supporting the Manchurian policy, and on the last day of the session of the Diet, June 14, there passed unanimously a resolution calling on the

[61] See Neville's analysis, May 20, 1932, *F.R.*, *1932*, IV, 690–91; "Japan Calls Upon Admiral Saito," *Christian Century*, June 1, 1932, p. 691.

[62] Grew to State Dept., June 13, 1932, *F.R.*, *1932*, IV, 77–78.

[63] Reported in *New York Times*, June 22, 1932, and in almost all other major American newspapers, conveniently collected in the Grew Papers, "Clippings, April–June 1932."

[64] *Christian Century*, June 1, 1932, p. 691.

government to emulate the United States' example in Panama in 1903 by recognizing the new state of Manchukuo.[65]

Saito's government was not yet ready to extend official recognition to the new nation. It chose to await the outcome of the investigations of the Lytton Commission as it had pledged to do when the commission was set up, but it gave the new nation every assistance in consolidating its nationality, reorganizing the currency, building new railway lines, developing trade, and supplying advisers. What the new nations needed most of all was money, which Japan could not so easily provide. The alternative was for the Manchukuoan government to seize the customs collected by the Chinese Maritime Customs Service at its ports, chiefly at Dairen, which had hitherto been sent to the Chinese government at Nanking. Without the support of the Japanese garrison, such a move would have been impossible since Japan was party to an international agreement guaranteeing the inviolability of the customs. At the time, Japan denied any complicity in the matter, stating it was a move taken by an independent nation. Protests by the United States, Great Britain, and France were brushed aside. The whole world suspected, however, that the decision was made in Tokyo, and revelations at the War Crimes Trials provided ample proof.[66]

Stimson's policy did not seem to be working very well. His protests and threats apparently were not deterring Japan. True, the last troops left Shanghai, but only to be moved to Manchuria and to press the campaign there against the remnants of the army led by General Ma Chan-shan. In the new state, the Japanese had virtually taken over—recognition or integration into the empire would only change things legally. As for fearing American action, all reports from the Far East indicated that the opposite was true. In a long memorandum to Admiral Pratt, Admiral Taylor on June 10 made this point very clear.[67] All that Stimson seems to have accomplished was that to the Japanese, the United States appeared the great

[65] *Japan Times,* June 23, 1932; also report of American commercial attaché in Tokyo to Commerce Dept., June 17, 1932, D/S 893.01 Manch/436, and Takeuchi, p. 388.

[66] See chief of staff, Kwantung army to vice minister of war, June 24, 1932, IMTFE, Exhibit 227.

[67] Taylor to Pratt, June 10, 1932, Taylor Papers, Box 269.

obstacle to their legitimate expansion and the "motive power" behind the positions taken by the League to thwart Japan. Neither Great Britain nor France would do anything without American prodding. Indeed, no sooner did Stimson leave Europe than Simon went back to his former pro-Japanese behavior, despite his willingness to protest the customs seizure. Hornbeck noted this to the Secretary when he wrote, "Except they specifically and unequivocally promise, no reliance can be placed upon them." He went on to say further, "We can count on no other great power as a firm 'ally' or associate." [68] Unhappily, the observation was accurate. The United States was alone in facing the foe across the Pacific. From many sources and directions Stimson was being urged not to step out ahead of the other powers and to stop sulking and nagging. His colleagues in the department offered the same advice.[69] The Secretary himself was not very happy. To his diary he confided on June 23, apropos of the Ishii speech and the seizure of the customs, that he feared he would have the Far East on his hands again.[70]

What he had to deal with was the state of affairs in Manchuria, which, Castle noted in his diary, were "going from bad to worse." [71] Bad was the seizure of the customs from which China drew 15 per cent of her import duties. Worse was the imminence of the recognition of the new nation by Japan. Pressure on the Saito government for immediate recognition was coming from almost every section of Japanese opinion, with the army spearheading the drive. It was following a suggestion by War Minister Araki on July 1 that the seven leading Tokyo newspapers printed identical editorials calling for recognition. A few days later, a mass meeting in Tokyo attended by high-ranking army officers clamored for action. Shortly after that, the vice chief of staff informed the Emperor that Manchukuo had to be recognized, lest it appear that the nation was divided, the civilians not supporting the

[68] Memorandum by S. K. Hornbeck, June 27, 1932, D/S File 893.51 Funds/ 128; also *Christian Century*, May 11, 1932, pp. 596–97.

[69] *Rochester* (New York) *Times-Union*, June 27, 1932, and *Christian Science Monitor*, June 29, 1932; also memorandum by Allen Klots, June 23, 1932, D/S File 893.01 Manch/330, and Stimson, Diary, June 25, 1932.

[70] Stimson, Diary, June 23, 1932; K. Radek, the noted Soviet publicist, made the same observation in "The War in the Far East," *Foreign Affairs*, X (July 1932), 553 ff.

[71] Castle, Diary, July 14, 1932.

military.[72] The government could hardly resist the pressure, and it appeared that it would not wait for the report of the Lytton Commission. Count Uchida told Lord Lytton, who was then in Tokyo, and the American and British ambassadors that recognition was at hand, regardless of what the League of Nations or the powers said or did.[73] Defiance could not have been more complete or more arrogant. Preparation for recognition was accomplished with the appointment at the end of July of a supreme representative of Japan to Manchukuo, General Muto Nobuyoshi, who was also to serve as commander of the Kwantung army and governor general of Kwantung. This appointment signaled the subordination of the Foreign Office to the army and the approval by the Cabinet of an aggressive policy of recognition.

In the face of all these moves and indications, Stimson knew not what to do. He had protested the customs seizure but to no avail. When the Chinese asked him for advice or how best to treat the customs seizure, he replied in a long communication which occupies three and one-half pages of print in the *Foreign Relations* volume but which said, in effect, only "be of stout heart." [74] It distressed him not to be able to give aid to China; to give them "stone in place of bread." [75] They regarded him, he knew, as their one true friend. They had nowhere else to turn in their plight and their plight was bad indeed: the Japanese from the north; rebel Cantonese from the south; communism in the middle. The Nationalist government barely was existing.[76] But what could Stimson do? As for the rumor of early recognition of Manchukuo, again, he was helpless. Grew from Tokyo and his advisers in the department urged him to say nothing lest a protest precipitate action by the Japanese and hasten recognition. All Stimson did, therefore, was instruct Grew to say, should the Japanese ask him America's view on recognition, that Washington disapproved.[77]

[72] Kido, Diary, July 20, 1932; Grew to State Dept., July 15, 1932, *F.R., 1932*, IV, 143–46; "The Advance of 'Shokokurabu' to Manchuria," June 27, 1932, JFOD, S5.1.1.0–33, p. 77.
[73] Grew, *Ten Years*, p. 31.
[74] *F.R., 1932*, IV, 165–68.
[75] Castle, Diary, July 14, 1932.
[76] Nelson T. Johnson to State Dept., July 12, 1932, *F.R., 1932*, IV, 137–40.
[77] Grew, *Ten Years*, p. 31; Grew to State Dept., July 16, 1932, *F.R., Japan, 1931–1941*, I, 93–95, and Stimson to Grew, July 19, 1932, *F.R., 1932*, IV, 172.

Stimson's frustration mounted as July waned. He had already decided, after dining with Senator Borah on July 20, to invoke the Nine Power Pact should the Lytton Commission report prove ineffective,[78] but that was more than a month away. He felt the urgency for making known immediately his displeasure. He did prevent Admiral Taylor early in August from paying a courtesy visit to Tokyo on his flagship, but that was too mild and indirect.[79] Something strong and positive, direct and sharp, in the spirit of the nonrecognition note and the letter to Borah was desirable. The time had come, Stimson believed, for a major pronouncement on American policy.

Ever since his return from Europe he had been toying with the idea of clarifying the position of the United States in a war between the League of Nations and a country branded an aggressor by the League. One of the most persistent questions European statesmen had directed at Stimson during his visit to the Continent was whether the United States would remain neutral in such a conflict, thereby, in effect, helping the aggressor nation by permitting it to purchase the sinews of war from American factories and farms. It was a most important question, for if Washington were to remain neutral, League action against an aggressor would be impossible. As early as July 14, he began to think about the possibility of a major speech on this question in terms of an implementation of the Kellogg-Briand Pact. "An authentic speech on it," he noted in his diary the same day, "would help tremendously over in Europe at this time." Soon after, he spent odd hours working on an address which gradually took shape, in his own mind, as his "magnum opus." Securing a podium was not difficult. At his suggestion to Walter Lippmann, the Council on Foreign Relations in New York extended him an open invitation. By the end of July, the ideas had been hammered out, refined by Allen Klots and James Rogers, and lacked only presidential approval. This was not so easy to get because Hoover was heavily occupied on the home front with the usual cares of office, plus the election campaign, then getting under way. Finally, on July 28, the President approved, but not before deleting certain references which he believed com-

[78] Stimson, Diary, July 20, 1932.
[79] Castle, Diary, Aug. 5, 1932.

mitted the United States to too close an involvement with the League of Nations.[80]

On August 8, Stimson journeyed to New York, where, in the evening, before a distinguished and select audience, he delivered his address. It was his first speech on foreign affairs in eighteen months and it was a notable one: strong, direct, positive, forceful. In it he combined his two current objectives: to chastise Japan and to take America close to the enforcement machinery of the League of Nations by way of the Kellogg Pact. As was his wont, he minced no words. The United States, he said, was committed to consulting with the other signatories of the pact to voice disapproval of a violation of the pact. Implicit in the pact was not only the pledge to consult but a firm promise to take sides—against the transgressor. The United States, he continued, would not remain a neutral bystander. Indeed, since the signing of the pact, neutrality had been impossible. "Under the former concept of international law when a conflict occurred, it was usually deemed the concern of only the parties to the conflict. The others could only exercise and express a strict neutrality alike toward the injured and the aggressor. . . . But now . . . such a conflict becomes of concern to everybody connected with the pact. . . . Hereafter when two nations engage in armed conflict . . . we no longer draw a circle around them and treat them with the punctilio of the dueller's code. We denounce them [the wrongdoers] as lawbreakers." It was clear from the next few paragraphs that he considered his position toward Japanese expansions in Asia a reflection of his concern with violations of the pact. America had not stayed neutral but had instead taken the lead in branding the aggressor. Unmistakable was his reference: "A nation which sought to mask its imperialistic policy under the guise of defense of its nationals would soon be unmasked." Japan stood condemned.[81]

[80] The development of the speech from conception to birth may be followed in Stimson, Diary, July 14, 18, 23, 25, 26, 27, 28. Hoover recalled his fears to Castle some weeks later when the latter visited the President at his summer camp. See Castle, Diary, Aug. 20, 1932. Hoover's objections to the speech were, at least in part, political. He feared alienating the Hearst press, whose support he sought in the election, by too "international" a position.

[81] The speech was reported verbatim widely. A convenient text is that in the *New York Times* of August 9, 1932.

It was not surprising that the speech created a great stir at home and abroad. It was a revolutionary pronouncement, a departure from the injunction of the Founding Fathers, from the long tradition of the American people, and from the policy of the Administration and its two predecessors. Neutrality had become the basic ingredient of American foreign policy, and here was the Secretary of State announcing its demise. Lack of concern with political events in Europe and elsewhere had become the hallmark of the American attitude, and here was the Secretary of State heralding a new dispensation. Some hailed the speech presaging the new order as a great landmark and milestone, an end of splendid isolation and a contribution of the highest importance to world stability. The world, said a circular letter emanating from the League of Nations Association, will never again have to wonder whether America would stand aloof in a crisis. In a future crisis, Washington will follow Stimson's course of action regarding Manchuria, speak out in defense of the sanctity of treaties and the rule of law, and consult with the other powers. Dozens of congratulatory messages poured into the department.[82]

Others regarded the speech as provocative and inflammatory, as nothing short of a harbinger of trouble. Said the rabidly isolationist New York *Daily News:* "[Mr. Stimson] is the most dangerous man in the Hoover government. He doesn't like war. Therefore Mr. Stimson insists on telling others they shall not fight. And by so doing he is dragging us even closer to the day when some fighting cock of a nation will knock the pacifist chip off our shoulder and say, 'Well, so what?' Mr. Stimson has just picked on the twentieth century's prize fighting cock—Japan." More soberly and less archly, many observers regretted that the United States was playing moral policeman, Sunday School teacher, and spokesman for the world. The vision of eternal meddling in other nations' business worried many people. "Stimson's Doctrine Proclaims 'Meddling' as National Deity" editorialized the *New York*

---

[82] New York *Evening Post,* Aug. 10, 1932; *Jersey City Journal,* Aug. 9, 1932; *Hartford Courant,* Aug. 10, 1932. The League of Nations Association circular is in D/S File 711.0012 anti-war/1312; the messages are in Stimson Papers, Box 18, Letters Received; see also National Council for the Prevention of War *News Bulletin,* August 1932, p. 5.

American, while the *Camden Post* asked whether Stimson had forgotten the injunction of George Washington, the lessons of World War I, and the repudiation of the League of Nations by the American people. Countless others feared an irritated and provoked Japan lashing out in anger and blindness.[83] Most distressing was the fact that Stimson was getting himself and the country into a dangerous situation by speaking loudly and carrying a small stick. Neither public opinion nor the navy were in a position to back the bold stand of the Secretary. Stimson, through his earnest desire to support the treaty structure and place his country in a position of leadership, where, he believed, it belonged, tended to rashness, and those in charge of America's defenses were frankly worried.[84]

To Europeans the address was of the greatest moment and the new American policy was on the front page of every metropolitan newspaper. In Geneva, the speech caused elation. The link between the United States and the League of Nations seemed to have been forged at last.[85] Woodrow Wilson at last had his vengeance over Henry Cabot Lodge. In London, Liberals rejoiced at the apparent renunciation by America of its traditional isolationist position. With the abandonment of neutrality and the promise to consult in the event of a breach of the peace, said the London *News Chronicle,* the United States no longer will look the other way in a crisis but will march in step with the other nations. As the veteran journalist Wickham Steed pointed out in a letter to the London *Times,* the speech bolstered the whole international-security structure by telling aggressors beforehand that they could no longer expect America to remain neutral. Even the London *Times,* arch Tory journal, representative of the Cliveden set, and whose owner, Major Astor, and whose editor, Geoffrey Dawson, wanted to have little to do with involvement and entanglement, could not resist commenting favorably on the momentous implications for world peace of Stimson's pledge to consult with the other powers. One other feature of the speech received wide acclaim in Great Britain. The abandonment of neutrality by the United States finally

[83] New York *Daily News, Waterville* (Maine) *Sentinel, Camden Post,* New York *Herald Tribune, Detroit Free Press,* Aug. 10, 1932; *Chicago Tribune, New York American,* Aug. 15, 1932; *Financial Chronicle,* Aug. 13, 1932, p. 1046.
[84] Castle, Diary, Aug. 20, 1932.
[85] Gilbert to State Dept., Aug. 18, 1932, D/S File 711.0012 anti-war/1313.

laid to rest the one great remaining source of friction between the two English-speaking countries. The question of the freedom of the seas, which had plagued both powers since 1793 and over which they had fought once and almost had come to blows on two other occasions, now had no relevance. There could be no American neutral rights for the British belligerent to trample upon.[86] In Paris, every important newspaper commented on the address, and, in most instances, favorably. The focus was on the pledge to consult and on its bolstering of the European security system. Even the rightist press, hitherto most articulate in supporting Japan in the Far East as a bulwark against Soviet communism and strongly opposing any effort to censure her, viewed with satisfaction the implications of the new American policy for the maintenance of the Versailles settlement. As the Nazis increased their power in Germany and unabashedly announced their aim to rectify the injustice of the peace settlement, Japan began to appear farther and farther away and American support began to appear more and more attractive.[87]

The Chinese could hardly be displeased with Stimson's stern warning to Japan, but they would have preferred some statement as to how the United States planned to stop Japan. There had been, since September 1931, three notable statements—the January 7 note, the letter to Borah, and now the August 8 speech—but the effect on Japan so far was not apparent. Lo Wen-kan, the Chinese foreign minister, whose sense of humor was well known in diplomatic circles, jocularly remarked to the American consul general at Nanking that he was now waiting to hear some details of the American implementation of the policies announced in the three statements.[88] Of course he expected none. Neither did the Japanese.

The effect of Stimson's speech in Tokyo was to stiffen the resolve to continue the forward policy on the mainland.

[86] London *Times,* London *News Chronicle, Manchester Guardian, Edinburgh Evening Dispatch,* Aug. 9, 1932; Wickham Steed's letter is in London *Times,* Aug. 12, 1932.

[87] French press comment, with analysis, is in Edge to State Dept., Aug. 9, 10, 11, 1932, D/S File 711.0012 anti-war/1277, 1278, 1320; also Armour to State Dept., Aug. 22, 1932, D/S File 793.94/5493.

[88] *Peking Times, Tientsin Times,* Aug. 12, 1932; *Peking Chronicle,* Aug. 13, 1932; Willys Peck to Nelson T. Johnson, Aug. 18, 1932, Johnson Papers.

Neither the Secretary's indictment nor his warning fazed the Japanese. The press expressed great indignation, calling the remarks "malicious propaganda," "highly improper," "impudent utterances," "vile and provocative," and the outbursts in the capital were violent and would have been worse except for a terrific heat wave in Tokyo at the time. But it was a façade. The Japanese were not really distressed, and there was no weakening of the will. They did not frighten easily, and in this instance they did not frighten at all because they did not believe Stimson would translate his words into action. The Foreign Office was convinced America would not fight because of the depression, naval weakness, public apathy, and absence of economic interests.[89] The Japanese were, in a sense, becoming accustomed to his statements. His threat in the letter to Borah months earlier to break the shackles of the naval limitations had never materialized. If they entertained any fears, these were quickly dispelled when President Hoover, on August 11, formally accepted renomination by the Republicans in a speech in which he said: "We shall, under the spirit of that [Kellogg] Pact consult with other nations in times of emergency to promote world peace. We shall enter no agreements committing us to any future course of action or which call for the use of force to preserve peace." If this were not enough, the President went on to emasculate Stimson's nonrecognition doctrine by stating that the United States would not recognize title to possession of territory gained in violation of the Kellogg Pact. This stand was somewhat different from Stimson's, which had included any situation, treaty, or agreement contrary to the pact. The President's interpretation virtually relieved Japan of any onus of wrongdoing because, after all, she was not seeking title to possession of territory.

No, the Japanese feared naught. Indeed, most of the excitement was cooked up by the Foreign Office's notorious press chief, Shiratori, who released an inaccurate and highly inflammatory version of the speech to arouse anti-American sentiment, which had been quiescent, to whip up annexationist fervor, which had been lagging, and to direct the populace from the harsh economic realities of unemployment, inflation,

[89] See the paper "Josei Handan" ("Situational Analysis"), Japanese Foreign Office, April or May, 1932, by Itagaki Seishiro, cited in Nakamura, p. 236.

depressed farm prices, and low industrial output.[90] If anything, Stimson's words stirred the government to greater defiance. Four days after his speech, the Cabinet formally approved recognition of Manchukuo, and on the twenty-fifth
of August,[91] Count Uchida, the foreign minister, so informed
the world in an address to the Imperial Diet. Japan, he said,
would brook no interference from the West. Regardless of
what the Lytton Commission might report, the decision remained unalterable. What had been done could not be undone. Manchukuo was here to stay. It was quite clear from
Ambassador Grew's reports that the Japanese meant business.
He believed even that the army would have welcomed intervention by the West to test its strength in a war.[92] Mori Kaku,
chief secretary of the late Inukai cabinet, said as much publicly in a speech in the Diet on August 25.

On September 15, representatives of the Japanese Foreign
Office in Changchun, the Manchukuoan capital, initialed a
protocol which sealed the relations between the two countries
and formalized recognition by Tokyo.[93] The world was
shocked. By refusing to wait until the Lytton report was
delivered, the Japanese insulted the League of Nations and
violated their own pledge given at the time of the commission's appointment. They also forfeited the trust of the
world.[94] Former sympathizers fell away rapidly. Even the
French conservatives, hitherto so decidedly pro-Japanese, bitterly attacked the action. *Le Temps,* in an editorial, labeled
the act discourteous and likened it to contempt of court.
Premier Herriot, who was strongly pro-League and liberal
anyway, took measures to prevent some small French banking
houses from floating loans either to Japan or to the new
nation. Rumors of a Franco-American deal were now re-
placing those of Franco-Japanese agreements. It was being

[90] Grew to State Dept., Aug. 19, 1932, *F.R., 1932,* IV, 198–99, and Aug. 13,
1932, *F.R., Japan, 1931–1941,* I, 99–100. For an interpretation of the Hoover
speech, see "What is the Hoover Doctrine?" *Christian Century,* Aug. 31, 1932,
pp. 1047–49.
[91] IMTFE, Decisions of the Cabinet, pp. 174–75. On September 13, the
Privy Council approved. IMTFE, Decisions of the Privy Council, p. 177.
[92] Grew to State Dept., Aug. 26, 1932, *F.R., 1932,* IV, 702–5; see also the
analysis in *U.S. Naval Institute Proceedings,* 58 (October 1932), 1511.
[93] Copy in *F.R., 1932,* IV, 253–54.
[94] Norman Davis to Stanley K. Hornbeck, Sept. 19, 1932, Davis Papers, Box
11 (Personal-London and Geneva, Confidential, Oct.–Dec. 1932 Folder).

said that in return for easement on the French debt to the United States, France would give support in the Far East.[95] British Tories similarly branded the action as a challenge to the League.[96]

Emboldened by this reaction of the powers, China sought to invoke Article VII of the Nine Power Pact, which called for an exchange of frank and full views among the signatories in case of a threat to the pact. While not expressly calling for a conference, that is what the Chinese wanted, a vehicle for condemning the Japanese action in separating Manchuria from China. An inquiry in Washington, however, discouraged the Chinese. Speaking for the Department of State, Stanley K. Hornbeck advised them to sit tight until after the Lytton report. Nothing, he believed, should be done until then. That report was the cardinal and official action by all the powers. In this position the British and French concurred.[97] So the world sat back and waited for the report, which was due early in October.

Only the Japanese did not wait. The Lytton report hardly interested them. The Privy Council, with the Emperor in attendance, put the seal of approval on the Cabinet's decision. Nothing was left to be done except implement the agreement with Manchukuo: take over control of national defense, the railroads, harbors, foreign affairs, and other important areas. Satisfaction was universal. Viscount Ishii remarked, "The present Japan-Manchukuo treaty will prove effective in fully maintaining and expanding our special rights in Manchukuo and Mongolia on the one hand and in elevating, on the other hand, Japan from a position of predicament full of troubles at home and abroad to a triumphant one." Not an ounce of remorse or guilt was felt. Recognition, said Count Uchida, is not a violation of the Nine Power Pact. Manchukuo was already an independent state when recognized. Such national self-delusion usually accompanies international robbery. As for any of the powers disturbing the settlement, Uchida told

[95] See Edge to State Dept., Sept. 8, 1932, D/S File 861.77 Chinese Eastern (Loan) 1932/8, and Sept. 19, 1932, D/S File 763.72119 Military Clauses/79; *Le Temps*, Sept. 15, 1932; Norman Davis to Stanley K. Hornbeck, Sept. 19, 1932, Davis Papers, Box 11 (Personal—Oct.–Dec. 1932 Folder).

[96] London *Times*, Sept. 16, 1932; also London *Sunday Times*, Sept. 18, 1932.

[97] The story of the interchange is in *F.R., 1932*, IV, 207–209, 228, 232–33, 255–56, 267—68.

his colleagues that they had nothing to fear. Without American leadership, no action would be taken and he had been assured by Ambassador Debuchi that Stimson would do nothing.[98]

Debuchi, of course, was quite right. At that very time, Stimson was warning his minister in Switzerland to discourage the League from looking to the United States for leadership. Initiative, he said, must rest with the League.[99] He had done enough, he believed, in rousing world opinion and spearheading the nonrecognition resolution. Unfortunately, in Japanese eyes he had done too much. To them he was the sole obstacle to their domination of the Far East. The author of the January 7 note, the letter to Borah, and the August 8 speech was the stumbling block.

Distrust and hatred for Stimson were rife—so was anti-Americanism. The Japanese press kept up a steady barrage of propaganda against the United States. The army used America as the hypothetical enemy in order to whip up a war psychosis and to indoctrinate the recruits. The patriotic societies also spread the poison. A steady stream of copy in the newspapers kept the imminence of war with the United States in the news. Reports circulated of American carriers in the Kuriles, of new bases in the Aleutians, of American bombing planes and aircraft instructors with the Chinese air force, and of the leasing of bases in Kamchatka. When in early September some employees of the National City Bank of New York photographed buildings in downtown Osaka as part of a business survey, a great spy scare was let loose, with the Japanese press accusing them of turning the photographs over to the War Department to facilitate bombing. The United States assistant military attaché in Tokyo reported the numerous books and articles published in Japan describing or predicting a war in the Pacific.[100] No wonder many Americans were gravely concerned over the possibilities of war between the two nations. It was dangerous, wrote Newton D. Baker to Roy Howard, for the United States to get so far

[98] See IMTFE, Exhibit 241 and Decisions of the Privy Council, pp. 73–80.
[99] Stimson to Wilson, Sept. 23, 1932, *F.R., 1932,* IV, 271–72.
[100] Grew to State Dept., Sept. 10, 21, 1932, *F.R., 1932,* IV, 240–42, 705 ff.; also Grew, *Ten Years,* p. 39; see the attaché's report, Sept. 9, 1932, *F.R., 1932,* IV, 711.

in advance of world sentiment as to risk a war by Japan on the United States alone. Howard agreed that the danger was real if the United States continued to step out ahead of the other powers. And to Robert Cromie, publisher of the *New York Sun,* Baker lamented Stimson's assumption of the role of enforcement officer for the world. It was not America's job, he said, to bring Japan to heel alone. He wondered what Stimson himself thought of the situation.[101] It was no secret that the Secretary was worried. On September 16, with Admiral Hepburn, he "talked over the underlying danger in the Far East and the absolute necessity of keeping the Navy in such a condition in which it would be airtight against any sudden attack by the Japanese." [102] It was tragic, indeed, that Henry Stimson's action, which stemmed from courage, nobility, and strength of character, should have resulted in placing his country in jeopardy. A diplomatist, unhappily, cannot indulge those virtues.

[101] Baker to Howard, Sept. 19, 1932, Baker to Cromie, Sept. 17, 1932, Baker to Howard, Sept. 27, 1932, Baker Papers, Box 122.
[102] Stimson, Diary, Sept. 16, 1932.

CHAPTER SEVEN
In which
Stimson leaves office frustrated

Any hint of force, either military or economic, I believe, would completely overwhelm the more moderate influences which are working beneath the surface to restore Japan to its former high place in the Council of Nations.
JOSEPH C. GREW, DECEMBER 3, 1932

In the final analysis, neither words nor formulae, neither rules nor regulations nor law nor treaties are decisive where a country is embarked upon a course such as Japan has followed. The deciding factor is that of force— in some form or forms.
STANLEY K. HORNBECK, FEBRUARY 14, 1933

In this sense, our Government believe that any plan for erecting an edifice of peace in the Far East should be based upon the recognition that the constructive force of Japan is the mainstay of tranquility in this part of the world.
COUNT UCHIDA, JANUARY 21, 1933

O N SEPTEMBER 4, 1932, at eight o'clock in the evening, after more than six months of labor, thousands of miles of travel, hundreds of interviews, and countless hours of deliberation, the five members of the Lytton Commission—Lord Lytton, General Henri Édouard Claudel, Dr. Heinrich Schnee, Count Luigi Aldrovandi, and Major General Frank R. McCoy— affixed their signatures to their final report and left Peking for home. The report itself was placed in the hands of a special messenger who set out at once for Geneva by way of Siberia. The Great Adventure [1] was past, and a terribly difficult one it had been. To unearth the facts about the Manchurian incident from the welter of conflicting evidence and testimony was hard enough; for five people of diverse background, training, experience, and predilection to arrive at unanimous conclusions and recommendations was more difficult. But it was done, and the world waited for the results.

The commission, it will be recalled, was created by a resolution of the Council of the League of Nations on December 10, 1931. It took more than a month for the Council to decide on the membership because of the difficulty of agreeing on the criterion for selection; some thought it should be individual qualities, others the power of the nations represented.[2] The two were finally joined: experienced and wise persons from the five leading countries—the United States, Great Britain, France, Italy, and Germany. By January 14, 1932, the selections were completed.

The chairman, Victor Alexander George Robert Bulwer Lytton, second Earl of Lytton, was a distinguished Briton both by lineage and accomplishments. Fifty-six years of age, grandson of the author of the *Last Days of Pompeii,* and son of a viceroy of India, he had been in his nation's service since youth. Educated at Eton and Cambridge, he had served in the Admiralty, the India Office, as governor of Bengal, and briefly as viceroy of India. He enjoyed a considerable literary reputation as the author of a biography of his grandfather and

---

[1] The words are those of G. H. Blakeslee to Stanley K. Hornbeck, Sept. 14, 1932, copy in Stimson Papers, Box 19, Letters Received. Blakeslee's analysis of the Commission's deliberations is a most important eyewitness account, and I have printed it in its entirety in Appendix.

[2] Charles G. Dawes to State Dept., Dec. 1, 1931, *F.R., 1931,* III, 610–11.

of other works. General Henri Édouard Claudel of France, five years orlder than Lytton, was a professional soldier. A graduate of St. Cyr and a veteran of the late war, in which he had commanded colonial troops, he had most recently seen service in Africa as an inspector general of colonies. The Italian, Count Luigi Aldrovandi, Lytton's age, was a career diplomat of aristocratic lineage and wide experience, having served in Vienna, Sofia, Cairo, and Buenos Aires. Most recently he had been ambassador to Germany. Dr. Heinrich Schnee, sixty years old, a lawyer and political scientist, had made a distinguished record in Germany's colonial administration. He had held posts in Samoa, the Bismarck Archipelago, in the colonial ministry, and as governor of German East Africa. The fifth member of the commission was Major General Frank R. McCoy. Fifty-eight years of age and a graduate of West Point, he had had assignments in many parts of the world, from Cuba to the Philippines, including long years of staff work. In 1928, President Coolidge had appointed him to supervise a presidential election in Nicaragua, and the following year, he chaired a committee of inquiry investigating a dispute between Bolivia and Paraguay.

Early in February, the commissioners, except for McCoy, who was not in Europe, left Geneva for the Far East, reaching Tokyo, where McCoy joined them, on the twenty-ninth. There they remained for eight days, interviewing various people, then on to Shanghai, Nanking, and Peking during March and April. On the twenty-first of April they got to Manchuria, where they stayed five weeks and heard reports from all kinds of people, observers of and participants in the events since September. On June 5, they returned to Peking for the remainder of the month, then to Tokyo on July 4 for almost two weeks of interviewing Japanese officials. On July 20, they went back to Peking, laden with millions of words of testimony, to prepare the report.

Everywhere they went in China, the commissioners received the most cordial treatment, both personally and officially. Almost daily they were wined, dined, and entertained by prominent citizens and officials and important foreigners—diplomats, businessmen, and service personnel. In Japan, however, and in Japanese-controlled Manchuria, their reception was less cordial. In Harbin, for example, the commissioners found themselves so circumscribed by guards that they could not move about freely to collect information and inspect sites. In Tokyo, Japanese officials gravitated between oily smoothness and outright hostility. In neither case could the commission get anywhere near an unvarnished narrative of the course of events. Uchida's tone was usually harsh and uncompromising, and toward the end of the stay he quite bluntly informed Lord Lytton that nothing the commission or the League or the Nine Power Pact nations might do would deter Japan from its course on the mainland. The independence of Manchuria, he said, was irrevocable and its recognition by Japan inevitable.[3]

The writing of the report turned out to be a prolonged and trying task. Before beginning the investigation, the commissioners had viewed their mission as uncovering the facts alone, of "lifting the curtain," without comment or recommendations and certainly without coming to any judgment on the question of responsibility or on the merits of the rival claimants; as Lord Lytton put it, "to tell the world the true facts," unbiased, objective, and complete.[4] But after examining the evidence, the commissioners could not avoid concluding that Japan was at fault. They agreed unanimously that Japanese explanations of the events in Manchuria were untenable. They also agreed unanimously on a solution to the Manchurian issue. What caused the difficulty in preparing the report was the fact that they differed on language and tenor. Lord Lytton was inclined to indict Japan in tone and words in every chapter; the others, no less convinced of the injustice of the Japanese position, wished to soften the indictment and avoid giving any unnecessary offense to the Japanese people and government. A nagging and painful illness which Lord Lytton suffered and which put him in the hospital for six weeks made him frequently irritable and obdurate, causing further difficulty. His insistence that he alone write the final report, so that its style would be uniform and literary, was thoroughly objected to by the others. They expected the drafts prepared

[3] See *F.R.*, *1932*, IV, 159, 163–64, 169, 175–76; also Kido, Diary, July 18, 1932.
[4] Lord Lytton to Lady Balfour, May 23, 1932, copy in Stimson Papers, Box 19, Letters Received.

by the commission's experts to be submitted to each of them for revision and then worked on by the entire commission for the final report. Lord Lytton, however, wanted all the drafts sent to him alone for editing and polishing and then to the others for approval.

Between General Claudel and Lord Lytton there was the greatest strife. The general tended to greater leniency toward Japan and took exception most strongly to specific sentences and expressions Lytton used as unduly harsh. His suggestion that the independence of Manchuria be accepted as a basic fact of international life and used as a basis for a Far Eastern settlement was unacceptable to Lytton. His threat to append a minority report incorporating his suggestion blighted the deliberations. It was General McCoy who turned out to be the peacemaker and conciliator. Tactful and patient, constantly striving for harmony, he led the way out of many difficulties by proposing either a postponement, a recess, or a compromise. To him belongs "the greatest share of the credit for bringing about a unamimous agreement." [5]

Finally, on August 30, after forty tense, dramatic, and often stormy days of discussion, argumentation, and disagreement, of revision, redrafting, and rephrasing, the report was finished. It fell between Lord Lytton's and General Claudel's positions. It was restrained and objective yet positive and definite; expert, thorough, and realistic. It would not recognize the validity of the Japanese conquest, yet it did not advocate return to the conditions prevailing before September 18. It attempted to effect a reconciliation between a demographically bursting Japan and a disordered, politically chaotic China. It called for tactful, calm, and dispassionate negotiation. Both sides were assessed blame, the greatest amount to Japan.

The more than one hundred thousand words of the report were divided into ten chapters: three on the background (China, Manchuria, and relations between China and Japan over Manchuria), one each on events at Mukden and at Shanghai, three on Manchuko's formation and development, and two dealing with conclusions and recommendations. As a doc-

---

[5] Blakeslee to Hornbeck, Sept. 14, 1932, copy in Stimson Papers, Box 19, Letters Received; also Nelson T. Johnson to State Dept., Sept. 1, 1932, *F.R.*, *1932*, IV, 220–21, and Nelson T. Johnson to Hornbeck, Aug. 30, 1932, Johnson Papers.

umentary record, it was most impressive—replete with facts and figures, authentic and complete. It concluded that the Japanese military action could not be considered self-defense, although the military on the spot may have believed it; that the formation of Manchukuo was not the result of a spontaneous and indigenous movement but a Japanese creation; that the people there did not on the whole support the regime; and that the recognition of the country would be in violation of international obligations incurred under the Washington treaties and the Paris pact. The recommendations for a solution were reasonable and equitable: that an autonomous regime be set up in Manchuria within the Chinese Republic by the Chinese government, that it be demilitarized, and that Japanese rights there should be guaranteed; that an advisory conference representing China, Japan, Manchuria, and neutrals be convened to prepare a plan for the governance of the area, to include the powers delegated to the Nanking government, the appointment of a chief executive and of foreign advisers, and the establishment of a constabulary; and that Sino-Japanese treaties be negotiated outlining the rights of the Japanese and the duties of the Chinese.[6] The only question was whether Japan would accept the report. If it would, a basis for a stable peace in the Far East could be achieved. But would the militarists yield? Would they relinquish their hold on Manchuria? Could they undo twelve months of blood and sweat? Could they write off the lives lost and the treasure spent? Could they retreat? Could they dissolve the fervent patriotism whipped up by the victorious campaign? Lytton and his fellow commissioners thought they could and would, if not at once, then certainly within a few years when the bill for the war came due. They were all, unfortunately, dead wrong.[7]

On October 2, the League of Nations Secretariat released the report to the member states and to the United States. At once the Japanese requested a six-week delay before its consideration by the Council to permit, they said, a careful review

[6] A convenient, chapter-by-chapter summary of the report is in *Pacific Affairs,* November 1932. Clarence Streit has a brilliant analysis in "The Far Eastern War in Geneva," *Asia,* 33 (February 1933), 78 ff.; a brief summary is in *International Conciliation,* January 1933, pp. 58–87.

[7] Blakeslee to Hornbeck, Sept. 14, 1932, copy in Stimson Papers, Box 19, Letters Received.

of each detail. But no one was fooled. That Japan would reject categorically the recommendations was universally expected. Manchuria would never be surrendered, even in exchange for an international guarantee of Japanese rights. This had been decided by the Cabinet as early as July, when rumors emanating from Geneva indicated clearly that Japan would be blamed for the fighting in Manchuria and for the establishment of a new nation. Indeed, it was for that reason that the Japanese extended recognition to Manchukuo before the release of the report, to present the world a *fait accompli* which could not be undone. The wish for a delay was merely to buy time to consolidate their position in Manchukuo before blasting defiance at Geneva and the world. The Japanese made no secret of their anger and disgust with the report and their determination to hold fast to their position on the mainland. A storm of protest swept through the islands. The press denounced the commission and on October 4, at a Cabinet meeting, General Araki made known the army's dissatisfaction while Count Uchida expressed the government's displeasure. Although the economy was foundering, with the yen sinking, securities dropping, short-term foreign loans due, revenue from taxation diminishing, savings accounts shrinking, trade balance unfavorable, and the budget at a deficit, the navy asked for and got 550,000,000 yen for 1933–34, almost triple the budget for the previous year. So the government made known its intentions.[8]

What could the League of Nations do under the circumstances? The only honorable course was at once to approve the report and then hold Japan to its recommendations. But that, of course, was an impossibility because it demanded firmness by the leading members, Great Britain and France, and by the United States, which was not forthcoming. Under the leadership of Édouard Herriot, France definitely leaned away from Japan. Although rightists continued to look upon the empire as the spearhead of anti-communism in Asia, as the justification for French exploitation of Yunnan, and as support for France's bid at the disarmament conference for a

[8] See Grew's analysis to State Dept., Oct. 8, 1932, *F.R.*, *1932*, IV, 716; also the statement by the secretary of the Japanese embassy in Manchukuo on October 4, 1932, reported in *ibid.*, 290–91. Marquis Kido noted the navy's firm attitude in his diary on October 18, 1932.

large army, their voice and authority had gone out with the Tardieu ministry in June.[9] Herriot was determined to range France on the side of maintaining the sanctity of treaties, not only for the effect on the European power structure, but also for the future of the League of Nations and world order.[10] It was not surprising that he unhesitatingly rejected Japan's firm and formal offer, made early in October, of commercial concessions in Manchuria for a military alliance,[11] but this did not mean that the premier wished to hold Japan strictly and immediately to the report in Geneva. Indeed, he suggested that the Council grant Japan the six weeks' delay to avoid inflaming the Japanese militarists and to permit cooler heads to prevail.[12]

In England, similarly, there was no wish to bring Japan to the dock at once. The prime minister, Ramsay MacDonald, supported by Labourites and Liberals, had no patience with Japan and would have preferred taking the strongest action against her in the League and in co-operation with the United States, but he realized that his country could do nothing. Deeply exhausted by the late war and immobilized by the depression, Britain should, he believed, shrink from entanglements, adventures, or trouble. The Tories in the National Government, led by Stanley Baldwin, Lord President of the Council, Lord Hailsham at the War Office, Samuel Hoare of the India Office, and Bolton Eyres-Monsell, the First Lord of the Admiralty, continued their faith in Japan as guardian of British interests in the Far East and their belief that a Japanese regime in Manchuria was better than a Chinese. They were frankly embarrassed by the Lytton Commission Report and regretted that a Briton had headed the commission. Sir John Simon, the key figure, vacillated between his Tory allegiance and conservative inclination and his wish to join America in common action, but so eager was he to become prime minister

---

[9] *Literary Digest*, October 15, 1932, p. 16, cited *Paris Temps;* also H. K. Norton in New York *Herald Tribune*, Sept. 11, 1932.

[10] Norman Davis to State Dept., Oct. 10, 1932, *F.R., 1932*, IV, 296. Ambassador Claudel to Castle, conversation on Oct. 10, *ibid.*, 295; Gilbert to State Dept., Oct. 29, 1932, *ibid.*, 318.

[11] Claudel to Castle, conversation Oct. 10, 1932, *ibid.*, 296; also memorandum by Norman Davis of a conversation with Herriot, Nov. 28, 1932, D/S File 500A15A4 Steering Com/227.

[12] Edge to State Dept., Sept. 19, 1932, *F.R., 1932*, IV, 265–66.

that he dared not alienate the Tory die-hards.[13] The result was to abdicate leadership to the United States, with a promise to support any action Stimson might take but meanwhile urging the League to give Japan the desired six weeks in the hope that something would happen to end the unpleasantness.[14]

As for the United States, Stimson did not take up Simon's suggestion of leadership. Quite the opposite. He suggested to Simon that because of proximity and greater interest, Great Britain should take the lead in formulating a course of action.[15] Stimson was doing only what his advisers, public opinion, and the mundane exigencies of a presidential campaign suggested: hands off. He could not overcome those insuperable obstacles. As early as July, when word trickled to Washington from General McCoy that the commission's report would condemn Japan and be in line with the American position, the department's experts began to urge Stimson not to step out ahead of the other nations. When the report became public, reactions in the United States were uniformly favorable. There was hardly a single dissent to the view that the report was impartial, just, practical, and helpful. The leading newspapers and men like A. Lawrence Lowell, James T. Shotwell, and Hamilton Holt applauded it without reservation as one of the outstanding events of world history and considered it excellent as a basis for an Asian settlement. But they counseled against the United States' taking independent action or assuming special responsibility for chastising Japan.[16] Castle summed up the prevailing opinion most accurately: "One thing is certain . . . nobody in America wants war with Ja-

[13] See the analysis by E. H. Dooman, Nov. 12, 1932, D/S File 793.94/5624.

[14] The British position may be followed in the astute comments by Norman Davis to Hugh Gibson, Oct. 10, 1932, Davis Papers, Box 26, Gibson File, and to Hornbeck, Sept. 17, 1932, *ibid.*, Box 11; also *New York Times*, Aug. 16, 1932; Sir John Simon to Norman Davis, Oct. 10, 1932, *F.R., 1932*, IV, 296; and Gilbert to State Dept., Oct. 29, 1932, *ibid.*, 318–19. The British Liberals were very pleased with the Lytton report. Wickham Steed called it "the weightiest and most significant contribution to international knowledge of a dangerous dispute that has ever been made under the auspices of the League." Wickham Steed, "After the Lytton Report," *Contemporary Review*, 142 (1932), 650.

[15] Stimson to Norman Davis, Oct. 14, 1932, *F.R., 1932*, IV, 300.

[16] A. L. Lowell to Newton D. Baker, Oct. 31, 1932, Lowell Papers, World Peace Foundation Box, Baker Folder (Harvard College Library); Philip C. Marsh, director of League of Nations Association, to Mrs. Corliss Lamont, Oct. 7, 1932, American Boycott Association Papers.

pan whatever the Japanese may do in Manchuria." [17] The *Financial Chronicle* called for "scrupulous aloofness," and Raymond Leslie Buell pleaded for assuaging Japan by returning the scouting force to the Atlantic, ending the immigration restriction, and reducing the tarriff.[18]

Nobody at this time made any claim to militant action. The seasoned diplomats, above all, urged the Secretary to move slowly and follow rather than lead the League. From London, Norman Davis cautioned Stimson not to advise any of the European nations on what they should do, lest the onus fall on Washington, and from Geneva, Hugh Gibson noted that America had already done too much, so that, unhappily, everyone believed the Sino-Japanese conflict to be really a dispute between the United States and Japan. From Tokyo, Ambassador Grew wrote that the only hope was to encourage the moderate elements in Japan by giving them time and by the United States' adopting a non-belligerent attitude.[19] The presidential campaign, if nothing else, would have made virtually impossible American leadership in the settlement. Stimson and all the other principal Republicans in the government were busy in the hustings and had little time for such remote places as Asia or Europe. Indeed, when on September 26 the Secretary read to the Cabinet a long and thoughtful analysis of the Lytton Commission Report by George H. Blakeslee, McCoy's adviser on the commission, there was hardly a flicker of concern.[20]

Stimson, although himself judging the report "comprehensive and intelligent in treatment and as judicial in tone . . . a magnificent achievement," [21] drew back from following his

[17] Castle, Diary, November 8, 1932.

[18] *Financial Chronicle*, Nov. 26, 1932, p. 3576, and R. L. Buell in New York *Herald Tribune*, Nov. 20, 1932. Hornbeck disapproved privately the Buell suggestion in that it would be interpreted as weakness by Japan. See his memorandum dated Nov. 25, D/S File 711.94/751. Sidney L. Gulick, secretary of the Commission on International Justice and Good Will of the Federal Council of Churches of Christ in America, made a suggestion similar to Buell's. See his letter to President Hoover, Nov. 25, 1932, D/S File 711.94/743.

[19] Davis to Stimson, Oct. 28, 1932, *F.R., 1932*, IV, 315–16; Gilbert to State Dept., Oct. 29, 1932, *ibid.*, 317–21; Castle, Diary, Oct. 8, 1932; Grew to State Dept., Oct. 8, 1932, *F.R., 1932*, IV, 719; Grew, *Ten Years*, p. 67; memorandum by J. E. Jacobs, Oct. 28, 1932, D/S File 793.94 Com/4791/2, and one by Hornbeck, D/S File 793.94/5603.

[20] Stimson, Diary, Sept. 26, 1932.

[21] *F.R., 1932*, IV, 287.

natural inclination and strong conviction to speak out sharply, advise the League, and lead the onslaught against the transgressor by demanding Japan's acceptance of the recommenda- tions. To Davis, Gibson, Wilson, and Gilbert he stated the policy. The problem, he said, was one between the League and a member. Let the League formulate a policy and then ask for America's support. Under no conditions must Geneva look to Washington for guidance. He hoped, "by refraining from initiating suggestions, to bring the League States to a realization that the responsibility for formulating a course of action upon the report of the Lytton Commission to the League rests with them." Nor did he wish the League to shift that responsibility to the signatories of the Nine Power Pact.[22]

Stimson, it appeared, had grown tired of leadership. He apparently had had enough. His firmness had resulted only in building up a resevoir of ill-will and animosity in Japan against the United States. He was prepared to agree with Grew that any more provocation would be useless and might even lead to hostilities; that coercive measures would weld Japan more firmly in opposition to the rest of the world; that peace might best be served by moving gradually rather than precipitously.[23] Not that he censured Japan any less, but rather that he began to comprehend the futility and danger of going it alone—indeed, of going it at all without the physical means and the popular will. And, of course, after November 8, he was a lame duck, just biding time until his departure from the helm with his defeated Republican Colleagues.

It was inevitable that the League Council grant Japan the delay: no other course was possible. The plans laid back in July to consider the report promptly upon its arrival in Geneva were scotched. At a conference on October 23, Lytton, Eric Drummond, Norman Davis, Sir John Simon, Anthony Eden, and Ray Atherton agreed to convene the Council on November 21 to consider the report, thus giving Japan ample time to cool off and perhaps to work out a face-saving method of con-

[22] Stimson to Davis, Nov. 14, 1932, Davis Papers, Box 2, Atherton Folder; also Nov. 21 in Box 17, Confidential Memorandum Folder; also Stimson to Gibson, Nov. 19, 1932, *F.R., 1932*, IV, 342–43 and 347—49. A Chinese request that Stimson take a strong position to prevent delay by Japan was turned aside by Hornbeck. See *ibid.*, 362.
[23] Grew, *Turbulent Years*, p. 934, n. 9 (diary entry, Nov. 28, 1932); Grew to State Dept., Nov. 28, 1932, *F.R., 1932*, IV, 372–73.

forming to the report. The alternative was to press Japan to conform at once, which surely would mean her withdrawal from the League. Lytton was sure that Japan would eventually give way, especially with affairs in Manchukuo deteriorating. And deteriorating they were—disorders, bandits, floods, famine, trade diminished, currency wildly fluctuating. Already, he noted, the great industrial houses exhibited reluctance to put their money in the new state. Soon the Japanese would be only too glad to wash their hands of the affair.[24]

The powers seemed satisfied with this solution to the problem, even China. The Chinese had at the outset objected to the report because it did not recommend a return to the pre–September 18, 1931 situation. Realizing, however, the futility of such a dream, Wellington Koo announced in Geneva on October 9 that China accepted the recommendations as a basis for settlement. There was no denying it, dispassionate Chinese had to admit some responsibility for the difficulties in Asia.

The autumn of 1932 found European affairs in a turmoil—involved in debts and reparations, disarmament, and crucial elections in Germany which were to decide that nation's future direction. That unhappy continent was heavily preoccupied with its own miseries, yet it had to find time and energy to watch extracontinental events which were of utmost importance to its destiny, chiefly, the American presidential campaign and the Far Eastern crisis. The former, if terminating in a Democratic victory, might well presage a reorientation of American foreign policy and more direct participation by Washington in Europe's political life; the latter, if terminating in Japan's successfully defying the Nine Power Treaty, might be the signal for the end of the Versailles settlement, and if terminating in Japanese withdrawal from the League, might well spell the doom of international organization.

So Europe watched Japan during the delay granted by the League as her statesmen cast about for some means to reach a face-saving accord with the Mikado's representative to the League which would enable Japan to accept the Lytton Commission Report. But Matsuoka Yosuke was adamant. No so-

[24] Hugh Wilson to State Dept., July 23, 1932, *ibid.*, 182; Norman Davis to Stimson, Oct. 28, 1932, Davis Papers, Box 11, Telegrams Sent, October 1932 Folder.

lution would be acceptable which did not take into account the existence of Manchukuo and its recognition by Japan, said the fiery delegate. He was not a reasonable, mild, and conciliatory man as was his predecessor, Matsudaira. Matsuoka was intimately associated with the military at home and had been, as vice-president of the South Manchurian Railway, one of the leaders of the September attack. He would not relent. To retreat from Manchuria and to undo the past was unthinkable.[25] Norman Davis and Hugh Wilson worked particularly hard at Geneva to achieve some compromise before the Council convened, and despite Matsuoka's intransigence, they expected him to come around. They figured on the empire's shaky financial condition and attendant economic and social distress; on the considerable popular opposition to a series of assassinations planned by the Tenkokai (The Society of Heavenly Action), the Dokuritsu Seinensha (Independent Youth Society), and the Kokuryukai (Black Dragon Society); and on the reluctance of the government to leave the League.[26] They were aware of the uneasiness felt in Tokyo by the presence of the United States Fleet in the Pacific.[27] All these factors, they believed, invited moderation by the Nipponese.

They were, of course, to be sorely disappointed. Japan would not yield, and when the Council met on November 21, the situation was no different from what it had been six weeks earlier. Matsuoka spoke passionately, reviewing the chaotic conditions in both China and Manchuria in justification of Japan's actions there and excoriating the Lytton Commission for its unrealistic and unhistoric approach to the situation. He recalled America's similar action in Mexico in 1916 and 1917 and ended with a plea for recognition of Japan's service to civilization in Asia. The Chinese delegate sought to refute each of Matsuoka's points in reply, but Matsuoka would not weaken. For three days a colloquy went on between the two. It became clear to all the representatives that an impasse had developed, yet no one of the major nations wished to break it. All sat attentively but passively. Finally, on the twenty-fifth, Beneš of Czechoslovakia suggested referring the whole matter to the Assembly, a suggestion eagerly

[25] Wilson to State Dept., Nov. 19, 1932, *F.R., 1932*, IV, 351–52.
[26] Grew to State Dept., Nov. 28, 1932, *ibid.*, 373.
[27] Castle, Diary, Nov. 15, 1932, and Stimson to Grew, *F.R., 1932*, IV, 325–26.

accepted by the others, except for Japan, which preferred the lethargy of the large countries in the Council to the determination of the small ones in the Assembly.[28]

When the Assembly met on December 6, the lesser powers took command at once. Delegates from Sweden, Ireland, Norway, and Czechoslovakia urged immediate adoption of the Lytton Commission Report, censure of Japan, and non-recognition of Manchukuo. They warned that the very existence of the League of Nations was at stake. Should it fail to uphold its commission of inquiry, its usefulness would be ended. Switzerland, Guatemala, Uruguay, Denmark, and the Netherlands gave strong support to the movement. Emboldened, the Chinese representative called for a declaration branding Japan the violator of the Covenant of the League, the Pact of Paris, and the Nine Power Pact.

At this point, Sir John Simon felt constrained to apply a brake to the rising emotion, which he realized could lead only to punitive measures (invocation of Article XVI and of sanctions against Japan), to Japan's withdrawal from the League, and, very possibly, to war. He therefore urged moderation and referral of the whole matter to the Committee of Nineteen without Assembly action. It took a rousing and defiant speech by Matsuoka on the eighth to take the wind out of the smaller nations' sails. When he announced that nothing would budge Japan from Manchuria and hinted at walking out of the League, they were not so sure they wanted to take the risk. So they supported Simon's course and the following day, without considering the report, the Assembly passed the question to the Committee of Nineteen. It was clearly a matter of preferring "nineteen" to "XVI." [29] That committee convened promptly and appointed a small subcommittee to work out specific measures for reconciling Sino-Japanese differences. It was empowered to invite an American and a Russian to join its deliberations and to render a report by March 1, 1933. The Committee of Nineteen then adjourned.[30]

The entire procedure disappointed and disgusted Secretary Stimson. He saw the Assembly's action as leading to Japan's

[28] League of Nations, *Official Journal*, Vol. XIII:2, pp. 1871 ff.
[29] League of Nations, *Official Journal*, Special Session of the Assembly, Supplement No. 11, pp. 21 ff.
[30] *F.R., 1932*, IV, 414–15 and 432, describes the work of the committee.

getting off too easily.[31] He had fully expected the Council and the Assembly to accept the Lytton Commission Report and, in its spirit, to reiterate the March 11 nonrecognition resolution, this time with specific reference to Manchukuo.[32] More than that he neither looked for nor desired. But at least the Japanese would stand censured at the bar of the world tribunal and the commission of inquiry would have had some meaning. Before the Council was to meet, he had instructed Davis and Wilson to get Herriot and MacDonald to pressure the other members of the Council to pass the nonrecognition resolution before any conciliation attempts were made.[33] When Wilson reported such action to be unlikely, Stimson fumed. After the Assembly's action, he would not even permit an American to sit with the conciliation subcommittee. To Wilson he wrote: "When questions of principle and procedure have been adequately dealt with by the League under its own constitution, the time will have arrived for discussion of participation by the American government in machinery and processes which may be suggested by the League for conciliation as such." [34] In other words, the United States would give no help until the League showed some spine. Stimson could not "put more punch into those damn mushy cowards," [35] however, and soon, realistically, he accepted the invitation for an American to join the committee.

His ire he vented on Sir John Simon—"for weaseling." [36] It was Sir John's speech that had turned the tide in the Assembly, a speech which drew attention to those parts of the Lytton Commission Report favorable to Japan and which caused Matsuoka to remark that the foreign secretary "had said in half an hour in a few well chosen phrases what he had been trying to say in his bad English for the last ten days." [37]

[31] Stimson, Diary, Dec. 12, 1932.
[32] Castle, Diary, Dec. 2, 1932.
[33] Stimson to Wilson, Dec. 4, 1932, F.R., *1932*, IV, 386, and Dec. 5, 1932, *ibid.*, 388.
[34] Stimson to Wilson, Dec. 15, 1932, *ibid.*, 428–29.
[35] Stimson, Diary, Dec. 16, 1932.
[36] Stimson to Wilson, Dec. 9, 1932, F.R., *1932*, IV, 406.
[37] The *Manchester Guardian*, on December 8, 1932, noted Matsuoka's remark. The Japanese were quite pleased with Simon's friendliness and really did not fear any strong action by the British Tories. See Ministry of War, Research Section, *Attitude of the Powers With Regard to the Manchurian Affair*, pp. 25–27, cited by Nakamura, p. 233, n. 619.

It was Britain's opposition that had caused the small powers to hesitate, squirm, and submit. Prentiss Gilbert put it neatly when he wrote Stimson from Geneva: "The contest is really no longer between China and Japan but between Great Britain and the League of Nations." [38]

The Chinese were, no less than Stimson, bitter and frustrated. They saw their last hope for help from the League vanish in the Assembly's action. Sir John Simon's speech had announced Geneva's bankruptcy.[39] Nothing could come of conciliation. From the United States, only "helpful but negative" aid could be expected.[40] By themselves, they could do nothing; the country was in the greatest chaos. Chiang Kaishek and the Kuomintang were virtually powerless outside the Yangtze provinces. In the north, south, and west, the provinces were practically independent of the central government, rural military chiefs controlled armies, regional war lords usurped revenues.[41] In desperation, Nanking turned to the Soviet Union and on December 12 announced the resumption of diplomatic relations with Russia.[42] Perhaps the Communists would be willing to rush in where the capitalists feared to tread.

The Japanese reacted sharply to the Assembly's action. Instead of being gratified for having avoided official censure and welcoming the additional delay, they petulantly rejected the whole idea of a conciliation committee and made quite clear their hostility and disdain for the Lytton Commission Report. They were plainly defiant. Their reply to the recriminations in the Assembly and to their isolation by the Sino-Soviet agreement was more aggression. Reports from Asia indicated the beginning of a new military thrust to and then through the Great Wall into North China. Rumors of an elaborate plan to place Pu Yi on the throne of a kingdom carved out of North China and joined to Manchukuo were widely circulated. And instead of loosening the hold on Manchuria, the Cabinet voted to assume complete control over

[38] Gilbert to State Dept., Dec. 20, 1932, *F.R., 1932*, IV, 451–57.
[39] See Nelson T. Johnson's report to State Dept., Dec. 11, 1932, *ibid.*, 411–13.
[40] Hsu Mo, Chinese vice minister of foreign affairs, to Nelson T. Johnson, Dec. 5, 1932, Johnson Papers, Conversations.
[41] Johnson provided an able summary of China's internal situation. See Johnson to State Dept., Jan. 5, 1934, *F.R., 1933*, III, 490–93.
[42] H. Moore, *Soviet Far Eastern Policy, 1931–1945* (Princeton, 1945), p. 19.

the entire Manchukuoan communications system.[43] As usual, and unfortunately, the United States was singled out as the culprit, the source of Japan's woes, this time as the broker for the Sino-Soviet *rapprochement*. As the Osaka *Nichi Nichi* observed, "the Washington government instructed Mr. Johnson to . . . do this . . . to hold Japan in check." [44] On the third of January, infantry units based in Manchuria advanced southward toward Shanhaikuan, in the southeast corner of Jehol Province where the Great Wall runs into the sea and through which the Peking-Mukden railroad ran. Two days later, the city fell, and the army pushed on to Jehol, the provincial capital. Peking lay only eighty miles away on the other side of the Great Wall. Domination of North China seemed the goal.

The whirlwind operation did not have much effect on the course of international affairs. The subcommittee of the Committee of Nineteen continued its deliberations and search for a formula for conciliation. The League did not call the Assembly into special session. The date for the committee's report was not advanced but permitted to remain the sixteenth of January. The reason for the apparent lethargy is quite clear. Everybody knew that if strong objection were to be taken to the newest Japanese thrust, it would lead directly to the invocation of Article XVI with war the likely consequence.[45] The British shuddered at such a probability. Sir John Simon made quite clear Britain's intent to take no notice of the attack. Liberals and Labourites deplored the foreign secretary's December 7 speech and the whole trend of the government to close its eyes to Japanese wrongdoing and urged a clear-cut courageous stand now that "the eleventh hour has struck." [46] The bulk of opinion, however, was reflected by the *Daily Telegraph*'s comment that "no report by the League which was calculated to wound Japan and compel her withdrawal from the League would find the requisite unanimity at Geneva. Japan, once outside the League,

[43] IMTFE, Decisions of the Cabinet, Dec. 9, 1932, p. 176. Hallett Abend of the *New York Times* reported the Pu Yi rumor to the U.S. consul in Dairen; see *F.R., 1933*, III, 65–66.
[44] Quoted in Martin Sommers, "What Jehol Means to Main Street," *New Outlook*, 161 (February 1933), 26.
[45] Gibson to State Dept., Jan. 10, 1933, *F.R., 1933*, III, 48–49.
[46] Lord Cecil's words in letter to London *Times*, Jan. 1, 1933.

would be far less subject to restraint than she is within the Geneva areopagus; and the threat of a Japanese march on Peking, with a real Sino-Japanese war to follow, would then take on a substance it does not possess at present. Britain, at any rate, has no reason to embroil herself with an old and proud friend and former ally, who is rightly regarded as the main bulwark against Bolshevism in the Far East." [47]

The French similarly cringed at the thought of hostilities. Although many on the left clamored for sanctions or a break in relations, the main body of opinion, as seen in the Paris rightist press, favored turning the other cheek. Certainly, Joseph Paul-Boncour, who had replaced Herriot, was no passionate proponent of righteous indignation. [48]

Across the Atlantic, Secretary Stimson was in no position to court involvement. He was greatly upset by the Japanese move and lashed out at Ambassador Debuchi in an interview on January 5, suggesting very bluntly that if Japan could not behave decently, she ought to get out of the League of Nations and out of any other arrangements governing the conduct of nations. [49] But beyond that he could not go. In the twilight of his official life, he could not commit the nation. Even if he were able to do so, the American public clearly wanted no part in the affair. Arthur Brisbane, one of the most popular and widely read columnists of the day, reflected the popular sentiment when he said it should not be the business of the United States to go roaming over the world telling nations to live up to treaties. [50] The passage of the Philippine Independence bill in Congress, overriding Hoover's veto, manifested the same attitude. The bill had originally passed both houses in 1932. On January 13, 1933, Hoover vetoed it on a number of grounds, among them the dangers to the islands arising from "the pressure of those immense neighbor populations for peaceful infiltration or forceable entry into this area. . . . The Filipino people alone will be helpless to pre-

[47] *Daily Telegraph,* Jan. 4, 1933; also Atherton to State Dept., Jan. 6, 1933, D/S File 793.94/5871.
[48] Edge to State Dept., Jan. 5, 1933, *F.R., 1933,* III, 14, and Jan. 10, 1933, D/S File 793.94/5975.
[49] Memorandum by Stimson of a conversation with Debuchi, Jan. 5, 1933, *F.R., Japan, 1931–1941,* I, 107–108.
[50] Arthur Brisbane, "Today," in *Spartanburg* (South Carolina) *Herald,* Jan. 20, 1933.

vent such infiltration or invasion." His warning fell on deaf
ears. For days later the bill again went through successfully,
and in the debate in the legislature and in the public forum,
the role of the islands in the political equilibrium in the Far
East received scant attention.[51]

Stimson would not even make a statement, as he had one
year earlier under similar circumstances and in response to
another Japanese thrust, although the Chinese government
and the League of Nations were urging him to do so, the
former for moral support, the latter for guidance.[52] Indeed,
at that very moment his statement of the previous year was
under heavy attack by President Lowell of Harvard, who
blasted Stimson's nonrecognition policy in a speech on January 7 before the Foreign Policy Association in Boston. Lowell
pointed out the dangers of a policy which provoked and irritated but did not achieve the objective. He assailed mere expressions of disapproval without some kind of sanction as
idle threats, ineffective and dangerous.[53] Stimson agreed, privately, that another statement might seem only to irritate
Japan and gain nothing. It would have been generous to give
China moral support, but it was not worth the risk. As for
the League, it needed no guidance. Its course was patently
clear: approve the Lytton Commission Report and vote nonrecognition of Manchukuo.[54]

Stimson did believe, however, that it was important for
the Japanese and the world to know that the nonrecognition
policy was not a temporary Republican party policy but an
American one and that the Democratic administration would
continue to refuse to accept the Japanese conquests as legal.
He did not want his silence to be interpreted as presaging a

[51] Hoover's veto message in H. Doc. 524, 72nd Cong., 2nd sess. See also
Ten Eyck Associates, *American Public Opinion and the Philippines Independence Act* (New York, 1933).
[52] Nelson T. Johnson to State Dept., Jan. 13, 1933, D/S File 793.94/5743,
and Arthur Sweetser to N. H. Davis, Jan. 10, 1933, Stimson Papers, Box 21,
Letters Received.
[53] The address is printed in the *Boston Herald*, Jan. 8, 1933. Letters com-
mending Lowell are in Lowell Papers, "Addresses and Magazine Articles,
1933–34." Hoover and Stimson knew beforehand of Lowell's plan to talk on
the subject and sought, with Walter Lippmann's help, to head him off. See
Stimson, Diary, Dec. 21, 23, 1932.
[54] Stimson to Wilson, Jan. 13, 1933, *F.R., 1933*, III, 61–64.

change by the new administration. He was pleased, therefore, when at a long conference he had with Franklin D. Roosevelt on January 9 the President-elect stated his complete agreement with the Republican policy toward Manchuria.[55] On the seventeenth, he made it public in his first formal statement on international affairs.[56]

The Japanese were considerably surprised by Roosevelt's statement. They had welcomed his election in November as the harbinger of a new policy—more liberal, more conciliatory, more realistic; less academic, less legalistic, less idealistic. They were delighted to see the passing of Stimson, to whom they ascribed all their troubles, and the seating of the Democrats, whom they considered less aggressive and imperialistic than the Republicans.[57] They were undaunted, however, by the prospect of continued pressures from the United States. Retreat was unthinkable, capitulation not even contemplated. They kept a steady course of aggression. They would consider no conciliation proposals which did not accept the independence of Manchukuo.[58] Talk of withdrawing from the League of Nations was heard everywhere, and positive steps were taken to build a league of Asiatic peoples to replace it. On January 26, a preliminary conference, which high-ranking military and civilian officials attended, was held in Tokyo to lay plans for the organization of such a league. Much of the discussion rotated around the necessity for creating an institution similar to the Pan-American Union to knit the Asians into ethnic and geographical solidarity and to increase their trade and cultural interchange.[59] The projected independence of the Philippines provided an impetus to the movement in that America's withdrawal helped the "Asia for Asiatics" program and left the field to the Japanese. They were perfectly willing and ready to assume the leadership of

[55] See the record of the conversation in Stimson Papers, Box 21, Letters Received.

[56] See *New York Times*, Jan. 18, 1933, and "Mr. Roosevelt Will Carry On," *Christian Century*, Feb. 1, 1933, pp. 142–43.

[57] Grew, *Ten Years*, p. 55; see reaction to election in the Tokyo press for Nov. 10, 1932: *Nichi Nichi, Kokumin, Jiji, Chugai Shogyo*.

[58] Grew to State Dept., Jan. 6, 1932, *F.R., 1933*, III, 16.

[59] Grew reported the meeting to the department; see his dispatch, Feb. 9, 1933, D/S File 790.94/34.

a Pan-Asian movement. Indeed, they were basking in the international limelight and were reveling in the attention the world was showering upon them.[60]

But if Roosevelt's position did not affect Japan, it seemed to have been quite an important catalyst for the League of Nations. There is some evidence that the assurances by the new administration prompted the Committee of Nineteen to take action. When it met on January 16 as scheduled, it knew full well that conciliation was impossible. The *sine qua non*, Japan's withdrawal of recognition of Manchukuo and admission of the illegality of its establishment, Tokyo would not accept. The smaller nations on the committee were prepared to act, and the knowledge that the United States would not turn its back on Geneva after March 4 canceled any hesitancy generated by the lukewarm attitude of France and Britain. After almost a month of listening patiently to Japanese justifications and excuses, meanwhile reading daily reports of the successes of the troops in Jehol, the committee voted unanimously on February 14 to recommend to the Assembly the adoption of the Lytton Commission Report as the only basis for a settlement and the nonrecognition of Manchukuo. The committee's report, drafted by a subcommittee of nine (Belgium, France, Germany, Italy, Spain, England, Sweden, Switzerland, Czechoslovakia), ran to fifteen thousand words. To avoid Article XVI, it did not brand Japan the aggressor or the violator of treaties. It did, however, unequivocally condemn that nation's whole course since September 1931.[61] The Japanese replied to the report with a demand on China to evacuate its troops from Manchukuoan soil and a renewed drive on Jehol.[62]

On the twenty-first, the Assembly met to consider the committee's report. After three days of debate, the report was adopted by forty-two of the forty-four nations present—Siam

[60] This pride in the attention centering on Japan can be seen in the publicity put out by *Trans-Pacific* in soliciting subscriptions. For the Japanese reaction to the Philippine Independence bill, see Tokyo *Asahi*, Jan. 17, 1933, and *Osaka Mainichi*, Jan. 19, 1933.

[61] The events can be followed in the reports of the American diplomats. See *F.R.*, *1933*, III, 92–93, 95–97, 111, 137–38.

[62] Sources in China indicated that the Japanese planned to take Jehol on March 1, the first anniversary of the establishment of Manchukuo. See Nelson T. Johnson to State Dept., Feb. 17, 1933, *ibid.*, 184–85.

abstained, Japan voted no. In his speech rejecting the report, Matsuoka was remarkably restrained, dignified, and confident: no saber-rattling, no threat, no dire predictions. He merely pointed out that the members of the Assembly did not understand the true situation in Asia, did not appreciate the chaos in China and Japan's difficulty in conducting negotiations under such a disorganized state, and ignored Japan's good work in bringing peace and order to Manchuria. After the address, the entire Japanese delegation left the room, and the headlines around the world reported "Japan Bolts League." [63]

Japan, of course, did not leave the League that twenty-fourth day of January. She could not withdraw except after giving official notice and not until two years after that. But the press was quite correct if it meant that Japan left the League except for the legal formality. And the world was shocked and surprised. Although there had been much speculation and prognostication that Japan might leave, the most knowledgeable people did not believe it would happen. Japan, they said, would not jeopardize her mandated islands, would not burn her most important bridge with the outside world, would not cut herself off from the society of nations. Ambassador Grew, who, despite his short residence in the island, had come to understand the Japanese character, recorded in his diary on February 14 that it was doubtful Japan would withdraw from the League.[64]

The fact is that at the very time he was making the entry, the army clique had decided to break with Geneva if the Assembly adopted the committee's report and was in the process of convincing the prime minister and other members of the Cabinet. The civilians in the government did not convince easily. The prime minister had hopes for some compromise with the Chinese, perhaps a pledge by the Chinese to suppress the anti-Japanese boycotts in exchange for recognition of Chinese sovereignty over Manchuria by an annual flag-raising ceremony. Makino Shinken, Lord Keeper of the Privy Seal and a former foreign minister and minister of the Imperial Household, shared the same view. But they could

[63] See Prentiss Gilbert's report of the proceedings in *ibid.*, 206–208.

[64] On February 20, Grew recorded: "My own guess was wrong; until recently I did not think they would do it."

not withstand the military, who had Count Uchida and the war and navy ministers on their side all the time. On the nineteenth of February, Prime Minister Saito, having capitulated, called on Prince Saionji, the last of the Genro, for his consent, which the old man gave reluctantly. The die was cast and orders went to Matsuoka to walk out.[65]

If Japanese defiance of the League of Nations caused great concern among the nations, censure by the civilized world did not chasten Japan. Walter Lippmann was wrong when he wrote: "It would be a stupid cynicism to deny the deterrent effect." Joseph C. Grew was right when he reported that the moral obloquy had served only to strengthen Japan's determination to push ahead. The Japanese loved nothing more than a heroic fight against odds. They were now more than ever resolved not to retreat and were ready to fight for Manchuria and beyond for all of Asia. The army and navy, Grew wrote, were in a state of high efficiency and becoming more arrogant, more bellicose, and more self-confident. Public opinion was mobilized and looked upon a war with Russia or the United States as inevitable.[66] No wonder the world was troubled.

The British Tories liked it not at all. Sir John Simon had been carried along on the tide of enthusiasm and by the courage of the Committee of Nineteen when he had voted for nonrecognition of Manchukuo.[67] Now Japan's stiffening attitude frightened him. He was not spoiling for a fight. On February 27, he announced in the House of Commons: "Under no circumstances will this government authorize this country to be a party to the conflict." On the same day, he attempted indirectly to soften the blow against Japan and head off a possible League embargo against that nation alone by proclaiming an arms embargo against both China and Japan.[68] Winston Churchill also tried to ameliorate any

[65] Hugh Wilson to State Dept., Feb. 9, 1933, *F.R., 1933*, III, 160; Grew to State Dept., Feb. 17, 1933, *ibid.*, 185, and March 6, 1933, D/S File 894.00 PR/63; also Takeuchi, p. 412.
[66] Lippmann in New York *Herald Tribune*, Feb. 22, 1933; Grew to State Dept., Feb. 23, 1933, *F.R., 1933*, III, 195–96, and *F.R., Japan, 1931–1941*, I, 110–11
[67] The change in British policy delighted the other League members. See Prentiss Gilbert to Nelson T. Johnson, Feb. 8, 1933, Johnson Papers.
[68] *Parliamentary Debates*, House of Commons, Fifth Series, Vol. 275, p. 59.

Anglo-Japanese animosity. "We do not want to throw away our old valued friendship with Japan," he said at a public lecture in London.[69] Most bitter was Sir Francis Lindley, the British ambassador in Tokyo, who poured out to Grew his resentment against his bungling government and the League of Nations for laying down "dogmatic theories without regard to facts." The whole matter, he claimed, could have been settled by direct negotiations. It was a local affair of no concern to international organization.[70] For much the same reasons, the French right also deplored the censure of the League.[71]

And what of the United States? Henry L. Stimson may well have been pleased by the Assembly's action. It had followed his lead; he had blazed the trail. He was responsible for applying the nonrecognition principle to the Far Eastern situation. It was his bold idea, while the other powers hung back, to hold Japan to strict accountability. The debt the League owed Stimson was not lost on observers. Hugh Wilson wrote him on the eve of the Assembly's vote: "The Assembly is about to vote the Report on Manchuria, a judgment on Japan by the nations of the world. More than any one man you have contributed to make such action possible within the peace structure. The Kellogg Pact has a vitality and reality which would not have been dreamed of without your energetic interpretation." [72] Many other people, both at home and abroad, considered the Secretary's leadership to have been noteworthy. There was much praise for his qualities of mind and character. "A high-grade intellect and a high-grade conscience," wrote Newton D. Baker, who had known in his day another noble figure.[73] Some who earlier had dubbed him "Wrong Horse Harry" and considered him slow witted and awkward had changed their views of him and characterized him as a man of honesty, deep sincerity, and moral earnestness.[74] There was a feeling among many that he had acted

[69] Bassett, *Democracy and Foreign Policy*, p. 564, and *New York Times,* Feb. 25, 1933.
[70] Grew, Diary, Feb. 22 and 24, 1933.
[71] New York *Herald Tribune*, Feb. 26, 1933, digest French press opinion.
[72] Wilson to Stimson, Feb. 23, 1933, Stimson Papers, Box 22, Letters Received.
[73] Baker to Walter Lippmann, May 26, 1932, Baker Papers, Box 49.
[74] "Rough Diamond," *Collier's*, Dec. 5, 1931, p. 45.

with great courage and had represented a strong moral position.[75]

But there were also many people who considered Stimson to have damaged America's position irretrievably. By "thrusting out our chin . . . unnecessarily fast and far," [76] by practicing reckless rhetoric and belligerent pacifism,[77] and by unsupported bellicose statements,[78] Stimson, it was said, succeeded only in alienating the Japanese without increasing the love of the Chinese and in leaving the United States vulnerable in the Pacific. America might well "get a world war out of that miserable business," lamented one correspondent.[79] Stimson's trouble was attributed to his legalistic approach. A lawyer turned diplomat, noted Admiral Montgomery M. Taylor, is a bad thing. Lawyers are unconcerned with execution of the verdict, a task left to the sheriff. Diplomats must have the means for implementation.[80]

It was true, of course, that much of Stimson's attitude toward international affairs derived from his legal training. As his recent biographer has pointed out, he approached treaties and their violations as a prosecuting attorney approached an individual who transgressed municipal law.[81] What he did not seem to realize was that in international affairs there was no clear-cut, categoric right or wrong as there was in the domestic realm. There was no "law" against which the conduct of nations could be assessed. In diplomacy, he seemed to have forgotten, if he ever knew, that one cannot let emotion or morality be the only guide of conduct. One must neither hate nor love, only calculate and weigh.

On the eve of his departure from office, Stimson, it appeared, had some misgivings about his policy. He seemed more aware of the danger of carrying censure and ostracism too far and of driving Japan into a back-against-the-wall posi-

---

[75] Bertram Hulen to Nelson T. Johnson, Sept. 1, 1932, Johnson Papers.

[76] Edward Price Bell to Ruth E. Campbell, Sept. 3, 1933, Bell Papers, Box "1931–34 Outgoing."

[77] Hamilton Butler, "A New Deal in the Pacific," *North American Review*, 235 (June 1933), 485–97.

[78] Admiral Montgomery M. Taylor to Colonel J. R. M. Taylor, Feb. 25, 1933, Taylor Papers, Box 269.

[79] Bell to J. L. Garvin, Feb. 13, 1933, Bell Papers, Box "1931–34 Outgoing."

[80] Taylor to Taylor, Feb. 25, 1933, Taylor Papers, Box 269.

[81] Elting E. Morison, *Turmoil and Tradition: A Study of the Life and Times of Henry L. Stimson* (Boston, 1960), pp. 273–75.

tion. He hoped something could be done to show a measure of good will and an absence of hostility, possibly a letter from the President to Congress requesting a change in the immigration laws to remove the restrictions against the Japanese. He hoped that there would be no drastic action or even implied threats or displays of strength.[82] His policy of bluff, which once had been so dear to him and which years later he considered to have been responsible for maintaining the peace,[83] did not in the spring of 1933 look as attractive. For after all, what had it achieved? All Stimson really handed on to his successor was the implacable enmity of the Japanese. His policy had not in the slightest deterred the Mikado's forces.

The tragedy of Henry Stimson was that he wanted desperately to call a halt to the wanton and reckless conduct of an international lawbreaker who ignored every norm of decent conduct and who broke the bonds of civilized restraint. But he could not marshal support at home or abroad. The President and Undersecretary Castle both held him in check, the former because of his fear of the warlike consequences, the latter because he did not really believe Japan to be the international brigand his chief portrayed her to be. And the vast majority of the American people wanted no part of Asia's, or, for that matter, Europe's, woes. Even the peace groups shied away from a belligerent stand lest their basic convictions be compromised. As for European backing, Britain and France simply could not be depended upon, as Walter Lippmann has pointed out. The British had a very real affinity for Japan which began at the turn of the century with the Anglo-Japanese Alliance and which persisted, in Tory circles, after its abrogation. France did not wish to jeopardize the security of French Indo-China. Both powers feared communism in Asia, against which, they believed, only Japan stood as the bulwark.

Stimson, finding the desirable impossible, was satisfied at the outset with eschewing the desirable. Soon, however, his moral sensibilities outraged, he elected to give vent to his ire by brandishing the pistol, which, unhappily, was not loaded, thereby transgressing the cardinal maxim of the statesman and placing his country in jeopardy. And yet it was, per-

[82] Stimson to Hornbeck, Feb. 1, 1933, D/S File 711.94/770.
[83] *The Far Eastern Crisis*, pp. 137–38, and *On Active Service*, p. 242.

haps, too much to expect Stimson, stern and reverent, nationalist and patriotic, to remain mute. Perhaps a nation as great as the United States, with roots deep in international morality, should have had the courage to voice the shock of civilization. Would the outcome have been different had Stimson remained silent? No man can tell.

APPENDIX
Blakeslee to Hornbeck,
September 14, 1932

_____

Honolulu, September 14, 1932.

Dr. Stanley K. Hornbeck,
Chief of the Division of Far Eastern Affairs,
Department of State,
Washington, D.C.

Dear Stanley:

The Great Adventure is past. The Commission has agreed upon a unanimous report. And its findings and recommendations, I am confident, will be gratifying to the Secretary of State and to your own good self.

When I left Peking, on the afternoon of August 31st, the members of the Commission were happy in the realization that they had at last surmounted all of their real difficulties and had only routine work to do for a couple of days in order to prepare the Report for final signature.

The findings are clear-cut and definite on the vital issues of the Manchurian controversy: (1) The military action of the Japanese on and subsequent to September 18th was not justified by the principle of self-defense, although the possibility is not excluded that the military on the spot on September 18th may have believed that they were acting in self defense (a clause added to satisfy General Claudel); (2) Manchukuo was created by Japanese: "It is perfectly clear that the 'independence movement', which had never been heard of before September, 1931, was conceived, organized and carried through by the Japanese, and was only made possible by the presence of Japanese troops". Official responsibility for this action is placed by clear implication upon Japan: "The evidence received from all sources has convinced the Commission that, while there were a number of factors which contributed to the creation of Manchukuo, the two which, in combination, were most effective, and without which, in our judgment, the new State could not have been formed, were the presence of Japanese troops and the activities of Japanese officials, both civil and military". "For this reason the present regime cannot be considered to have been called into existence by a genuine and spontaneous independence movement". Finally, the Japanese control Manchukuo: ". . . the main

207

political and administrative power rests in the hands of Japanese officials and advisers . . . in the case of all important problems these officials and advisers, some of whom were able to act more or less independently in the first days of the new organization, have been constrained more and more to follow the direction of Japanese official authority".

(3) The people of Manchuria as a whole do not support the new regime, but regard it as an instrument of the Japanese: "After careful study of the evidence presented to us in public and private interviews, in letters and written statements, we have come to the conclusion that there is no general Chinese support for the Manchukuo Government, which is regarded by the local Chinese as an instrument of the Japanese".

(4) A recognition of Manchukuo would violate international obligations: "It must also be clear from what we have said in the two preceding chapters that the maintenance and recognition of the present regime in Manchuria would be equally unsatisfactory (as the restoration of the status quo ante). Such a solution does not appear to us compatible with the fundamental principles of existing international obligations, nor with the good understanding between the two countries upon which peace in the Far East depends. It is opposed to the vital interests of China. It disregards the wishes of the people of Manchuria, and it is at least questionable whether it would serve the permanent interests of Japan".

The recommendations of the Commission are along the lines I suggested in an earlier letter: the maintenance of the territorial and administrative integrity of China, the organization of an autonomous regime for the Three Eastern Provinces, with foreign advisers having adequate powers, the demilitarization of Manchuria, the guaranteeing of Japanese rights, and the preservation of peace by boards of arbitration and of conciliation.

In terms of the machinery suggested, the Commission recommends a Declaration by China establishing an autonomous regime for Manchuria, and three Sino-Japanese Treaties. To carry out this program the first step would be an agreement between the Governments of China and Japan upon the main outline of settlement.

An advisory Conference would then be summoned, com-

posed of representatives of China and Japan and of two dele-
gations from Manchuria, one to be selected in a manner to
be prescribed by the Government of China and the other in
a manner prescribed by the Government of Japan. Neutral
observers might also be present, should this be agreeable to
the Chinese and Japanese Governments. This Advisory Conference would draw up the details of an autonomous administration for the Three Eastern Provinces, but should points of
difference develop which the Conference could not settle,
these would be referred to the Council of the League. After a
detailed plan had been agreed upon, it would be embodied
in a Declaration which the Chinese Government would send
to the League and to the signatories of the Nine Power
Treaty, and which would have the force of an international
obligation.

The main provisions suggested for the Declaration are:
(1) A statement of the powers to be reserved to the Chinese
central Government, which would include: control of general
treaty and foreign relations; control of Customs, Post Office,
Salt Gabelle, and possibly other agencies—with an arrangement for an equitable division of the net income between
the Central Government and the Three Eastern Provinces;
the power of appointment of the chief executive—the person
to be appointed would probably be agreed upon by the members of the Advisory Conference. (2) The establishment of
a constabulary and provision for demilitarization. The constabulary would then be the only armed force within Manchuria, and when adequately organized, all regular troops,
including Japanese Railway Guards, would be withdrawn.
(3) The appointment of Foreign Advisers. A substantial proportion of these advisers should be Japanese. Two foreign
advisers, of different nationalities, would have practically
complete control of (a) the constabulary and (b) the fiscal
administration.

A Sino-Japanese Treaty would be negotiated relating to
Japanese rights and interests in Manchuria. It is suggested
that this treaty should grant to the Japanese the right to settle
and to own land throughout all of Manchuria, but with some
modification of the principle of extraterritoriality, and some
additional judicial safeguards, such as the appointment of at
least two foreign advisers—but not of the same nationality—

to the Supreme Court of Manchuria. As for railroads, it is recomemnded either that a system of cooperation should be established through the appointment of a railway board, similar to the American Interstate Commerce Commission, or that the South Manchurian Railway and the Chinese roads should be almagamated through a holding company, according to a plan worked out by Colonel Hiam, the Commission's Railway expert. In carefully guarded phraseology it is stated that, in view of this mutually advantageous treaty, China might find no difficulty in recognizing all of the definite grants made to Japan by such treaties and agreements as those of 1915. As a matter of fact, the Chinese have stated definitely that they are now willing to recognize these alleged rights.

A second Sino-Japanese treaty would deal with conciliation and non-aggression. An Arbitration Tribunal would hear disputes regarding the interpretation of the Declaration and of the three Sino-Japanese treaties, and a Board of Conciliation would assist in the solution of any difficulties between the Governments of Japan and China which diplomatic negotiation had failed to settle.

By the terms of this treaty the Governments of China and Japan would agree to maintain no soldiers in Manchuria, but should either side commit an aggression by sending troops into the Three Eastern Provinces, or should a third state (U.S.S.R.) do so, the other state or states would be free to take whatever measures might be advisable. (That is, should the U.S.S.R. send troops into Manchuria, Japan might at once take similar action).

A third Sino-Japanese Treaty would provide for favorable commercial relations and would contain an undertaking by the Chinese Government that it would take all measures within its power against the anti-Japanese boycott, but without prejudice to the individual rights of Chinese consumers.

This summary gives merely the main provisions of the Commission's plan of settlement. The quotations are from drafts which were regarded, on August 31st, as final; but before the Report was signed it was reread in its entirety, and it is possible, though not probable, that some modifications were made in the sentences quoted.

The Report contains an introduction and nine chapters: chapter I, the Chinese background; chapter II, the general

Manchurian background; chapter III, the specific Sino-Japanese issues regarding Manchuria before September, 1931; chapter V, the events from September 18th to the establishment of Manchukuo; chapter V, Manchukuo; chapter VI, the principles and conditions of settlement; and chapter VII, recommendations. This was the chapter numbering up to the day I left Peking, but two additional chapters had been prepared, one dealing largely with the boycott, and the other with certain phases of the economic situation. These will be placed somewhere in the middle of the Report, and will change the numbering of some of the later chapters. There will be voluminous appendices.

The attitude of the Report is objective and judicial; its tone is restrained and conciliatory; yet it is positive and definite upon the vital issues of the controversy. The first three chapters, as well as the one on boycotts, are so written that they will arouse little discussion. But chapters IV to VII inclusive will be highly controversial.

To understand the process by which the Report was formed, to appreciate the difficulties met and overcome, and to sense the dramatic situations which developed, it is necessary to know the men who composed the Commission.

The Earl of Lytton, as Chairman, sat at the head of the conference table. Distinguished in lineage and in public service, tall and dignified, he appeared an impressive figure, especially on those formal occasions when he stood wearing the insignia of his various orders and his many decorations. In the literary field, as well as in Governmental posts, he had won a high reputation, and he possessed a charm of literary style which came naturally to a son and a grandson of two of the leading authors of England. A courteous gentleman, he presided at the Commission's meetings usually with tact and ability. But much of the time he was a sick man, occasionally dangerously sick, with the result, inevitable in the case of his malady, that he showed, now and then, an irritability which he would not have felt had he been in his normal health. He worked intensely and continuously, read all the essential documents and papers, listened to the many witnesses who appeared before the Commission, and came to the conviction that the Japanese were completely unjustified in their actions in Manchuria. As Chairman, it was his wish to write

a report for the Commission which should express these conclusions with the literary clarity and force of which he was
an acknowledged master.

But, at the other end of the table from Lord Lytton and
separated from him in every other respect by more than the
table length, sat General Claudel. As characteristically French
as the Earl of Lytton was characteristically British, he was
genial, even effusive at times, with a lovable strain in his
character, highly emotional, expressing himself in conversation or at the conference table simultaneously with voice, face
and hands. One of the most interesting sights at the Commission meetings was to watch the play of sunshine and shadow
across the face of the distinguished French general. Suddenly
the fascinating smile and the winning expression would disappear and grim, hard lines would take their place, as if once
again he were in some desperate battle of the World War.
General Claudel, as Lord Lytton, was convinced that the
Japanese were unjustified in their Manchurian adventure,
that they had created and controlled Manchukuo and that
an ideal solution of the issue in Manchuria must be one
which would maintain the sovereignty of China. But in many
of his views and in his emotional attitude he differed from
the Chairman. As he expressed it in one of the Commission
meetings, he desired, in Manchuria, as little Chinese sovereignty as possible. While intellectually forced to condemn
the Japanese, he was sympathetic with them and wished to
drape the naked truth regarding their actions with the flowing
phraseology of a pleasing and somewhat illusive literary style.
He was opposed to any expression which appeared to be an
indictment of them. The whole problem he seemed to view
sympathetically from the Japanese point of view. He spoke
and understood only French, which Lord Lytton also spoke,
though not with ease. As the days passed these two men mis-
understood each other more completely and the gulf between
them continually widened.

Between Lord Lytton and General Claudel sat the three
other Commissioners. Their views were somewhat similar.
They agreed with Lord Lytton in wishing to express with
clarity the convictions in which the entire Commission
shared, but they also agreed with General Claudel in part,

for they were insistent that the tone of the Report should be entirely judicial.

Dr. Schnee was typically German, combining much of the "Deutsche Gemutlichkeit" with a Prussian precision of mind. There were no effervescent emotions in either his manner or his character. He was quiet, thorough, dependable and genuine. Everyone came to like him, and to like him all the time. With the background of his colonial experience, he was a valuable member of the Commission, especially in his insistence upon accuracy in statements and in figures. Woe to any incorrect date or bit of statistics which strayed into a draft chapter. Dr. Schnee would dart at it as a hawk would pounce upon a wayward chicken. He spoke English in the Commission's meetings. The others could depend upon him to express sound judgments and to favor reasonable compromises which would lead to a unanimous report.

Count Aldrovandi, a former Ambassador at Berlin, could be unusually charming in the courtly, gracious Italian manner; but usually he appeared the cold diplomat with clear head and keen mind. He had a fine sense of correct legal phraseology. Statistics did not seem to disturb him, but if a word or a clause in a draft did not express with precision and exactness the idea intended—and there were many such—he detected it instantly and supplied the correct equivalent. Of the three Commissioners who made up the middle group, he was somewhat more sympathetic with General Claudel than the others; and in part for this reason, and in part from his perfect command of French, the language in which he usually spoke at the conference table, he served as the bridge from the rest of the Commission to General Claudel. In the last days at Peking he did an invaluable service in inducing his French colleague to accept a draft which brought agreement upon the one important issue then outstanding, and which made possible the unanimous Report.

General McCoy possessed a rare combination of qualities desirable in a member of an international commission: keen insight, inflexible purpose, good judgment, and abiding patience and tact. He would analyze accurately the factors in any given task and after determining the chief aims, would work constantly to obtain them, never permitting secondary

considerations, or irritations, or personal issues to swerve
him from his purpose. He would make a careful study of the
means best adapted for reaching the main objectives and of
the exact stage in the progress of events when these means
should be used, for he had rare ability in forecasting the
probable unfolding of a situation. Always, too, he was thinking ahead and planning moves in advance. He was ready
enough to compromise, in fact he believed that compromises
on a commission were necessary and desirable—provided they
were not compromises on essentials.

He became convinced that the chief objectives of the Commission were clear-cut conclusions on certain vital issues and
a unanimous report. And later, when it was evident that the
Commissioners were agreed upon these particular conclusions, he worked constantly for complete unanimity. The
Report, he felt, should be judicial in tone and attitude, which
led him frequently to criticize the Chairman's drafts. While
convinced that the Japanese were wrong on the Manchurian
issues, he understood their point of view and wished the
conclusions of the Commission, necessarily critical of the
Japanese, to be as little offensive to them as possible. He had
many friends among the Japanese leaders, and showed his
own breadth of sympathy by the comment, which he often
made: "The best people in every country are much alike".

In the Commission's meetings he was the most thoro-
going, constructive critic, and presented a number of drafts
and outlines to improve various chapters under consideration.
Possibly his foremost aim was to maintain harmony among
the Comissioners, which, for the most part, meant between
Lord Lytton and General Claudel, for he realized the importance of the human factor and of the personal equation,
and many were the expedients which he adopted to this end.
He exerted a great influence over Lord Lytton, and, certainly
for a time also, a measure of influence over General Claudel.
It was his suggestion which led Count Aldrovandi to prepare
with General Claudel the draft which finally brought a unanimous report. He won and held the confidence and the high
regard of the other Commissioners. Kind, considerate, never
up-set, he was outstandingly loyal to both cause and to person.
It was due to his sense of obligation to the Chairman in his
illness, as well as to his instinctive desire to be of service,

which led him to give up his cherished plan of a return trip through Russia, in order to accompany Lord Lytton on his long sea-voyage to Europe.

To General McCoy, all factors considered, probably more than to any other man, the Commission owes its unanimous report.

These five Commissioners were in complete agreement, as has been pointed out, in their analysis of the main factors of the Manchurian issue. This is remarkable, when one considers the different backgrounds and the divergent personal characteristics of the men; and is the strongest possible indication of the correctness of their conclusions. They all agreed, too, upon the ideal solution of the Manchurian issue. They differed only in the way in which they would state their unanimous conclusions and in the extent to which they would recognize and build upon the admittedly illegitimate political creation—Manchukuo.

But these differences became important, toward the close of the writing of the Report, so much so that the great issue before the Commission was whether their conclusions and recommendations would be unanimous, with all the weight they would then carry throughout the world, or whether there would be two reports, or a report with reservations, which would, in large measure, destroy the value of the work of the Inquiry.

The basis for a unanimous report had been laid shortly after our return to Peking, on June 5th, from the investigations in Manchuria. Three outlines of a final Report were presented to the Commission by Lord Lytton, General McCoy and Mr. Hass, the General Secretary. These were harmonized so far as possible and were united in a single draft. This draft, however, did not include the last chapter, which was to deal with the recommendations, since it was felt that it would be unwise for the Commissioners to give even a preliminary approval to any recommendations until after they had completed their visit to Japan. But the outlines of all of the other chapters, including one dealing with the principles which should underlie the final settlement, were carefully considered by the Commission and were tentatively adopted. The outline contained statements that the Japanese were not justified in their actions in Manchuria and that they had created and were controlling Manchukuo. Under these circumstances there appeared good reason to believe that the Commission would in all probability be able to present a unanimous Report.

But greater difficulties developed than had been anticipated. Soon after the return from Japan, on July 20th, Lord Lytton and the experts turned in the first drafts of various chapters, and the Commission undertook the task of studying and discussing them. These drafts were subjected to a searching criticism, were revised and sometimes completely rewritten. For the most part the changes made involved no conflict in fundamental principle between any of the members of the Commission; but such conflicts soon began to develop, in part between Lord Lytton and the other four members of the board, and later between Lord Lytton and General Claudel.

These differences were rendered more acute by Lord Lytton's illness. He had recurrent attacks of an infection which centered in kidney or bladder and which made him pathologically irritable. When we landed at Tsingtao, upon our return from Tokyo, he had to be carried on board the train on a stretcher. Some days later, in Peking, there was a sudden recurrence of the trouble in an acute form which made it necessary for the Commission to meet without him. This situation gave rise to various misunderstandings between him and the other Commissioners.

A divergence of view arose as to the best method of preparing the Report. The four other Commissioners seemed to take it for granted that Lord Lytton and the various experts would write draft chapters, which the Commission as a whole would then criticize, amend if necessary, and finally adopt. They voted at one time during Lord Lytton's absence that all drafts of the experts should be submitted to each Commissioner in their original form.

But Lord Lytton had a different plan. He insisted that he was to write the Report. He wished it to be in a uniform literary style, readable, interesting, and a very human document. He also realized, although he refrained from saying so to the Commission, that the conclusions and recommendations would be known as the Lytton Report, and he naturally wished it to do credit to a family as distinguished as his own for literary ability. This view led him to regard the draft chapters, written by the experts, as prepared primarily for his own use. He wished to revise or rewrite them before they should be circulated to the Commissioners. The latter, however, desired to read for themselves the unexpurgated opinions of the experts. They felt, too, that if Lord Lytton should himself write the entire Report, it would lead to unnecessary delay.

This difference was increased by Lord Lytton's desire to direct the work of the Commission even when he was unable to be present at its deliberations. On one occasion he asked me to see him at the hospital, and when I called, gave me a memorandum which among other items contained the following: "I do not wish the Commission to discuss chapters Vi or Vii".

There were, not unnaturally, some tense moments when these differences were discussed in the Commission shortly after Lord Lytton had resumed the chairmanship but before he had recovered from the debilitating effects of his severe illness. "If you wish to help me", he would say, "you may do so and so. I shall write the Report. If any other Commissioner wishes to write his own report, he may do so". It seemed to the other Commissioners somewhat as if Lord Lytton regarded them as his assistants rather than his colleagues; but they showed a magnanimous spirit, and, under the constant leadership of General McCoy, they would say to each other that they should realize that Lord Lytton was a sick man. They finally decided to allow him as free a hand in the writing of the draft chapters as circumstances would permit.

But circumstances did not permit Lord Lytton to carry out to the full the ideas he had fought for in the Commission. He himself drafted certain of the final chapters, but others went to the Commission for consideration without his previous revision. The Commission went over each chapter, page by page, discussing every point brought up by any of the members. Sometimes they would agree upon a desired phraseology, but more usually they would decide the substance of what should be said and would leave the phrasing to the Drafting Committee. Lord Lytton therefore, with the help of the other members of the Drafting Committee, had the opportunity of putting the finishing touches upon all chapters before they were included in the final Report. And he took the liberty himself of making small changes which would not affect the sense but would improve the style.

Differences over methods of procedure were less difficult to deal with than those concerning the chapters which Lord Lytton himself had drafted. He chose to write upon some of the most controversial subjects, such as the Incident of September 18th and the Shanghai Affair, and he drew up the conclusions regarding Japan's actions in Manchuria, and presented the principles which should govern the settlement. Whatever he wrote was well written, but believing strongly, as he did, in the injustice of Japan's case, he was inclined to present an indictment of Japan upon every count, and to express this with occasional evidence of feeling and, in addition, now and then a bit of sarcasm.

The other Commissioners were opposed to this method, and wished the Report, however damning might be its conclusions against Japan, to be expressed in a judicial spirit, with no show of emotion and no word which would cause unnecessary offense to the Japanese Government or people. And so the other four descended upon the Chairman's drafts. Not only did they remove all evidence of an effort to indict Japan and all expressions of feeling, but in the case of the chapters upon the Incident of September 18th and upon the Shanghai Affair, they rejected the drafts themselves, disapproving of his Lordship's method of treatment. In regard to Shanghai they desired to express no judgment upon Japan's action, on the ground that that affair did not fall within the scope of their Inquiry. As to September 18th, Lord Lytton, in his draft, had argued in favor of the greater plausability of the Chinese account as against that of the Japanese. This was deemed unsatisfactory, and, at General McCoy's suggestion, the Commission made a summary of the conclusions regarding the Incident to which they were all willing to subscribe.

These conclusions were ample to condemn Japan for its actions upon that eventful night. But the Commissioners, after all their study of that event, after all the evidence they had read and the witnesses they had heard, including the leading Chinese and Japanese participants, still remained uncertain as to just what did happen on and near the railway tracks. They exchanged views at one meeting, and found that their several surmises were widely divergent. They all agreed that there was an explosion—the Chinese stated that there was one but they regarded it merely as a signal for the Japanese attack—but the majority of the Commission at least, as I remember it, did not believe that there was any explosion between ten and eleven o'clock which injured the railway track. At any rate, they were all convinced that the Japanese account, in its entirety, was untrue.

It was General Claudel, however, who was the most severe and most sweeping critic. On more than one occasion, after a Commission meeting had been called to order, he read in French a statement regarding some chapter of Lord Lytton's which was before the Commission for discussion. He stated that it was entirely unacceptable, not only because of objectionable sentences and expressions, but because of its whole tone and spirit, as well as on account of certain of its conclusions. Sometimes Dr. Jouvelet, the General's interpreter, followed with an English translation of the criticism.

Lord Lytton met these attacks with a rare magnanimity, but with a magnanimity which was marred by occasional evidences of irritation and lack of poise, due, at least in large part, to the effects of his severe illness. There were certain objects which he wished to obtain: the writing of the report by himself, definite conclusions upon both the vital issues concerned and the main recommendations, and a unanimous agreement by the Commissioners. If he could obtain these objectives he was willing, if necessary, to throw overboard everything else. A number of times he said to General Claudel, "If you will only tell me what you want, I will try to put it in the Report". And so his Lordship would accept, with apparent equinimity [sic], the radical revision and even the complete rejection of draft after draft which he had presented to the Commission.

One can hardly praise adequately the devotion to his task shown by Lord Lytton. For six weeks in the hospital, at times on his back with severe pain and a high fever, whenever he was able to sit up—and at times when he was not fit to do so—he would work at the Report. He was continuously reading and writing and in Commission and Committee meetings, from morning until night. Often he would reach the limit of his strength. A couple of times, after our Drafting Committee had been in session for three hours or more in the afternoon, and I had queried whether we should not adjourn, he said: "Yes, I must stop. I cannot work any longer." And even during the night, as he confided to me on one occasion, he would wake up and would plan how he could satisfy General Claudel.

And so the earlier chapters were rewritten, revised, and put into final form. On one or two occasions the concessions made to General Claudel reached the innermost fortifications which defended the vital conclusions of the Commission, and from which there could be no further withdrawal, whatever the result. But unanimous agreement was finally obtained upon all the chapters up to the one on Recommendations.

For that final chapter General Claudel made a proposal which threatened and actually came near to preventing a unanimous report. He believed that the Japanese were not justified in what they did upon, and subsequent to, September 18th, and that they had created and were controlling Manchukuo, and he agreed, too, that the settlement recommended by the Commission was in theory the best possible, and that it would have been satisfactory some months previously. But since the creation of Manchukuo, and in view of the impending recognition of its independence by Japan, the draft plan of settlement was, in his judgment, idealistic and largely impractical. "Manchukuo is an illegitimate child", was the way he expressed it at one of the Commission meetings, ["]but we have it on our hands. What are we going to do with it?" Even when the Commission was in Manchuria General Claudel had in mind the idea that the recommendations of the Commission might take the existing Manchukuo Government as a basis, and attempt to modify it in order to make it acceptable to the League of Nations. Count Aldrovandi shared this idea, at least for a time and in some degree, although toward the end he impressed me as standing nearer to General McCoy and Dr. Schnee than to General Claudel. There appeared some danger, however, that if General Claudel should insist upon signing the Report with a reservation, Count Aldrovandi might join him. This would have greatly weakened the effect of the Report, and would have been hailed as a partial victory for Japan.

During the last few days in Peking General Claudel presented a formal statement to the Commission, urging certain suggestions and drafts, and stating, "I must request very strongly that they be taken account of in our Report, in order that I may not be compelled to add to it, on some points, the expression of my personal opinions". In other words, this statement was in the nature of an ultimatum—accept my ideas or I shall make a reservation to the Report.

His most important proposal was that a draft should be included in the Report recommending to the Council of the League that it should take cognizance of the probable recognition of Manchukuo by the Japanese Government, and suggesting that in such a contingency, "the maintenance of peace in the Far East, as regards Manchuria, might best be secured not by the simple recommendation of our Plan, but preferably by a compromise between the theoretical principles embodied in that Plan and the principles which are now in course of realization in the Manchukuo". Then followed a paragraph which seemed to imply that it would be satisfactory if the Manchukuo authorities should modify their constitution so that it would be "based upon the wishes of the people". General Claudel's draft concluded: "By making certain recommendations regarding the future Constitution of the 'Manchukuo State', the Council, taking account of realities, may find in this fact a means of assuring a durable peace in the Far East". (English translation circulated to the Commissioners).

In other words, if Manchukuo should modify its constitution, it might be recognized as an independent state. The illegitimate child, as a matter of practical convenience, would have the taint of illegitimacy removed. The Commission could never accept this proposal, although it was willing to recommend the utilizing of the existing machinery and the personnel of Manchukuo so far as consistent with the adoption of its own plan.

After General Claudel's ultimatum it seemed probable that the Commission would be unable to present a unanimous Report.

During the discussions over this issue, as well as over the other serious problems before the Commission in its last two or three weeks in Peking, there was many a tense moment and many a dramatic situation. The Commission meetings were usually held in the German hospital, in a small bare room next to the one in which Lord Lytton lived and worked. Many a session was all sunshine, and whatever suggestions were made by General Claudel, as well as by others, if they related to detail, were willingly accepted. But other days the storm clouds would gather, and sometimes they would break. This was apt to happen when General Claudel presented a prepared statement. With a beautiful voice, an unusual charm of manner, a facile and emotional countenance, he would speak to the Commission. At times his hands would press his breast, and he would exclaim, "Principle is involved; honor is at stake; I cannot yield on this point".

When Lord Lytton attempted to reply, he would sometimes forget the principle of conciliation which he attempted to follow and would say, "I will accept as much as possible, but such and such points I will never accept. You can write your own report". When his Lordship spoke, a transformation would take place in General Claudel's face; it would become at once like New Hampshire granite in winter.

Lord Lytton felt, and with much justification, that he had made extreme concessions. At one of our Drafting Committee meetings, he was asked what he would say at Geneva if an inquiry arose as to the real meaning of a certain phrase adopted at the request of General Claudel, and he replied, "I would tell them it meant—the price of unanimity".

When the tense moments arrived it was usually General McCoy who led the way out, either by proposing a postponement of the discussion or by arranging for a short recess. At the close of the session he would often remain for a few minutes alone with Lord Lytton, who clearly relied far more upon his advice and counsel than upon that of anyone else. And General McCoy would tell his Lordship, with friendly frankness, that he should stop saying that he would not agree to this, that, or the other proposal, or that others could write their own reports. And a little later he would take occasion to speak to General Claudel, expressing his approval of some particular suggestion the latter had made—for he made many good suggestions—thus trying to prevent the two extremes on the Commission from getting too far apart. It was part of his strategy, too, to keep postponing a final decision on the dangerous issues until the Commission had reached an agreement upon most of the points in the Report. And he constantly stressed the importance of a unanimous decision. When it seemed probable that General Claudel would write a dissenting reservation, and Mr. Haas, the General Secretary, was preparing for this development by saying in small committee meetings that it would make no difference in Geneva should General Claudel make a reservation, General McCoy took him somewhat vigorously to task, "Whatever may be the effect in Geneva, it will make a tremendous difference in America whether the Report is unanimous or not".

And when the critical session arrived and General Claudel delivered to the Commission what appeared to be his ultimatum, it was General McCoy who saved the day by the wise recommendation that Count Aldrovandi should meet with General Claudel and attempt to draw up a statement which the Commission could accept. Count Aldrovandi undertook the task and was successful in producing a draft which both he and General Claudel approved. It was in French, but at the next morning's meeting of the Commission a hurried English translation was handed to other members. Lord Lytton reserved judgment until he could study the French original. To me at least it seemed that the English text could not possible [sic] be accepted by the Commission. I think Lord Lytton held the same opinion, judging fomr [sic] some comments he made to me after the meeting. But in the afternoon the prospect looked brighter. Lord Lytton had a session with Count Aldrovandi, and it turned out that the hurried English translation was extremely misleading, and that Lord Lytton regarded the French text as satisfactory. They agreed upon an English version which was acceptable to all.

And so a unanimous Report was achieved. Everyone knew that the rest of the Commission's work, some three days of it, related to mere detail. I do not know how General Claudel felt on that August 30th afternoon, but those of us on "our" side, felt almost hilariously happy. The Commission of Inquiry had been worth while. These five men, representing the leading states of the world, had agreed unanimously upon every one of the great issues in this international controversy, and upon a just and equitable settlement.

The Aldrovandi-Claudel draft, which will be included in the middle of the last chapter, states in substance (for I do not

have the text with me), that should Japan recognize Manchukuo, the Commission believes its Report would remain
unimpaired; that the Council would find in the recommendations suggestions which would still be helpful in solving the
Sino-Japanese issue; and that the Council of the League might
be able to suggest the utilization of some of the administrative
machinery and some of the personnel of the Manchukuo
Government in order to effect the object aimed at by the
Commission.

There is no recommendation, suggestion, or intimation
that Manchukuo should be recognized, or that it would be a
satisfactory solution to accept Manchukuo as a basis for a
settlement. There is an intimation that should Japan recognize Manchukuo, some of the recommendations of the Commission might no longer be of value, but this intimation is not
clear, and is well worth the price of unanimity. The expression to the effect that some of the administrative machinery
of Manchukuo might be utilized, is entirely unobjectionable
from our point of view. Obviously, should the Commission's
plan of settlement be adopted, some of the Manchukuo administrative machinery and personnel would undoubtedly be
taken over.

As I have already pointed out, it is General McCoy who
is entitled to a great share—probably the greatest share—of
the credit for bringing about unanimous agreement. And,
unknown to the other Commissioners, he held in reserve a
final proposal, which he had carefully thought out, and which
he planned to use in a last attack in the fight for an un-
broken report. But the victory was won without calling up
his reserves.

According to the findings of the Commission, it is evident
that Japan has violated the Pact of Paris, the Nine Power
Treaty, and the Covenant of the League of Nations (Article
X). To be sure, the Report does not make this statement in
these words, but it does say: "the maintenance and the recognition of the present regime in Manchuria . . . . does not
appear to us compatible with the fundamental principles of
existing international obligations". Further, it presents the
conclusions, already described, that Japan used military measures in Manchuria which were not justified by the principle
of self-defense; and that Japan's army and officials were the

chief factors in creating and maintaining Manchukuo, which has severed all territorial and administrative ties with the rest of China. These actions were inconsistent with the obligations of the Pact of Paris, and of the Nine Power Treaty and of Article X of the Covenant of the League. It is clear, therefore, that in the judgment of the Commission, Japan has violated these multilateral treaties.

With the Report signed and on its way to Geneva, the query naturally arises whether the Chinese and Japanese Governments will probably accept it. In the opinion of the Commissioners and of the staff, if I sensed it correctly, the probability is that the Chinese Government will accept it, although reluctantly so as far as some of the points are concerned. But it seems certain that the Japanese Government will, at first, refuse to follow its recommendations. The Japanese Government appears determined for the present to carry through its program in regard to Manchukuo.

But some of the Commissioners, as well as others, are still hopeful that after some time has passed, possibly a couple of years, Japan will decide to abandon its Manchukuo experiment and accept the general plan of settlement recommended by the Commission. The considerations which lead to this conclusion are that Manchukuo is costing Japan an immense sum of money, both directly on account of military expenditures in Manchuria, and indirectly on account of the anti-Japanese boycott in China. Japan is not in a financial condition to support for long the luxury of an expensive foreign military enterprise, and is even thought by some to be in danger of an economic catastrophe in the near future. Under these circumstances, and possibly faced, as she might be, by the condemnation of world opinion, it is believed that there may take place in Japan a revulsion of feeling and a change in convictions which would lead the Japanese to the conclusion that it would be both wiser and more to their own interest to accept the Commission's plan. There is already a basis in Japan from which such an opinion might develop. Although vocal Japan appears unanimous in favor of the Manchukuo policy, many influential older statesmen are opposed to it, as well as a large proportion—some of my Japanese university friends say a majority—of the Japanese professors.

For the immediate future, however, and so long as Japan

continues to recognize and maintain Manchukuo, the important problem concerns the relations between the United States and the League, on the one hand, and Japan on the other.

According to the findings of the Commission, it is evident that Japan has violated the Pact of Paris, the Nine Power Treaty, and the Covenant of the League of Nations (Article X). To be sure, the Report does not make this statement in these words, but it does say: "the maintenance and the recognition of the present regime in Manchuria . . . does not appear to us compatible with the fundamental principles of existing international obligations". Further, it presents the conclusions, already described, that Japan used military measures in Manchuria which were not justified by the principle of self-defense; and that Japan's army and officials were the chief factors in creating Manchukuo, and thus in severing its territorial and administrative ties with the rest of China. These actions were inconsistent with the obligations of the Pact of Paris, and of the Nine Power Treaty, and of Article X of the Covenant of the League. It is clear, therefore, that in the judgment of the Commission, Japan has violated these multilateral treaties of which she is a signatory.

It is also evident that if the United States and the states which are members of the League of Nations should accept the conclusions of the Commission, they cannot consistently grant recognition to Manchukuo. The United States would be debarred from doing so by the note of January 7–8th, and the members of the League by the vote of March 11th.

Now that Japan has formally recognized Manchukuo and has established intimate legal relations by treaty, the refusal of the United States and the League powers to extend recognition will create a situation which of itself will doubtless lead to generally unsatisfactory relations with Japan and to recurring friction. The announced intention to abrogate extraterritorial rights—to take but one issue—will naturally, if carried out, cause frequent controversy.

But it is hardly to be expected that the powers will do nothing more than passively to decline to recognize Manchukuo. When the Report is discussed at Geneva, in October or November, a heated and protracted debate is expected. The Report will undoubtedly be accepted and supported;

and many of the delegates, if not the League as a whole, will attempt to marshal world opinion against Japan in an effort to force her to undo the wrong committed in Manchuria. With this effort, of course, the American Government and people will be in sympathy. The Secretary of State will doubtless continue his policy of cooperation with the League, so far as possible, and will take some suitable occasion to express publicly his support of the Report of the Commission, much as he gave his public approval to the Resolution of the Council providing for the Commission's appointment.

Under these circumstances the judgment of the world as a whole will probably express itself in severe condemnation of Japan, with the result that relations between Japan and most of the other nations will be severely strained. There is a possibility that the United States may be regarded by the Japanese as the outstanding leader in this opposition, and that the largest measure of resentment may be concentrated against our country.

The situation now developing promises to furnish a severe test of the efficacy of world opinion when pitted against a great military power determined to carry through a certain course of action. If world opinion, combined with internal economic and financial distress in Japan, should be successful, it would be a triumph for the League and especially for the United States. But if Japan should persist in its present course, and be able to maintain it, there is a possibility that, after some time, many states, under the leadership of France, might recognize Manchukuo, and leave the United States to be the one great power in opposition to Japan. The position of the United States might then be further embarrassed by the possibility—I do not say probability—that the Chinese Government might sign a treaty formally recognizing the independence of Manchukuo.

This analysis is based upon the probable and possible course of events in the future. As to future developments, you are doubtless well provided with opinions from the Embassy in Tokyo and the Legation in Peking; but I will add a summary of probabilities as viewed by Chinese, Japanese, and foreigners.

The forecast of the Japanese is based upon their interpretation of Chinese history and Chinese character. They believe that they can establish in Manchuria peace and order and resulting prosperity. They admit that it may take some time to do this, but as soon as the kaoliang is harvested, which should be within a few days now, they hope to make a good start in suppressing the larger bandit or volunteer forces, and to complete this work probably within a year. After that it will take much longer to stamp out the smaller bands; General Honjo's estimate, as I remember it, was from three to five years, while General Doihara, according to the press, suggested that it might be ten years before the task would be fully completed. However long it may take, the Japanese are convinced that they can bring about substantial peace and order; that when that is done the inhabitants of Manchuria and the Chinese Government at Nanking will acquiesce in the independence of the Three Eastern Provinces; and Manchukuo will be permanently established as an independent state. It is the Chinese way, they claim, to recognize a fait accompli. The great majority of the Chinese in Manchuria, Ohashi told me, have no interest in government, and will support any regime which will protect them in earning a living. The Japanese point especially to the contentedness of the Chinese under Japanese rule in the Leased Territory. They assume further that under these circumstances the powers would eventually recognize Manchukuo. It is obvious that they are placing their hope upon France to lead the other powers in this direction.

It is, of course, conceivable that the Japanese have made a correct analysis of the situation. They may have the political astuteness—although there are no present indications of it—to mould Manchukuo into a state which would be fundamentally and genuinely Chinese, though with close political and economic ties with Japan, much like another "Cuba", a development which would make some of the powers more inclined to recognize the new state.

But this Japanese analysis, taken in its entirety, is rejected by all others than Japanese with whom I have discussed the situation. It is formally rejected by the Commission: "To cut off these (three Eastern) Provinces from the rest of China, either legally or actually, would be to create for the future a serious irridentist problem which would endanger peace by keeping alive the hostility of China and rendering probable the continued boycott of Japanese goods". An opinion commonly expressed is merely that China will never acquiesce in Japanese control of Manchuria. A more thoughtful judgment, but also typical, was given me recently in Peking by Dr. David Yui, who said that the Japanese view might have been correct had Manchuria been a country by itself, but since it is so closely bound to China geographically, it would be impossible for Japan to hold it without recurring military efforts by the Chinese to drive them out. There is an apparently unanimous conviction among the Chinese that eventually, no matter what may happen in the near future, Manchuria, with its nearly thirty million Chinese, must be Chinese politically as well as racially.

Many of these Chinese appear perplexed, however, when I ask them what they would do in the contingency that the Japanese Government should occupy Peking and Tientsin with its military forces, and should then announce that the Japanese troops would remain in occupation until China should recognize Manchukuo. Mr. Ingram, the British Chargé at Peking, told me recently that already some Chinese were coming to the conclusion that they should "liquidate their losses", as he said they expressed it, which meant that they should recognize Manchukuo for the time being, a step which they believed they could take with political safety since they were convinced that Manchuria would eventually, in any case, be a part of China. Dr. H. H. Kung, who happens to be one of the passengers on this steamer, gave me the estimate, in reply to a direct question, that 90% of the Chinese leaders would oppose recognizing Manchukuo under all circumstances. That is, Dr. Kung believes that some 10% of the Chinese leaders would favor recognizing Manchukuo, as a temporary measure, if Japan should use military pressure. Some of the members of his staff would place the proportion higher.

Among others than Japanese there is a difference of opinion as to the continuance of Manchukuo, should the Japanese permanently refuse to accept the Commission's plan of settlement. Some believe that it will last indefinitely, though with constant friction with China and clashes with Chinese soldiers, so long as Japanese troops maintain it. Others believe that the difficulties and the expense of supporting an independent state will gradually force the Japanese to annex Manchukuo, as they annexed Korea.

In any case, so long as existing conditions continue, the American Government will be forced to maintain its refusal to recognize Manchukuo.

In closing this letter, which has become substantially a report, I imagine that you may wish to know what my own work has been during these last weeks of the Commission.

In addition to assisting General McCoy, I was a member, with his approval, of two committees appointed by the commission, and did a certain amount of work for Lord Lytton. After returning to Peking from our month and a half in Manchuria, I served on a committee with Lord Lytton and Mr. Haas, the General Secretary, to harmonize the three outlines for the final report which had been submitted by Lord Lytton, General McCoy, and Mr. Haas.

After the visit to Japan had been concluded and the Commission had returned to Peking, General McCoy informed me that he had granted Lord Lytton's request that I should serve with him and Mr. Haas as a member of a Drafting Committee. So during August and a part of July I enjoyed the privilege of watching from the inner circle, and in a very small way of participating in, the moulding of the Report into its final form. Lord Lytton also asked me to attend the meetings of the Commission, which usually lasted throughout the morning. In addition, the Drafting Committee would sometimes meet three or four hours in the afternoon.

The work of the Drafting Committee was somewhat elastic. We prepared for the Commission certain of the chapters, especially the one on Recommendations. For other chapters, after the Commission had discussed them, the Committee would make changes to carry out the desires of the Commission, and in some cases would prepare them for resubmission to the Commission. Lord Lytton did more of the work himself than an ordinary chairman, and often called members of the staff to serve on the committee for the consideration of certain chapters. During part of this period I was asked to concentrate upon some drafting work which Lord Lytton had started but which he could not carry on, partly on account of illness and partly on account of pressure of time: this was to condense and in part to rewrite two of the historical chapters.

In conclusion I wish to add a final word in regard to General McCoy. I scarcely knew him when I received my appointment. But I have come to entertain for him not only a real affection but a genuine admiration. Due to the combination of qualities which I have already described, he is exceptionally gifted for a position on an international commission of inquiry. It has been a great privilege as well as a constant pleasure to work with him.

(Signed) George H. Blakeslee

A NOTE ON THE SOURCES

THE CHIEF sources for this study are the public records of the United States government, printed and manuscript, and the private, unpublished papers of the principal organizations, and persons prominent at the time, as follows:

DEPARTMENT OF STATE

Foreign Relations of the United States, 1931, 1932, and 1933.

The United States and Japan, 1931–1941 (2 vols.).

MS Diplomatic Correspondence, 1931–1933 (National Archives).

DEPARTMENT OF NAVY

MS Records of the Office of the Chief of Naval Operations, 1931–1933 (National Archives).

PRIVATE PAPERS

Jane Addams (Swarthmore College).

Newton D. Baker (Library of Congress).

Edward P. Bell (Newberry Library).

William E. Borah (Library of Congress).

Nicholas M. Butler (Columbia University).

William R. Castle Diary (in Mr. Castle's possession).

Norman H. Davis (Library of Congress).

W. Cameron Forbes (Library of Congress).

Joseph C. Grew (Houghton Library, Harvard University).

Hannah C. Hull (Swarthmore College).

Nelson T. Johnson (Library of Congress).

A. Lawrence Lowell (Harvard University).

Chester Rowell (Bancroft Library, University of California).

Henry L. Stimson (Yale University).

Montgomery M. Taylor (Library of Congress).

American Boycott Association (in possession of Mrs. Corliss Lamont).

American Board of Commissioners for the Foreign Missions (Houghton Library, Harvard University).

League of Nations Association (New York City).

Swarthmore College Peace Collection (containing correspondence, broadsides, periodicals, and newspapers of

numerous peace societies; Swarthmore, Pennsylvania).
Twentieth Century Fund (New York City).
World Peace Foundation (Boston).

The Japanese side of the story was gleaned from a number of
sources: the records (exhibits, proceedings, summaries) of the
International Military Tribunal for the Far East, Japanese Foreign Office Documents (microfilm), and the diaries (microfilm)
of Marquis Kido and Prince Saionji. The British diplomatic
records for this period in the Archives of the Foreign Office are
not open for scholarly research. A very small portion concerning
the Far Eastern crisis to December 1931 has been printed in
Chapters 9, 10, 11, and 12 of *Documents on British Foreign Policy,
1919–1939* (Second Series, Vol. VIII), edited by R. Butler and
J. P. T. Bury. Similarly, the private papers of the principal participants are not available, although the editors of the *Documents*
have made use of those of the Marquess of Reading and Sir John
Simon in compiling their work. Important clues to British policy
were, however, provided by debates in the House of Commons,
gleanings in the press, and observations by foreign diplomats in
London and Geneva. French documentary sources are not open.

INDEX

235